Hampson Thomas

Horwich

It's History, Legends and Church, 1893

Hampson Thomas

Horwich

It's History, Legends and Church, 1893

ISBN/EAN: 9783744704311

Printed in Europe, USA, Canada, Australia, Japan

Cover: Foto ©ninafisch / pixelio.de

More available books at **www.hansebooks.com**

PREFACE.

I HAVE been requested by Mr. THOMAS HAMPSON to write a short Preface to a work of his which is about to be published, entitled "Horwich: Its History, Legends, and Church."

That work is still far from completion, but the author has favoured me with a view of such portion of it as has appeared in print.

I think that his book will prove interesting and entertaining to many readers.

One statement I may make with great confidence, viz., that the zeal and diligence which the author has used in pursuing his task entitle him to every encouragement.

He has spared neither time nor labour.

He has had access to various documents, Church registers, and books of reference, and has been very persevering and industrious in his researches. The best commendation that I can give him may be expressed in the following short sentence: I wish him and his book all the success they merit.

HENRY S. PIGOT.

Horwich Vicarage,
    27th July, 1883.

RESPECTFULLY INSCRIBED,

BY KIND PERMISSION, TO

JOHN LONGWORTH, ESQ.,

THE KNOWLES,

Chairman of Horwich Local Board, &c.,

In virtue of his office, and as the representative of an ancient family long and honourably connected with the village, and a due acknowledgment of the valuable aid afforded in the compilation of this work,

By his humble Servant,

THE AUTHOR.

INTRODUCTION.

IN placing before our readers the subjoined contribution to local history, we do so with the hope that the imperfections of the work may not militate against its usefulness. The history of any village or hamlet in a county so rich in historic lore cannot fail to throw some shadow which collaterally must inspire some new thought, lay bare some important fact, or serve as an adjunct to demonstrative evidence. History has many bye-paths, and in journeying along some of these we may pick up some pebble, hear some faint echo that perchance may lead to the discovery of some important link. In the hope that some such may be found herein has been our object. How far we have succeeded we leave others to determine. In dealing with the "legends" of Horwich we have thought it best to give them with all their faults both as to date and incidental surroundings. Legends are in a great measure common property. Some there are that are more closely allied with certain districts, but, though thus associated, we should find that other districts have the same legend, sometimes under a different name. Legends lead us far away into the past, and though each generation may make such its own, the date of their promulgation is clothed in mystery. We have given one in which a former Incumbent of Horwich is associated. We have been favoured with a sermon by the same incumbent, and in juxtaposition our readers will conclude with us that a greater antiquity is attached than the story would show. To those who have so kindly aided us we tender our thanks, and if our task should be so far successful as to inspire a greater degree of local patriotism, or be a straw in the historic current, then our labour will not have been in vain.

Horwich, Oct. 11th, 1853.

HORWICH:

ITS HISTORY, LEGENDS, AND CHURCH.

CHAPTER I.

HORWICH, comparatively speaking, is a modern village, and yet its history is associated with the past, in more direct connection than many of those—its neighbours around—that can claim affinity in the more stirring events of national history. As we pass through its broad and dignified principal thoroughfare we see signs of modern architecture and modern requirements; here and there one or two old dwellings of a bye-gone period stand as landmarks to guide us in our investigations: but even here we are denied any evidence to prove any antiquated history. If we look for information to the silent testimony of the more ancient structures, we must direct our attention more to the boundaries of the village, than to the village itself; and this perhaps may be accounted for by tracing its history and associations.

Harewich, Horewhich, Horwick, Horwich, from *hore*, higher, and *wick* a village, higher village, would seem to indicate that the position of the village proper in more ancient times must be looked for outside of the area which now forms the more populous portion of the village of to-day. In this, perhaps, our readers will agree with our conclusions, though, in what must have been then a dense forest, certain residences may have existed, the position would seem to indicate their connection and use with the forest. As we proceed in our investigation we think it will be clear to our readers that a small colony might or were gathered within the confines of the forest itself. Horwich is a geographical anachronism; its modern aspect can scarcely be implied in its ancient name, and when we remember that much of the history of a place is found in its name, and can trace its connection only by the etymological aids embraced therein, and though sometimes these may be misleading and prove dangerous data, yet of all guides we may look upon them as the more sure and true. With this assumption, if we would gather evidence or records of the past, we shall be guided somewhat outside the area of what constitutes the more populous portion of the village of to-day. As a forest, regal in character, and magnificent in proportions, we could scarcely hope to find such a gathering of the more exalted animal—man—within its confines as would prejudice the lives and liberties of those animals of a lower type, for whose provision and protection the forest existed; so that if there be evidence of a village—a higher village—such village must have had its existence within the boundaries of the modern village, and yet outside the area which marks the present more populous path. In fact, many of the names which geographically would seem to be just outside the forest, would seem to strengthen our position; while its-cliffs and ascending "knolls," unsuited for chase, and unfitted for harbour, would still give a magnificent survey of the proud forest and adjoining localities. Harland, in the volume of the Cheetham's Society publications to which we shall refer, gives the derivation as follows: "Hor"(a) hoar, gray, and "wich" (Ger. wic), Anglo-Saxon, dwelling (village). In both of the definitions we have given, whether we take the prefix "hor" as referring to its aspect—hoar, gray—or we take it as referring to its geographical position—hore or higher—in both we find a striking and well-defined description of what we may conceive to be its ancient characteristic. Mr. Jabez Allies, in his "Ancient History of Worcestershire," refers to many localities the names of which end in "wic" and "wich," and observes that almost all those places are connected with high ridges of ground, or dorsal or background elevations, which in ancient times would be considered the most advantageous places for residence. Harland remarks that the old German form " wich " is preserved in only two places in this locality, "Prestwich and Horwich, both of these places being situate on high ridges of land." Following up this, the only safe guide that we can command, we must look for any evidence of the germs of modern Horwich outside the more stirring surroundings of the present. Its more ancient history, however, is contained in its forest, which was termed a "Royal Forest," under the care of the Lords of Manchester. In "Harland's Manchester," we find copious references to the royal forest, from which we also gather the fact that the Greslets, who held the barony of Manchester, only paid £6 yearly as fealty for the whole barony. Of Thomas, 6th baron, little is known; he seems, however, to have been a true Norman Seignior in his passion for the chase. He married a lady named Christiana Ledets. His refusal of aid to King Henry III. to carry on his war in Gascony, and means for the projected crusade in the Holy Land, doubtless led to the escheatment of the lands of the said Thomas in Manchester and Horewych Forest (1253-4.) Dr. Hibbert Ware refers to a grant and confirmation to the said Thomas Greslet "of 'freewarren' in Manchester and Horewych." Manwood, in his "Forest Laws," says that "a forest is the highest franchise of noble and princely pleasures; next in degree unto it is the liberty of free warren. Every complete forest holds within itself a chase, a park, and a warren; the killing, hunting, or hurting of any of the beasts or fowls, of chase, park, or warren, within the territory of the forest, is a trespass of the forest, to be punished by the laws of the forest only." These laws we shall hereafter refer to.

Considering the high estimate in which the chase was then held, it is not at all surprising that the Normans regarded the forest at Horwich as the most valuable appendage of the manor of Manchester. It is also rendered highly probable, from an examination of manorial records, that the Baron's chief residence was not in Manchester, but at a hunting-seat at or near Heton-under-the-Forest, which was the pointed name given to Heaton in ancient record. If we take tradition, and paraphrase the preceding sentence, we may conclude that just outside, you under the very shadow of the forest, the proud owner thereof had his residence. "Lord's Height" takes its name, we are told in the unwritten history of the village, from the fact that the "Lord of the forest" from its gentle elevation could command a view of the forest; and the notes of the horn, or the call to the foresters, could be better heard as it re-echoed from the back ground of rock and cliff. Whether, however, the "Lord of the forest" so far honoured the village as actually to build within it a baronial residence or not, certain it is that such a residence existed not far from its confines, and almost within its enclosure. When we remember that apart from the more dangerous sport of war, the more active exertions of the Norman nobles consisted in hunting and hawking, we may assume that the forest of Horwich would hold out superlative attractions. The forest of Horwich was extensive, and had within its jurisdiction a forest court, consisting of judge and other officers. This would have made the forest somewhat costly to the Grantee, and so he held it under the name of a Warren. The Lords of Mamcestre appointed three foresters to the forest of Horewich, and offenders against the forest laws within the forest were brought before the Court Baron or Court Leet for punishment. The forest is thus sketched in the "Survey of the Barony of Mamcestre:" There are eight vaccaries (cowgates or pastures) and one plot which is not a full vaccary and are worth xix[1]. The pannage (or swine feeding) of the same forest with the avery of sparrow hawks are worth yearly x[s]. There are three foresters who keep the forest and have escapia, and give yearly lx[s]. The sum or value of the forest is xxiiij[l]." (£24) which is a large yearly issue from a forest in the thirteenth century, and plainly testifies to the importance and worth of the forest at Horwich. This will be all the more striking when we note that the Greslets only paid £6 yearly as fealty for the whole barony, including the forest. In a commercial sense, if such a word could be applicable to those early times, the forest at Horwich would prove a valuable investment, and in those days its importance could not be neglected nor the revenue drawn therefrom be discarded by the Lord Robert, or his son and successor, Thomas de Greslet.

In one of the "Forest Statutes" the mode of a forester's walking and watching in the forest is strikingly pourtrayed. No modern sentinel or soldier on guard is surrounded with more exact requirements, nor mode of performing a course of duty regulated by stricter conventional law. "That the foresters rise early and going with their bailiwick shall there transact their customary duty till the 9th hour—*horan nonam*—the hour of noon or 3 p.m., and then gets dinner, and quickly after dinner returning into their bailiwick, viz., into those parts they had not been in before dinner, there go listening and lying in wait, that no one does ill there, until evening. Evening may be said canonically from 4 to 7 p.m., so he shall every day.' There is one word mentioned which may require some little explanation, viz., escapia, or the fines imposed for trespass. The law was as follows: "If any man's beast be found within the forbidden lands, or in the fawning time within the forest, every owner of such beast shall be amerced for every foot one penny; for a second offence the said amercement; and for a third the beast shall be forfeited to the lord of the forests.' "For the keeping of this forest (Horewiche) there ought to be three sworn foresters, who shall give for their bailiwick to the lord one year with another £4, and answer to the lord for all the agistments that have been made by the lord's bailiffs, or by themselves on their behalf, if they should be required by their lord." The forest of Horwich was at this time (1282, &c.), 16 miles in circumference, and contained eight vaccaries or cow leys, afterwards called booths, and 16 places of pastures, which pasture was composed of a mixture of wood and plain. Though much of authority is given relative to the forest itself, nowhere do we find any clear or well defined boundary to mark out its exact position. A view of the plain or valley in which Horwich is situated may give it, as seen from its rising summits, and there may be some truth in the old story, which ascribes the sign board to the "Squirrel Inn," as indicative of the wary little animal hopping from branch to branch on the last tree in a northern direction of the proud forest.

A forester was a sworn officer ministerial of the forest, and his duty was to preserve and watch over the vert and venison, and to make attachments and due presentments of all matters of trespassers done within the forest, attaching or arresting trespassers. In the forest of Horewich the forester also discharged the duties of district officers of the larger forests, called agistors, or the collectors of payment for cattle and swine feeding. Manwood says: "The number of foresters should be in accordance to the quality, and the ground of the forest—one forester or more in every walk or bailiwick of the forest, so that he may walk daily between nine and dinner, and dinner and evening the whole extent of his jurisdiction (bailiwick or walk). The three sworn foresters giving to the lord for their office a fee farm rent of £4." This paying for the position, instead of by virtue of holding and performing the duties of the position, being paid thereby, would seem to indicate that much of the value of the position depended on the foresters themselves, that perquisites and other aids must have been great, that the very circumstances surrounding their elevation to the position would given them power, scope, and necessity betimes of exercising their authority to the detriment of others. Perchance the almost worn-out legend of the "Robber's walk" within the forest itself—to which we shall hereafter refer—may have, if at all, its origin in the petty tyrannies of these foresters; for not only around the forest, but within the most rigid legal enactments abounded. In "Manwood's Forest Laws" we have the following "oath of the inhabitants of the forest, being of the age of twelve, as the same hath been accustomed and used of ancient time":—

You shall true liegman be
Unto the King's Majestie
You shall no hurt do
The beasts of the forest unto
Nor anything unto
That doth belong thereto

The offences of others you shall not conceal
But to the utmost you shall them reveal
Unto the officers of the forest
Or to them that may see the same redress
All these things you shall see done
So help your God at's holy doom

CHAPTER II.

Not only were the foresters in charge answerable to their lord for agistments, and bound to protect the forest from trespass, but a watchful care was to be exercised in the protection of the young, and a special supervision during the breeding season. They were surrounded with strict regulations relative to the forest and its keeping, which must have been of an irksome nature. "Pannage, herbage, minerals, honey of bees, aeries of sparrow hawks, herons, and eagles, vert and venison, and all issues of the forest by themselves and others, according to seasons, and according as the said agistments that have been made by the lord's bailiffs, or by themselves on their behalf, if they should be regarded by their lord, and they ought to be sustained through the entire year by the larger vills lying near the forest." These larger vills or villages, which ought to keep the foresters were Lostock, Rumworth, Heaton, Halliwell, Sharples, Longworth, and Anderton, and the division land in the respective villages for that purpose, was as follows: "Eight oxgangs of land in Lostock, fourteen oxgangs of land in Rumworth, four oxgangs of land in Heaton-under-the-Forest, three oxgangs of land in Halliwell, four oxgangs of land in Sharples, two oxgangs of land in Longworth, and seven oxgangs of land in Anderton, so that there are forty-two oxgangs of land which should sustain the said foresters with bread, drink, and victuals, as is aforesaid."

Such ample provision was thus made in order that the foresters might devote more exclusively the whole of their time to its necessities and protection, but, though surrounded with strict enactments, and bound by oaths which, in a superstitious age, must have exercised a powerful effect, yet in the multiform duties they were called upon to perform, any laxity, or any perversion of trust could be easily thrown on the shoulders of others; or any loss which a dereliction of duty might entail could with impunity be recouped by an exercise of the power vested in them.

Agistments, from the French "giste," a bed, consisted in the collection of a tax imposed for cattle and swine feeding within the forest and boundaries. Sheep, however, were not agistable, "because they bite so closely that they destroy the vert, the green hew of the coverts," and coverts were more needed for the requirements of the forest than the value of any tax which might be imposed upon them. But not only within the forest at Horwich, but in other large forests, did the duties of the Horwich foresters extend; the agistments in connection with other forests was collected by them. They had also to collect the pannage money for the swine feeding on beech mast and acorns, the grass money for cattle and horses agisted, the fees for working the quarries, for the taking of the honey of the wild bee, for the aëries or nests of sparrowhawks and hawks of various kinds, and of herons and eagles. They had also to collect issues of the vert-green hew or coverts, serving both for food, browse, and defence for the deer, as oaks, beeches, &c.; and for shelter and defence, as ashes, poplars, maples, alders, &c., or "nether vert," as the hawthorn, blackthorn, &c., brakes, gorse, heath, &c. All trees growing in the forest to feed deer were called "special vert," to destroy or to injure which was a great violation of forest law, which was most grievously punished.

But, though the duties of these foresters were great and widespread, they had certain privileges and powers, which gave them an amount of authority dangerous to the peace of others or otherwise as they might incline. To live on the confines of a forest, when the needs of society—if such a word be permissible—were few and simple, had within it much of the benefit which is supposed to arise from a near habitation to a market town in our own days, but in both instances the advantages have juxtaposite deterrents. In a later day to live within the charmed circle is to invite heavier taxation; to live within the approach of the forest was to be within call and invitation of these police of the forest.

The villagers of Lostock, Rumworth, Heaton, Halli-

well, Sharples, and Anderton were enrolled as special
constables, and when called upon were to undertake
certain duties, and we need not fear but that the principle of throwing upon others what might be a burden
to ourselves would be less acted upon then than now.
We know something to-day of the care which is exercised just before the August grouse shooting commences;
how nightly watchers vigilantly exercise supervision on
our moors and grouse coverts, how almost impossible it
is to break through the nightly vigils of these armed
watchers, and with what devotion and suspicion they
tend their charge. Go back to the time to which we
are now referring, and at certain seasons each villager
of the six taxed villages was called upon to assist the
foresters in the preservation and keeping of the forest
charge. "In the season of the year when the hawks
begin to build their nests, the aforesaid villagers, by
warning of the foresters, shall collect themselves in
Hore-wich-ley, and from thence, being sworn, they shall
go throughout the whole of the forest to see what nests
they have made, and from the time of this view the foresters
shall remain in the forest day and night themselves
until the Feast of St. Barnaby; and every one of the
aforesaid cowherds shall find in the time of their day of
guarding the nests six oaten loaves and one penny worth
of victuals to the said day of St. Barnaby. When the
hawks shall have hatched, the said villagers shall come
into the said forest to take the hawk chickens from the
nests, delivering every one to those foresters or to
the lord's bailiffs there present. And if in any article
of the said custom they shall make default they may be
put in plea by these foresters in the Court of Mamcastre
(Manchester) and there according to the law and
customs of ploughing, to wit, that they shall plough
every ox-gang of arable land of the old and not of
the new assart, as well as that belonging to Nicholas de
Longford, who is now defonct, as of all others in
Withington, Didsbury, Barlow, Chollerton, Denton,
and Haleton, in the township of Mamcastre, wheresoever they shall be assigned, each half an acre of ground,
if they shall have the plough of the owner of that ox-gang for that time, and he shall have one penny for the
work."

It is somewhat singular to note what modern customs are interwoven in ancient usages. The very punishments of the past have worked themselves into our social system. It has been said, and doubtless with some truth, that the prevalent custom amongst the farmers of the district in giving a half day's ploughing to the incoming tenant of an adjoining farm, takes its rise from this custom of mulcting the villagers for a dereliction of "forest law" by demanding of them this interchange of labour. We see no reason to doubt this assertion, for though the labour might exist as a punishment, the good resulting therefrom would be so obvious that by mutual consent this interchange of labour would doubtless be retained. So important was the position of the forester held to be that even his perquisites (so far as the law could determine) and his wages were prescribed. "The sustenance of a forester varied in amount and in character, being sometimes a money amount, and sometimes wholly in kind, when the latter was the case the temptations to the foresters were many and great."

In the middle ages the use of honey—wild honey—was very extensive; for domestic purposes it was all prevalent. Its present substitute—sugar—not being introduced into England until the fifteenth century it would be an article of extensive requirement: fruits to be preserved would require its aid; the more expensive beverages were made from it, and from the early days of the Saxons its use and necessity were much prized, but of the use of wax our early ancestors were entirely at bay. For such an important article there needs be a brisk demand, for whatever may be said of the simple habits of our forefathers, we have no proof other than that those habits of simplicity were more the result of necessity than of choice. Wherever opportunity was given for the exercise of more voluptuous display our fathers were not behind their more privileged sons. Honey would be an important article in the eyes of the foresters; a keen knowledge of the intricacies of the forest would be required to find out its profitable store, and under its time-mellowed boulders and overhanging cliffs, within its dangerous declivities, there the forester's harvest would be. Where, however, the forester was paid in money, his wages and aids were fixed with as much regularity as the nineteenth century labourer with his 3s. 4d. per day. Manwood says a forester in fee may claim to have 1½d. a day throughout the whole year. So a forester in fee might prescribe to have all the *mort bois* or windfall wood within the forest or throughout his bailiwick, and also all the browse-wood felled for browse for the deer in winter. He might also claim the umbles and skin of every deer killed in the forest. With regard to the word so often used to describe the forest animals or beasts of the chase, Manwood's definition of venison is both definite and pointed. "Venison," says that authority, "is that general word which old foresters and good woodmen do understand every beast of forest or chase and to none other, venison must always mean one of the five beasts of the forest or one of the five beasts of chase as a word of art proper to beasts of forest and chase. Thus hunting and killing a hare in the King's forest is a trespass; all trespass in this forest are either of vert or venison." In addition to the "aids" we have already referred to, there were other perquisites of which the foresters held a claim; these perquisites were valuable adjuncts to the office; for instance, he had a claim on "one or both shoulders of every deer killed within this bailiwick."

"Scot ales" were most directly connected with forest usages, being a kind of tax to prevent unauthorised persons from collecting and making unjust exactions. A statute enacted "That no officer of the forest should, by virtue or colour of his office, make any gathering of Scot ale, hay, oats, or other corn, lambs, young pigs," &c. Manwood explains "That Scot ale is when any officer of the forest keeps a public-house within the forest and, by colour of his office, cause men to come to his public-house, spend their money; or, where he keeps any game, or sells any ale on a certain day, and by colour of his office causeth people to spend money with him, there is also a Scot ale punishable by law." In short they were a kind of feudal truck or tommy shops. There were Scot ales that were lawful where held by tenure, by grant, or by prescription. In the first charter of King Henry 3rd, 1217, cap. 7, it enacts "That no forester or bedal shall for the future make any ale shots, nor collect sheaves of corn, or oats, or any grain, or lambs, or swine; nor shall make any gathering but by or on oath of twelve men regarders), and when they shall think reasonably suffice for the purpose."

Of the unauthorised gatherings of the ancient foresters "Scot ale" or "ale shot" was the most common. This was when a forest officer, under colour of keeping a house of entertainment, used his authority to procure custom of and from the tenants. If the fact was proved at the Court of Swanimote, the officer was fined and dismissed from his office. Scot (Anglo-Saxon) is a gathering or contribution, and Coke explains the Scot ales of the forest charter to be a collection made for the forest officers when they came to the house of any whereunto others are contributory within the perambulation of the forest, which was then called *Potura*—a drinking.

An Itinerary of Edward III., 1331, shows that this had become a more serious exaction. The "Fillenale" (ale feast or ale filling) is there stated to be a custom claimed by the foresters, and also by the bailiffs of the hundred, to receive provisions as well for themselves as for their men, horses, and dogs, such provisions being exacted from the tenants and inhabitants within the perambulation of the forest or the hundred to which they belonged. They exercised a kind of lien on the Inhabitants, who were called upon to provide such needs without any pay or return. We need not wonder that acts of petty tyranny were exercised by these privileged foresters. At a time when justice was administered by the lords of the forest, or by nominees, who by virtue of privilege, grant, or right, thought more of the preservation of the denizens of the forest than the more contumacious animal—man, it would prove an easy task for these foresters, for petty spite or malicious feeling, to lay information against an obnoxious individual that would prove dangerous to his liberty. A spirit of independence or rebellion against unjust exactions would create a desire for revenge, and around every forest, sometimes within its more intricate enclosures, would be found a band of outlaws, who were bound by the strong affinity of mutual protection, who would be alike enemies to the foresters and to their charge. Even in its modern aspect, positions suitable for such a combination may be readily conjectured; its winding cliffs and bush-entangled dells; its glens and picturesque valleys, with its knolls and overhanging ridges, may give scope for a free imagination as to the stirring events of this period.

CHAPTER III.

It was doubtless to this period that the old legend of the "Robbers' Walk," or "Thieves' Grave," has reference. Though the legend is told in various forms and almost forgotten, yet there are many still in the village who in their journeys to Rivington Old Grammar School in times gone by can remember how this ancient legend was associated with the spot over which they travelled. Most of our readers in Horwich and many outside, will know that within a very recent period the road leading to Rivington (Raventon—town of the ravens) via the racecourse, was formed of five ridges, or narrow ascending "pads." It was on these ridges or "pads"—footwalks—where centred the interest of the old legend, and though the story is preserved only in the traditional history of the village, and as such may differ in form, yet we venture to give it as told by a venerable representative of an ancient village family.

When Horwich was nothing but a wood there was a "lord of the manor," who treated his tenants with unjust severity. So fierce was he in temper, that even his favoured woodmen (foresters) trembled at his appearance; his very pleasure consisted in exercising despotic authority and showing his power in acts of petty tyranny. At the time when the will of the "lord" was virtually the law of the district, he was enabled to "lord his authority and work his mischief" with impunity. He was passionately devoted to the chase, and cruel and niggardly to his dependants, whom he denied the rights and privileges which were theirs by forest law and prescriptive authority. His niggardly disposition made him suspicious, and he watched the actions of his underlings with anything but lordly grace. Necessity compelled his foresters or woodmen to make up for his niggardliness; yea, a denying of their "just dues and demands," by turning products of the forest to their good. As his avaricious disposition increased the raid on the forest products grew in extent, till at length the lessening of the venison, the loss of agistments, and a famine of wild honey, roused the lordly owner to a rage. To shift the burden and remove the blame, the raids that had led to the partial depopulation of the forest and the robbery of wild honey, was laid to the charge of those who happened to be fated to live almost within the confines of the forest or within its jurisdiction. To show his sense of the want of vigilance on the part of his foresters, a number of them were discharged, and a decree issued from the lordly court that the offending inhabitants should come before the tyrant for judgment. But they knew what that judgment would be, and though innocent, they felt that a scapegoat could alone satisfy the desire of the tyrant. They determined to discard the summons and make common cause with the harshly treated foresters who had incurred his lordship's wrath. Thus within the forest itself were gathered a "band of outlaws who feared not its lord nor listened to his decrees," within the intricacies of the forest, or in rude dwellings upon the wide-spreading heather. These "cast-outs" were a standing grievance to the proud and haughty owner. From their vantage ground with unwarying spies to watch every movement, every effort of capture was frustrated, and at times, when an incursion was least feared and expected, this gang of desperadoes made their raids and seized upon cattle, pillaging and destroying, committing terrible havoc upon his lordship's preserves. Such exactions brought reprisals, and though the glens hidden by overhanging trees, and the very lairs of the foxes afforded them shelter, yet such was the desire for revenge upon these desperate destroyers, that armed patrols watched the forest and its approaches by day and by night. As a reward of these vigils one, the leader, was captured, and his body left to swing upon a tall oak tree, and his flesh left for the eagles and birds of prey.

Abutting the wood or forest his lordship dwelt, and thither had brought his wife and "children three." A sudden call from a higher authority led him from home, and having duly charged his servitors with the custody of children and his wife, he left home, but not without some misgivings as to the safety of those he was leaving behind. His journey led him through the forest, and the crackling underwood made him betimes to glance around, and though such an occurrence might be expected from a spot where animals "small and great" abounded, yet with each sound he turned with the conception that his progress was watched, and his journey noted. Once he espied a pair of keen and vengeful eyes looking out from a dense bramble bush, and, giving orders to his attendants, the bush was surrounded and beaten, but only resulted in despatching a weasel from under the protecting shelter of the bush. But a pair of keen eyes were there, burning with vindictive brightness, and lit up by a deadlier revenge, and not till the forest glade was reached and the shelter of its underwood denied protection, did those eyes cease to watch the lordly course.

Tyranny ever gathers divergent sympathies and affiliates opposing powers when the combination is needful for the protection or security of either, and though the action of the gang of outlaws was sometimes an offence and oft a danger to the foresters, yet in hatred of the one and the fear of the other there was inspired a sympathetic alliance which gave much in common to forester and outlaw. The absence of the "lord" was an event which could be improved; the sympathy of the attendants, yea, the passive aid of the foresters, was a power to be courted. Upon the tall oak still hung the bleached bones of their companion, denied of sepulture, and in their very whiteness seemed to point to heaven, and registered afresh the terrible vow of vengeance which its comrades had taken under its dread shadow. That night they gathered together, and wended their way to the almost unprotected dwelling of the forest lord. What an affinity of sympathy could not secure, an exercise of power could, and soon wife and children were helpless victims in the hands of a band whose very bosoms swelled with intensity of vengeful passion. The terrible scene need not be depicted, but the words of the wife and mother are as the words of prophesy, and the very core of the legend. Pleading in vain, in very agony of soul she cried, "Cruel murderers, to stay not in your blood-thirsty mission, where innocence pleads for mercy. Heaven shall mark your path, and your trail shall be pointed out." "Cut short her babbling," cried one of the gang. "No," said the leader, "would you render our revenge less sweet by denying to her lord the knowledge of the hands that have thus repaid his cruelty; rather let us take the 'brats' and hang them as company for our companion." The "track of retributive justice" was swift, and ere long they suffered for their crime, but even his lordship was ill at ease, and death overtook him, ere he knew the spot where his children lay. But the "peace of the grave" was denied the five desperadoes who had committed the deed. Innocence lay buried in an unconsecrated spot; the rites of religion had been denied them, and how could those five men rest so long as virtue and innocence had not been sprinkled by the holy incense of the church? Nightly these five spirits of darkness perambulated the spot, not far from a rising mound that marked those youthful graves, and not till years afterwards when a worthy divine sought counsel and conversation with these disturbed spirits, and performed the last rites of the church over the spot where the "sweet ones slept," did those perambulations cease? From that time the spot has been known as the "Robbers' walk," and a rising mound close by as the 'Thieves' grave," and never, said our venerable reciter, "hath it been permitted to destroy those ancient records of so terrible a story." Modern progress has, however, destroyed these ascending ridges, and though the story we have told has been varied in form, yet few will fail to notice some resemblance in each.

In more modern times in one of the more intricate "glens," there was an alehouse known by the name of "Tigers in the Wood." It has been said, and perhaps with some semblance of truth, that the spot where this beerhouse stood had been occupied by a still more ancient one. Judging from the regulations of the forest these alehouses would be tempting investments for the foresters, and be enticing avenues for increasing their gains. Modern regulations are looked upon much in the light of an infliction on the rights and privileges of a class, whose trade has ever been thought to be dangerous to a degree to the success of the outside community. But in modern legislation we find much that is only a revivified form of active, ancient customs. The very law which denies the power to sue for "aleshots" and debars modern landlords the right to "trust" with impunity, is only an exemplification of the charter of 1217, and in other and minor details modern legislation is not ashamed to borrow—without acknowledgment—many of the ancient laws of our forefathers.

Besides their regular allowance or fees throughout the year, the foresters, or keepers of Horwich forests, and the keepers of other forests in this part of the kingdom, had an allowance of victuals and drink in their perambulations, which we have before stated was termed *Potura*. This was claimed by custom, to take man's meat, horse meat, and dog's meat from the tenants within the perambulation of the forest. In some places this right, privilege, or custom was commuted by money payments, and many, to avoid the exaction which sometimes pressed heavily, readily made the commutation. Land subject to this custom was called *Terra Potura*. This tax is referred to in the following order of King Henry VII., 1502, and refers to a denial of arrear of *terra potura* as to four Lancashire forests.

"To our right-trustie and well-beloved father, the Erle of Derbie, George Stanley, Knt., Lord Strange, Sir Henry Halsall, Knt., Sir John Towneley, Sir Richard Sherburne, Knt., &c. Whereas of olde use and custome, the foresters and keepers of our forests of Penhull, Rossingdal, Accrington and Trawdon, have hadde of verrie right and duty, at c'taine tymes and dales, meate and drinke of the tennants therein and adjoining, the which is now called '*puture*,' otherwise forester fee, as is set forth in a boke, in which boke it also apperth that for divers displesours and annoyances that ye seide foresters com'itted agaynst ye seide tennants, ther wyves and s'vaunts, ye seide tennants made complaynt to our p'genitors Dukes of Lancaster, whereupon ye said tennants bound themselves, ther heyses and tenures, to our p'genitors to pay for tyme being yerely 12l. 13s. 4d. to seide foresters towards ther wayges, and in recompense of ther meate and drinke, called forester's fee, ye which was paid to ye first yeare of King Edward IV., in which yere by labour, and meanes made with him, ye seide poture was put in respite, so that 119*l*. 6s. 8d. is now in respite, which if it should be longer delayed would turn to our disherison, and ye utter destruction of our forests for lack of keeping; wherefore we will and desire and natheless charge you, and anie five of youe to call before youe, as well as our tennants now in being wi ye seide forests, and other most ancient persons adjoining, as ye in your discretion shall think most convenient, and enquire which of ye seide tennants ought to pay ye seide duties, and what some (sum) ev'y one of y'm, after ye olde usage and custom ther, and thereupon to compel them, and ev'y one of them to pay ye seide some (sum), and for defaulte to distreyn (distrain) them and ther tenures, and for utter refusing thereof to seaze on their tenures imediately, and admit such other p'sons as will bee content to pay ye seide duties."

CHAPTER IV.

From time immemorial forests have been devoted more or less to religious purposes. "The Temple of Jupiter Ammon rose up in the midst of a grove of palm trees, and the oracles of Greece were situated in groves." Many of the religious rites of the northern nations of Europe were performed in the forest, and in all countries we find evidence to prove that homage, yea worship, has been paid to particular trees. This feeling it is that even to-day clothes our woods and plantations with imaginary and supernatural beings. The Druids held nothing more sacred than the mistletoe and oak. In the early history of the country during the time of the "Britons" the forests of England were not only useful as giving means of subsistence, but a secure retreat from an enemy. Strabo, in describing a British town, says, "Forests were the only towns in use among them (the Britons) which were formed by cutting down large circle of wood, and erecting huts within, and sheds for cattle."

The first forest laws of which we have any record were passed in the reign of Canute the Great in 1016, and were extremely severe and savage. The reason why kings should have possession of forests as a royal privilege is given by John Manwood: "The king or sovereign governour of a realm is the most excellent and worthiest part or member of the body of the commonweal next unto God . . . And therefore in respect to his continual care and labour, the laws do allow to the king . . to have his places of recreation or pastime wherever he will appoint." It has been remarked by a very acute writer that "there is, after all, a dash of the savage even in the most civilised man," and the forest-hunting habits of our forefathers and sports of to-day are evidence.

With the advent of the Saxons, came a race that were hunters from their childhood; they fixed the boundaries of forests and made enclosures, and looked upon the trophies of the chase with as much glory as upon the trophies of war. A forest of the dimensions of Horwich could scarcely fail to command attention. Safely in possession of the capital of the Segantl (Blackrod), the proud forest at its base could scarcely fail to command and attract a race of hardy hunters; and to chase the wild boar and the deer through the primeval forest would be a temptation too great to be resisted. It is in the time of the Saxons that we first find any trace of the enacting of laws for the forests of England and the clear definition of their boundaries, and here it is required that we should explain what perhaps ought to have been explained at the very beginning of our reference to the forest, viz., the meaning of the word. Its etymology is obscure, but its legal meaning is thus defined by our old authority, Manwood, as given in his edition published in 1598: "A forrest is a certain territorie of wooddy grounds and fruitfull pastures, priviledged for wild beasts and foules of furrest, chase, and warren to rest and abide in, in the safe protection of the king for his princely delight and pleasure, while territorie of ground so priviledged is meered and bounded into irremoveable markes, meeres, and boundaries, either known by matter of record or else by prescription. And also replenished with wilde beasts of venarie or chase, and with great coverts of vert for the succour of the said wilde beasts to have there abode in; for the preservacion and continuance of which said place, together with the vert and venison, there are certen particuler lawes, priviledges, and officers belonging to the same, meete for that purpose that are onely proper unto a forrest, and not to any other place." Blackstone thus defines a forest: "Forests are waste grounds belonging to the king, replenished with all manner of chase or venery, which are under the king's protection for the sake of his recreation and delight." The Saxon noble had his large house or hall built in the forest, which supplied the timber of which it was constructed. Within the forest gathered the hetrogenous compound representatives of the national character. A wandering minstrel, a holy pilgrim, sang forth his lays, or told his sad story within the forest glade; and thither many a gang of outlaws, living by plunder, sought retreat yea, and many a holy man, disgusted with the world around, sought refuge there, where

> Far in wild remote from public view,
> From youth to age the reverend hermit grew;
> Remote from man, with God he passed his days,
> Prayer all h.s business, all his pleasure praise,

The foresters were, however, a privileged class, in that they were sworn to the fulfilment of duties, which alone comprised, outside the "revelry of war," the sole occupation and thought of the king and his nobles. The timber of the forest was little regarded, the chief object of care were the wild beasts by which they were inhabited, and for the preservation of whose lives no precautions could be too strict. The foresters themselves were protected by the most rigid laws, and their persons held each as being in charge of the king's deer. We know that authority sometimes is a dangerous power, and that legal protection is the reverse of moral restraint. A class such as the foresters, surrounded with all the immunity which a sport-loving monarch could give, must have proved a dangerous weapon to be used, either vindictively or otherwise as the occasion might serve. Ere we leave the forest let us glance at a few of the pains and penalties that were intended to protect these woodmen. "If any man offered force to one of them, he was, if a freeman, to lose his freedom and his property, and if a villain his right hand was to be struck off; and for the second offence the penalty was loss of life. It was death to kill a deer in a royal forest. Sometimes the offender had his eyes destroyed, and even if anyone, through sport or malice, should chase a deer until the deer panted, the lowest penalty was a fine of ten shillings—an enormous sum in those days." A code of laws of this draconian character, however pleasing it might be royalty and the nobles, could scarcely fail to prove of hardship to their dependants and the other inhabitants of the country. We have, however, nothing to show how far the rigidness of forest law affected the happiness of our forefathers, except here and there a thread of some traditiona story, yet we cannot doubt, judging from the history of other places, placed under similar conditions, that the comfort, yea, the rights of our forefathers were sacrificed to the arrogance of the nobles, and that to live on the confines of a forest was anything but paradisiacal in character.

From Harland's Mancestre, Cheeth. Soc. Pub., to which we have already referred, we find that "The wood (forest) of Horewich, comprising 16 miles in circuit, is worth yearly in pannage, avries of eagles, herons, and hawks, honey, minerals, millstones, and iron, or earth, for turning ashes and the like Issues 003, of which the verdure in oak, ashes, and the like great wood in covert 160 marks (£106 13s. 4d.), and the same wood is so several that no one may enter it with a licence. In which if any beast be found without license the owner of that beast shall give for that trangress 6d. of fixed custom." In forest-law the offence of trespass was a grave offence. Manwood thus refers to the law:—" If beasts or cattle of any foresters, a stranger dwelling outside of the forest, be found feeding, the cattle or beasts having by chance strayed into the forest, the owner or owners of such beasts or cattle was to be amerced (fined) for every foot 1d. or 4d. per head ; this fine or amercement only referred to the 1st and 2nd offence, for the third offence the beast or cattle became forfeited to the King." In the "Survey of the Manor of Mancestre," Cheetham's Soc. Pub., we find the following interesting references: —" In Horewich 16 plots of pasture not measured because of their largeness in wood and plain, of which 2 in wood and plain always make one vaccary, altogether eight vaccaries of which can supply 10 loads of hay." From the "Rental of the Manor of Mancester," 1473, we give the following:—

Rodus Radcliffee arnig' tenet vnám pasture aim in Horewiche de deo Dno p fine p'det r p Anm.

viijlí. xvjs. vi'jd.

Edwardus Hulme tenet vj mess cu p t lnen in Horwiche p'J vol O'Kenley gt t Annor et 2 p Anm.

xlí. llljs. ljd.

Willimus Heaton tenet tria mess on pt lnen in Horwiche voe, Ryddley wood, de It co Dno p t d fule 2 p Anmi xxs.

Horewiche some (sum) xxiijlí. xiiijs. ljd.

Examining still further the rent-roll of the Lords of Manchester, we find that in Horwich at that time land was held subject to certain service being rendered, and those holding the same were called "Knight fee tenants." Amongst the number we have the following: "Ralph Radcliffes one pasture in Horwiche by the said service, £8 16s. 8d.; Edward Grinhalgh Grynehaugh (Greenhalgh) four messuages in Horwiche Leigh rented at £4 6s. 4d., by the same service £3 13s. 4d.; Edward Hulme six messuages with appurtenances in Horwich, with appurtenances called O'Kenley £10 4s. 2d.

As we proceed it will be found that many names of places, localities, and individuals, are interwoven so closely with the past history of the village, that without a reference thereto, much mystification prevails. If we take the name "Greenhalgh," it is known the more ancient inhabitants persist, notwithstanding modern refinement, in calling it "Grinaw." Traditionary authority for the pronunciation is thus supplemented and supported by ancient documentary evidence. The main thoroughfare is equally grafted by significant reference to ancient names. Horwich, as we have before remarked, is a geographical anachronism; we may go a step further, and speak of it as a geological enigma. The large boulder stones, in their egg-shaped appearance, and possessing characteristics uncommon to the locality, and yet lying in rich profusion on its wild expanse of moorland, bespeak a visit in the far, far past, when those boulders moulded and shaped in their long journey over frozen seas and rivers, or by some terrible convulsion, when the aspect of surrounding scenery was changed, and in the powerful struggle of innate but opposing forces, its beautiful range of hills rose in their stern majesty. Nay, may not a geological examination warrant the assertion that its valley was once swept over by the "mighty deep," and the outstretched plain of which Horwich is a part, have formed a mighty river joining the Irish Sea? Perhaps few districts are so rich in evidences of such an existence as Horwich. From whence the long stretched beds of beautiful sea-like sand, which abounds. From whence the layers of pebbles, shells, and other fossil remains recently-exposed to view, at the "Dig Leechs." Creeping out to view on its hill sides, we have the coal measure and its valley, devoid of that useful and powerful adjunct of civilisation; as we gently walk down its sloping hills the coal measure is again found, at a little depth under ground, and on the borders of those hills and upon its ridge coal has been dug at a greater depth. But though coal may not exist in very large expanse and of sufficient thickness to warrant outlay, yet its solid phalanx of rock and its famed stone quarries proves "Nature to have been bountiful in her gifts." Perhaps we could not better describe the geological feature of the Horwich Hills than by quoting from a work entitled "Geology of Country round about Bolton," by Ed. Hull, B.A., F.G.S. :—

Section of Burnt Edge Colliery, Horwich.

	ft.	in.
1 Shale and flagstone	106	0
2 Top coal	0	10
3 Dark fire-clay (full stigmaria)		
4 Light fire-clay, with nodule of ironstone (kernals)	3	0
5 Hard silicious stone	1	0
6 Fire-clay	0	6
7 Bottom coal		
8 Hard, rough, and course grained grit	2	0

At Winterhill 15 feet of flags and shales, between the upper and lower seams, which thin out southwards. The fire-clay is valuable for pottery. In a pit sunk from the rough rock down to the two feet coal at White Gate (Mr. A. Mason's) the depth was found to be 125 yards, and contained the following series :—

	ft.	in.
Coal	1	0
Fire-clay	3	0
Coal	1	8
Clay	0	6
Grit	0	0

The highest point in Horwich is a small mound, situate not far from the boundary of the village, behind the Five Houses, it being 1,475 feet above the sea level, the relative heights of Rivington Pike and Two Lads being, the former 1,192, the latter 1,276, the lowest point in Horwich being close to where, in a narrow spot, Horwich joins Westhoughton, being 330 feet above the sea level.

CHAPTER V.

To what period must we ascribe the decline of Horwich Forest? Little now remains to tell of its primeval grandeur, and the time has long passed "when the Lacies and the Ferrers, followed by their vassals, plunged into the thickets in all the ardour of the chase, and emerged only at a distance of several miles to witness the dying struggles of the weeping deer" (Baines). In Dr. Hunter's edition of *Sylva*, published in York in 1786, we find the following very sensible note on this subject:—"In order to trace the history of the decay of our forest-trees, it will be necessary to remark that the first attack made upon them of any material consequence was in the 27th year of the reign of Henry 8th, when that monarch seized upon the church-lands, and converted them, together with their woods, to his own use. Ruinous as such an attempt might appear at first, it did not bring with it any pernicious consequences, as the whole kingdom, at that early period, was plentifully stocked with all kinds of timber trees, especially the oak. During the civil war which broke out in 1642, and all the time of the interregnum, the royal forests, as well as those of the nobility and gentry, suffered a great calamity, insomuch that many extensive forests had, in a few years, hardly any memorial left of their existence but their names." Tuffer, a versifier in the reign of Henry 8th, complains "that men were more studious to cut down than to plant trees." The old fable has it, "The axe said to the tree lend me of thy wood to make a handle; the request was granted, and the tree fell." Baines remarks: "This ancient forest, from its capacious dimensions and the abounding supply of timber for building purposes and for fuel, became a manufacturing station as early as the reign of Henry 8th, for at that period we read of cotton yarn spun at Horwich." As we proceed, we shall have to notice how many and varied are the places in Horwich which, at a very early date, were devoted to spinning, bleaching, &c., but we shall fail to discover any cause why, though the pioneer in the staple industry of the county, Horwich has been left so far behind in the wealth-producing race. Apart from its rich stock of fuel, there might be other causes for its then supremacy; its flowing rills and streams would suggest, by their flowing declivities, the use of water power, and this mode being of very ancient date, its introduction could not well be stayed in a place so fortunately situated as Horwich. In fact we have evidence to prove that perhaps the oldest factory in Horwich received its power through the water wheel. But the supply of timber fuel was early supplemented by the ("black stone")—coal—which projected from its hill sides, and the writer remembers an old village worthy, tracing the origin of the name "Coal fires," which is given to the lane leading to Mr. Peak's tile works, said that the name was given to the lane because it led to where the black stone was used instead of "wood fuel," the manner of its discovery being as follows:—" That once upon a time a gang of men had gathered at the base of the hill, and having lighted a fire, they were gathered around borrowing warmth from its glowing embers, when hearing a noise at considerable distance from them, they felt it due to their safety to seek refuge in flight, but the fire would prove a traitor and tell of their late presence there; to put out the fire and thus destroy all evidence that they had lately encamped there, they threw a quantity of earth and stone of a black nature upon the burning timber. When, however, from the higher summit of the hills they perceived their fear to be groundless, they returned, and to their surprise found a bright red glowing fire awaiting them." From that day the black stone was used by those dwelling on the hill sides, and as a contra distinction, the road leading thereto was called going to the "Coal Fires." We have already shown that a knowledge of the properties of coal was known at a still earlier date by our forefathers, and in ages preceding them (History of Blackrod), and how much of probability there may be for the story we care not to determine, but undoubtedly the name of the lane is both suggestive and instructive.

From "Lancashire Lieutenancy," Cheeth. Soc. Pub., we extract the following: "The money wch was sette downe for Boulton plsh, Deane, &c., either from collecting on the old rate or some mistake, the con^t. throughout the four parishes of Bolton division collected twice the amount of quota required, and paid over to Sir John Byrou ab 13 Feb., 1585, Horwich being thus referred to: 'Thoms Heaton, to be paied to the constable of Heatou, Halliwall ou Horwiche lij. xlx., x. ob.'

From the Shuttleworth Accounts, Che. Soc. Pub., we have the following reference :—

Oct., 1587. Spente in Manchester, when the rente of Horryche was paid, iiij.d.

Sep. 1588. To the Cunstablye of Hallywell a fifteni towards the makinge of souldiares in to Iereland xviij.d.

1591. Nycholas Mather, of Horwaghe, the laste p...ments which he undertooks to paye for Robert Greenshalge, his sonne-in-lawe, vi.L.

1592. For the rentes of Herwaghe, xj.L. v.s. vj.d., whereof was paied to Mr. Lassie (Lacy's) bailiffe, lord of the manor of Manchester, xj.L. v.d., and spente in Manchester iiij.d., soe remanethe of the , iiij.s. viij.d.

1605. To the tenents of Horwige for their expenses for karyege of xlv. loads of the tythe barley at Hulle, from Hulle to Gawthorppe, vis., v. score and fifteene mettes, xv.s. iij.d.

1682. The land was 1s. in the £. In "Gregson's Fragments," our reader will find an extended list. Heaton-cum-Halliwell £0 13s 0d, the usual fifteenth of every tounship within the cevaral hundreds, besides the deductions.

Oxe-lay, when the county has to pay £200, Salford hundred has to pay £23 ; when the county pays £5, Salford hundred pays 10s. 6d. This scale was agreed upon the 8th January, 1583 (25th Eliz.), by Henry, Earl of Derby and a number of J.P.'s of the County Palatine, when Bolton division pay 17s., Horwich, Heaton, and Halliwell pay 1s. The rate for the relief of the maimed soldiers and prisoners in the Marshalsea was settled at a general assize at Lancaster, 2nd April, 1601 (42nd Eliz.), Deane parish (Horwich included) paying 3d. weekly. Finally the county rate was fixed at a general meeting of the county justices, 11th August, 1624 (22nd James), so when Salford hundred pay £100, Horwich, Heaton, and Halliwell pay £1 14s. 1½d.

From "Lancashire Inquisitions" we have the following references to Horwich. "Inquisition taken at Boulton-on-the-Moor, 15 April, (1st James), 1612, after the death of Randle Barton, Esq., Smithells, it is stated that Randle Barton was seized in fee for 12 messuages, 400 acres of land, 80 acres of meadow, 500 acres of pasture, two acres of wood and underwood, 500 acres of moor moss and herbery in Horwich, he being so seized enfeoffed Will Fleetwood, &c. . . . and all those messuages, lands, &c., in Horwich (parcel of the premises in the tenures of William Dekens, Henry Dekens, and Henry Walker) . . The messuages, &c., in Horwich are held of James Anderton, Esq., in socage by fealty and rent of £8 16s. 8d. paid yearly at Michaelmas, and are worth per annum clear £3 6s. 8d." From the above we gather that the proud forest of Horwich was rapidly disappearing, and at the beginning of last century the forest, as such, had disappeared. Upon its ashes arose what might have been considered the beginning of a prosperous industry. In various positions—to which we shall make more extended reference as we proceed—cotton yarns and cotton products were well represented, and a future of commercial activity might have been prophesied for Horwich, but the light of hope was clouded ere the day dawn of the staple industry, and to-day we find the pioneer only sparsely represented in that great wealth-producing power of Lancashire. Why this should be might prove dangerous to conjecture, for in its natural advantages, in its abundant water supply and commercial surroundings, every facility is offered.

Horwich abounds with scenery at once striking, attractive, and romantic—rich in traditional lore. From the latter source we gather that upon the plains o heather stretching in wild beauty betwixt the "Two Lads" and the "Pike," a bloody struggle for supremacy took place in those changing and troublesome times, which marked the infant growth of the nation, and in proof thereof many of those tangible tokens of bye-gone battlefields are said to have been dug up. How far traditionary evidence may be accepted, and with what degree of safety we may trust to its guidance, we are not prepared to say, though we would not altogether discredit the tradition, remembering how much local and national history owes to this source. This much we will venture to say, that the position and surroundings are such as to inspire the thought that more stirring events have occurred here than are chronicled, when from the summit of the "Pike" the beacon fire was answered by the lurid blaze from Ingleborough and Pendle.

For swift to east, and swift to west, the warning radiance spread,
High on St. Michael's Mount it shone—it shone on Beechy Head.

Let us examine the situation, and the relative names given to the more prominent natural characteristics, staying here and there to gather up the lessons so silently, and yet so suggestively given us by the way, and perchance we may be benefited thereby. Perhaps we could not do better than take as our guide that eminent local antiquarian Dorning Rasbotham, "Sept. 12th, 1787, I went this day to visit a remarkable stone, and took with me the landlord of the alehouse at Moorgate (Horwich) as my guide. In this excursion, after having the Winter Lads some time on our left, we proceeded over Winter Hill in which situation was about south-west or north by south. The stone lies upon the declivity of a hill in the township of Turton. It goes by the name of the Hanging, or Giant's Stone. The tradition of the common people is, that it was thrown by a certain giant upon a certain occasion (the nature of which they do not specify) from Winter Hill on the opposite range to this point, and they whimsically fancy that certain little hollows in the stone are the impressions made by the giant's hands at the time he threw it; but I own I could not find out the resemblance which was noticed to me. It appears, however, to have long excited attention, for that it is a heavy, gray, moor stone; a rude mark of a cross, that about 7 inches by 6 inches, appears at a very distant time to have been cut upon it. It is elevated upon another piece of rock, and its greatest length is 14 feet, its depth in the thickest part 5 feet, and its greatest breadth upon the top, which is nearly flat, is about 9 feet. The height of the highest part of it from the ground is about 5 feet 8 inches. A thorough going antiquary would call this a Druidical remain. This stone is about three miles and a quarter north-east by north from Rivington Pike, and something more than three miles north-west of the Winter Lads. The range of hills is in the several townships of Horwich, Halliwell, Sharples, Longworth, Rivington, and Turton, and are of different altitudes. At the Winter Lads the horizon meets your eye above the summit of the building upon Rivington Pike, and upon Winter Hill considerably above the top of the Wilder Lads. In our ancient map part of the range is distinguished by the name of the Egbert Den, and in my walks crossed the remains of a very remarkable trench, to this day known by the name of Dane's Dike. It extends for the length of more than three miles in a straight line, running from the northwest to the north-east. It commences at or about 'Lomax's Wife,' in Halliwell, and is for some space the boundary between Smithell's estate in the township of Sharples, and from hence it reaches to the part of Winter Hill. Near the trench is an eminence which commands a view of its whole extent, and which is called by the people in the neighbourhood 'Counting Hill.' In these hills are mines of coal, particularly at the edge of Hordern, in the township of Sharples, and upon that part of it which belongs to the Smithell's estate, in Halliwell, and in the latter township some inconsiderable slate delphs have been opened, but neither the slate nor the coal appears as yet to have been worked to any considerable advantage. Under the peat in the township of Halliwell was found, a few years ago, marle (yellowish and bluish), which is cut out with the spade as easily as tempered clay may be, and which has produced good crops when it has been used as manure. As I passed over the brook in the valley it gave demonstration of the violence with which the floods after heavy rains came down; the channel was filled with rude fragments of rock, which had tumbled over each on other certain occasions. My guide told me that the water sometimes came down from the eminence above with so much violence as to form a cascade, the noise of which resembled thunder, and under which a person on horseback may ride without receiving any damage." Mr. Rasbotham continues, "To the right of the road from Bolton to Chorley upon the summit of Horwich Moor lie the Wilder Lads, two rude piles of stones, so called from the tradition of the country that they were erected in memory of two boys who were wildered (bewildered) and lost in the snow about this place. They lie about quarter of a mile S.E. by E. from Rivington Pike, and may be distinctly seen for a considerable distance as you pass along the road, from which when at Horwich Chapel they are something more than a mile distant. They are undoubtedly of very high antiquity, and were originally united by a circular mound, about three-quarters of which yet remaineth visible. Their circumference is about 24 feet and a half, and the passage between them about $6\frac{1}{4}$ feet. The remains of the mound are about four feet wide, but upon the east side for a space of 17 feet is entirely levelled. The account and drawing was taken in 1776, but they have been lately raised, I imagine by the proprietor of the common, with the view of their being more distinctly seen from his house."

The two pyramidial cairns that gave the name to the hill called "The Two Lads" have given rise to much conjecture. As to their origin, their object, and the story they would unfold, tradition is at variance, and hypothesis crippled for want of some link by which an investigation might prove probable. Of their antiquity none can question; their object, and the lesson they would teach, is the deepest mystification. One traditional story relates how those two boys, children of good Bishop Pilkington—whose memory is so far forgot today that his heritage for the poor is prostituted and claimed by the rich—were lost in the snow upon this spot, but there is nothing in proof, but rather to the contrary—except the coincidence that the Bishop had two children, both of whom died young. But might we not expect to find, considering the Bishop's character and position, some more extended and other than traditional record of so tragic an occurrence? But a still older tradition, and one that we have elsewhere referred to ("The Two Lads"), exists in the more ancient unwritten history of the village, that here lie the bodies of two children of one of the early Saxon Kings, whose parents died in battle; and when we remember that it was no uncommon custom for the ancients to bury their chiefs, Kings, and great warriors upon some towering elevation, and to mark the spot by some (to us) rude erection, sometimes a cairn of stones, a rude cross, or other symbol, our enquiry opens up a fair field for investigation, and a delightful one for our imagination. This view may be strengthened by the surroundings, which tell of Saxon supremacy, in "Edgar's Den," and the inroads of the Danes in the "Danes' Ditch." The author of the "Pictorial History of Lancashire" says, "Winter Hill, properly enough called on account of its wild appearance, and of its attracting so much cold and so many heavy storms, but it is also designated 'Edgar Hill,' so called from the circumstance of a petty Saxon King of the name of Edgar having hunted upon its sides." By some they are linked with the ancient religion of our country; by others they are viewed as simple land marks in a primitive age, but if the latter were their original purpose, why need there be two in such close proximity, and why such care exercised in their surroundings? But whatever their object, we cannot look upon them other than as connecting links with the far, far past, and be ready to anathematise those ruthless Vandals that have well nigh robbed us of these spiral monuments.

CHAPTER VI.

Few churches have had a more chequered existence than the one at Horwich, and none has risen like the Phœnix from its ashes with more renovated and vigorous vitality. Suffering purifies, and opposition strengthens that which in itself is noble and good. The history of this church is another proof to the many, if others were needed. As we proceed in our investigation our readers will gather sufficient to warrant our first assertion. We will now, as far as possible, trace its early history. In so doing we shall have to confess, notwithstanding every effort to trace the beginning of such history, that much is clouded and obscure, where we might have hoped to find some true guide. Chronological confusion, and a clear disregard of an important trust, are charges fully sustained against those to whom such records were entrusted.

Horwich Church, or rather Horwich Chapel, is known to have existed as early as 1565, for the "Commissioners for Removing Superstitious Ornaments" informed the Bishop of Chester "that they had taken away from Horwych Chappel vestment, albe, alter cloth, corporasse, and other idolatrous gear." Here we have the existence of the chapel clearly proved, but for how long it had existed there is no demonstrative evidence. We incline to the opinion that a much earlier date must be given thereto. The difficulty which ever encircles ecclesiastical questions meets us here. We have seen that Horwich formed the most valuable appendage to the Barony of Manchester, that its importance was duly acknowledged, and due care and provision made for its protection; that within the forest itself were gathered a number of foresters, and within the limits of its authority were the dependants, tenants, and others. At a superstitious age, and considering the polity of church government, and the influence of the clergy,

It would seem to violate history to aver that so large a number should be denied a privilege which we find even less numbers to have enjoyed at that period. The Lord of the Barony, however much he might disregard the physical needs of its dependants, had a superstitious regard for their spiritual wants. We have evidence to prove that in many districts where no spiritual provision was known to have been made, in reality such provision existed. Take the neighbouring village of Anderton, the comparatively recently erected Roman Catholic Chapel was stated to be the first place of worship erected in that truly rural village, but a chapel existed here when Rivington was known by its primeval name of "Raventon," and the "Pike," as "Raven-Pike," and throughout the country we find many names of places still extant that mark to-day an almost solitary spot where once stood a building set apart by the English people to worship God and dwell in peace, long before the ruthless Norman approached our shores. Henry of Huntingdon says of William, "That he caused churches and villages to be destroyed to make habitation for his deer. When, however, the thunders of the church shook even the throne of Kings, yea, when Christianity in its primitive simplicity gradually illumined the whole island, terrified by the anathemas of the church, or moved by the holy zeal which primitive Christianity inspired, every Baron and feudal lord, every petty chieftain or circumscribed King, were ready to bow to the church's decree, and almost every manor had its Solomon ready to build a house in which the Most High might dwell, and at the time of the Norman invasion the clergy had obtained possession of nearly one-third of the country, and in the most agreeable spots, amid shady woods and by silver rivers, had erected their religious houses." The Barons of Manchester, we have seen, were early attracted by the forest at Horwich, and a clergy that had made such an invasion on the land of the country as to own one-third, besides centering in themselves the national wealth, could scarcely fail to pay more than passing attention to so beautiful and yet so quiet and attractive a spot as Horwich. Yes, the very surroundings of the question would suggest an early introduction of the

Christian Church system into a place so favourable and so associated with the past national religion. However violent the change, and however strong the effort may be, there always exists some outward token, some visible sign, to speak of that which went before. The Reformation was a violent effort on the part of the more powerful to destroy the sympathies and eradicate from the minds of the many but less powerful and more yielding all traces of the past religion; but to do this with success required caution, the tendrils of the pre-Reformation period were so intertwined in the habits, sympathy, and growth of the nation that over-drastic measures would have ensured defeat, consequently we find much in common and little in difference betwixt the Church as it was and the Church reformed. It was only by a gradual process, when penalties and sufferings had failed, that the Church really was reformed. Man in all ages has kindred sympathies; there is an hereditary, an unacknowledged but powerful innate disposition that exercises despotic authority in the most democratic aspiration. The sympathies moulded and fashioned in childhood exercise a power in manhood, and society, in its integral parts, is a reflex, an index of society in the aggregate. To have pulled down the proud old structure, where sire and son alike had worshipped, would so far have wounded the susceptibilities of the national temperament as to have defeated the designs and objects of the spiritual marauders, and have rendered their task hopeless. We have already seen that in forest and grove the ancient Druids performed their mystic rites, that upon the Horwich hills are some rude stones which Dorning Rasbotham said "An antiquarian would call Druidical remains," and the Rev. W. Probert declares are rather monumental stones of some Saxon chief or king. We incline to the former, as their present position, considering the ruthless havoc that has defaced and partly destroyed so much of antiquarian interest, can be no safe guide for a true interpretation of their character. But in whatever form we incline to view these interesting relics, whether Druidical or monumental, they yet associate Horwich with the more early history of our country. If we take them as the former we may expect, yea, suggest, that

In the disuse of that Bardic temple another would rise, and in the destruction of the Druidical feasts the light of Christianity would shine. The very disuse would argue that a greater and more powerful agent would be called into existence. Deny as we may, it is utterly impossible for man to exist without religion, in the sense that religion is an act of homage, and any change is merely of object or mode. The existence of these relics in their monumental form, associated with the names given to surrounding characteristics, would be equally suggestive of an early religious history. But where, we may be asked, are any records? We can only answer that if the like conditions produce results exactly similar elsewhere, we safely claim that our argument is sufficiently fortified.

The existence of Druidism in any district would be a sufficient inducement to the enthusiastic missionary to go there and proclaim the simple Gospel plan, and when we remember how early the pioneers of Christianity exercised a power over the Saxon kings, we certainly may venture to suggest that a place so favourable to the hunting proclivities of the early Saxons must be equally early associated with the religious growth of the nation. We have said that the history of the Church has been of the most chequered character. We shall have to refer to a period when its enemies held sway over it, and Horwich Chapel, though ostensibly and legally associated with the Established Church, was virtually a Dissenting meeting house. That with the advent of these daring innovators, who regarded not her traditions, nor reverenced her ceremonies, much that was valuable was so far disregarded or treated as some Popish remnant: that undoubtedly much of that history for which we seek in vain has been for ever swept away. Truly may it be said of Horwich Church at the time of which we write, "My house is a house of prayer, but ye have made it a den of thieves." How much the antiquarian, or he who would unlock History's hidden page, may deplore the period when England had no king and religion was only a holy riot, let the archives of many of our old churches declare, and perhaps none with clearer and more convincing evidence than the one at Horwich. As we proceed we shall have still further to refer to this period.

In one of the Cheetham Society's Publications we find the following reference : " Horwich Chap. to Deane 4 myles distant ; Chapp. Val, nos maintainance but the benevolence of the inhabitants, a donation of £100, the profitts of it detained. Incumbent Henry Pendlebury, a painfull, godly preacher." Dr. Calamy says : " Henry Pendlebury, M.A., preached his first sermon in 1649, and continued there some time as probationer. He was set apart Oct. 2nd to the office of minister at Turton Chapel, after passing the probationary exercises before the second classics in Lancashire, who met ordinarily at Bury. He afterwards preached some time at Horwich Chappel, and then in 1651 removed to Holcombe, where he diligently applied h mself to his stu jies, from whence he was ejected in 1662. He died in 1695, aged 70 years." Another account says that he was instituted at Turton Chapel before several local divines, including the vicar and curate of Bolton, and his first appointment was to Horwich Chapel, where he remained 12 months, and was afterwards transferred to Holcombe Chapel, and afterwards removed to near Rochdale. When there he wrote a book called " The Barren Fig Tree," or a practical exposition of the Parable, Luke 13 chap., 6—9 verses inclusive. The book was printed in London in 1700. A copy is now in possession of Mr. J. C. Scholes, Newport-street, Bolton. The preface is not written by the author, " but by thy true friend and soul's well-wisher, G. S.," and embraces 183 pages. Other works are also by the same author, a list of which Calamy gives in a foot-note. From the " Lancashire Survey, Cheetham Society Publications " we find the following very suggestive reference :—" Horwich : certif(ied) by (the) vicar of Dean y^t there is about 9^l p(er) an(num) belong(ing) to this chap(el), being y^e interest of 190^l called chap(el) stock, but y^e trustees for this money being Dissenters they refuse to give an account of it, or to pay y$_e$ curate there." From the " Record Society Publications, Lancashire Survey, 1650," we extract the following :— " And wee doe likewise find and p'sent that their is two Chappells wthin the said pish of Deane, that is to

witt Horwich and Westhoughton, and that the said
chappell of Horwich is distant from the said Plsh
Church of Deane foure statute myles or thereaboutes,
wch chappell is supplyed every Saboth ordinarylie by
Mr. Henry Pendlebury, who is a painfull godly
preachinge minister, who hath not for the present any
mainteynance or sallery, but onely the benevolence of
the inhabitants of the said towne, but is to receive
twenty pounds p'ann out of the tythes wthin the plsh of
Deane, now received by Mr. John Tildesley p'sent incumbent of Deane, and that there was a donation of
the some of one hundred, heretofore given by the will
affected of that chapelrey (for the see of the same was is
in the hands of Richard Holt of Ashworth, who hath
detyned the same, and the issue and profitts thereof for
the space of five or sixe yeares last past or thereabouts),
and that Ellis Brook, Willm Greenehalgh, and John
Greenehalgh, whose names the bond for the pa'ment of
the same and interest therefrom the said Mr. Holt was
taken in—are in suite at p'sent for the same; And wee
thinke fit that the said chappell should bee made a
pishe, in regard it is foure myles distant from its plsh
church, and to have belongine vnto it about a third
pte of Heaton, and all the bamell of Lostock, together
wi Peter Roscoes, and Willm Holdens wthin Hallywell,
and Mr. Anderton, of Anderton, Roger Rothwells and
Willm Rothwells of the same lying neare therevnto to
be affixed and Joyned vnto the same." For the following further information we are indebted to "Cheetham
Society, Lancashire Survey" for the same date:—" It
was found in 1650 that Mr. Anderton of Lostock, then
sequestered for his delinquency, was impropriator of
the tithes of Deane, which were then paid annually to
Mr. John Tildesley (vicar of Deane) a painfull preaching minister." The tithes amounted to £154 3s. 8d.,
the proportion to the minister at Horwich being £20.

As to who was minister at Horwich Chapel when the
"Act of Uniformity" came into operation in 1662 there
is some doubt. Baines without question places the Rev.
James Walton as the ejected minister. Dr. Calamy,
in his biographical sketches, says:—" Mr. James
Walton. It is certain he was sometime minister at this
chapel, which is in Dean Parish, but it is doubtful

whether he was ejected here or at Shaw Chapel near Oldham. He was provided with no subsistence when ejected, and had several children. He was a laborious, faithful minister." Through the kindness and courtesy of the Rev. Henry Septimus Pigot, M.A., the present highly esteemed vicar, we have had every opportunity and facility given for the examination of the old church registers, &c., which as we proceed we shall lay before our readers; and here we would acknowledge the kind aid and assistance given us by Mr. Samuel Bentley, the courteous sexton. From one of these registers we extract the following notice, bearing date Nov. 9th, 1699 :—
" Wheras ther was a difference betwixt some of the inhabitants in the town of Horwich consernin the seats and forms in the Chappell, it is generally concluded and agreed upon AT A PUBLIC Meetin of the Inhabitants, that every person may have his seat set out by ye inhabitants according to his Paidable Rent in the year of our Lord God, 1699. V F."

Sir Charles Anderton, Bart., the High New Gate Farm, on the south side.

Methawe Highefton, on ye north side
James Hilton 2 form (two forms) sun side.
Thos Anderton, 2 form north side.
Augustus Green'ugh, 3 form sun side.
Lord Willowby, 3 form on ye north side.
Hugh Witle, Reb Pill, 4 sun side.
George Marsh, 4 north side.
Thos. Nightingale, nine on sun side.
Thos. Rothwell, 5 north side.
John Greenough, Bird Man, 6 sun side.
Will. Makinson, 6 north side.
Whittle Lowerhouse, 7 sun side.
Peter Gorton, 7 north side.
Richard Pilkington, 8 sun side.
Augustus Greenough, 8 north side.
Peter Boardman, 9 sun side.
John Knowles, 9 north side.
Will Jonson, 10 sun side.
Henry Walker, 10 north side.
Peter Longworth and Wilson, 11 sun side.
Hunts and Horrocks, 11 north side.
Thos. Knowles, 12 sun side.
Oliver and John Greenough, 13 sun side.
Nathan Markland, 13 sun side.
Rob. Pendlebury, 13 north side.

Adam Hodgkinson, 14 sun side.
Thos. Thomason, 15 sun side.
Boowls Bank, 15, north side.
Thomas Roscoe, 16 sun side.

Concluded and Agreed by us whose names are heare under subscribed—Thomas Briggs, — Hunt, Samll. Chesham, Rtch. Hattonble, James Hilton, Tho. Anderton, Augustus Greenough, his letters, Hugh Whittle, Peter Hampson." To give a list of the clergy at Horwich Church with any degree of exactitude in regard to the more early would be a matter of difficulty. The church records are silent, and the Rev. John Norcross is the first name to be found in the old registers. That for a lengthened period Horwich was devoid of any fixed ministry seems highly probable, and the "supplies" which administered the ordinances of the church were perhaps of so changing a character as to preclude any idea of that "decency and order" prescribed by apostolic injunction. We, however, venture to give our readers the following list, which in in its incomplete form we think may be accepted, our authority being the Precope MSS., &c. :—

CLERGY AT HORWICH.

Oct. 1621. Edward Tempest.
1650. Henry Pendlebury.
1682. James Walton.
Dec. 1731. Robert Harvey.
1749. John Norcross.
1788. Samuel Johnson, ob. 19 Mar., 1826.
1828. David Hewitt.
1853. Henry Septimus Pigot, M.A.

CHAPTER VII.

The Rev. Richard Hatton, whose name appears as one of the signatures to the arrangement of the seats in Horwich Chapel, was then vicar of the mother church at Deane, and evidently connived at the irregular proceedings which existed at Horwich. This will be more readily perceived from the following letter from his successor :—"Bolton, Sep. 22st, 1717.—Rev. Sir,— I thought it necessary to send you ye following account of Horwich Chappel, which I desire you to transmit to my Lord Bishop of Chester, and ye revenue belonging to it is commonly said to be about £9 or £10 per annum, being ye interest of about £200 belonging to it, and for a full proof ys I here give my following testimony. But in the first place it may be convenient to acquaint you yt ys chappel has for ye 20 years last been in the hands of ye Dissenters, thro' ye contrivance of ye late Lord Wiloughby and ye connivance of my predecessor (Richard Hatton) appointed vicar 1673, who refused to renounce the covenant, but was nevertheless instituted by Bishop Pearson. But when my Lord Bp of Chester was upon his visitation at Manchester I acquainted his Lordship with ys matter, and his Lordship commanded me to give Mr. Walker, ye Dissenting teacher, notice to desist, which accordingly I did, and he submitted to his Lordship y's commands. Immediately after this I put into ye chappel a Conformable clergyman, who has supplyed ye Cure ever since, wch is above one whole year, and tho' I gave him ye surplice dues of ye chappelry, wch is all yt belongs to me in yt part of ye Parish, and two pounds per annum besides, yet ye with his contributions, wch is all yt he has to subsist on thus far, has not exceeded £14. And when ye demanded ye interest of ye Chappel Stock during ye time of his incumbency, the trustees for ye money being Dissenters, tell him they will not pay it, till they be forced to do it. Now one of these trustees has told me and several

others yt ye Chappel Stock is one hundred and ninety
pounds, and about two months ago he shewed me some
ends yt was made unto him upon ye account to ye
sum of about £80. And there are several living Witnesses yt can and do testify yt ye interest of ye said
Chappel Stock was paid to Episcopal Conforming
Clergymen yt officiated at Horwich Chappel during ye
reigns of Charles ye 2nd and King James ye 2nd and
till some time after ye Revolution ; and though this, as
its said, was given to all intents and purposes towards
maintaining a curate yt should supply ye said Chappel,
yet both against justice and honesty these Trustees
have sent me word yt they will build a Meeting-house
with part of yt money and apply ye remaining part
towards supporting a Presbyterian Teacher ; wt now is
to be done in ye affair. I humbly desire my Lord
Bishop of Chester's opinion and direction with your
own, who am your most humble and most obedient servant, J. Rothwell. For Rev. Dr. Wroe, warden of
Manchester." (*Noticia Cestorensis*, vol. ii., page 42.)

It will be sufficient here to remark—as we shall have
to refer more copiously to the Willoughby family—that
doubtless the Lord Willoughby above referred to was
the Sir Thomas Willoughby who was erroneously sum-
moned to the House of Lords as Baron Willoughby of
Parham, and who, having married Eleanor, daughter
of Hugh Whittle, of Horwich, of stern Puritan proclivities, embraced the religious opinions of the Whittle
family. The title was ill supported by several Presbyterian Lord Willoughbys, who alone possessed the title
without the estate. The Hugh Whittle referred to
appears to have held a more than ordinary prominent
position in the village, his Presbyterian leanings making
making him an enemy to the Episcopal Church. In
1685 he held the position and office of overseer for the
poor ; and in 1734 another Hugh Whittle, probably son
of the above, is returned as able to serve the office of
constable and churchwarden. In the above some explanation may perhaps be given of the " Hugh Wittle,
Reb Pill," given in our last, which, considering the
obstinacy with which he held his views, he would undoubtedly be looked upon as a " Rebel" to ecclesiastical

authority. At this period the church at Horwich was virtually in possession of men whose surroundings were detrimental to the interest of the church. In the life of the Rev. Oliver Heywood, the Nonconformist divine, we have the following:—" Mary, his sister, married Nicholas Hunt, of Horwich. She died in 1648, leaving only one daughter, Esther, who married Jas. Worsley, of Rivington," the divine thus writing,, " Mary Heywood, my father's second daughter, married to Nicholas Hunt, in Horwich, in Dean parish. A precious, gracious Christian, that spent much time in prayer, very discreet, humble, peaceable, useful, left one daughter Esther Hunt, my brother Nath, and I were tabled there when we went to schoole to Mr. Rudall. She was a handsome, proper woman, something pock hold, but comely, adorned with many inward graces. She died when I was at Cambridg as I remember in the year 1648. Nicholas Hunt, of Harwloh, in dean parish, that married my sister, married again, had by the latter wife six or seven sons; an orderly man in his conversation, and I hope truly religious, lived in widowhood several yeares after his second-wife's death, his daughter Esther Hunt keeping house for him — my sister's daughter. He died about feb. 2, 1673." The divine must be wrong in the date given, as in the registers under date of 1674 we have buried " Nicholas Hunte, of Horwich, Jany. 25th. Space denies any further reference to the position of the church at this period, only to just refer to the fact that in the unwritten history of the village this perversion of church property and alienation therefrom it is most pointedly referred to. Nonconformity was once a power supported by the influence and aid of the more influential, and Horwich Church was possessed of little power and opportunity for good.

The first register in the church bears date 1660, but judging from an old gravestone in the church yard—bearing date 1648—it may be presumed that some of an earlier date are wanting. Considering the chequered history of the church, this irregularity may perhaps be accounted for. During the confusion consequent on the civil war in the reign of Charles the First, in the blind bigotry of Puritanical fanaticism much that was valuable in our churches was swept away, and perhaps the fact that Horwich registers begin in the year of the restoration may be both suggestive and demonstrative. We have already seen that Horwich existed prior to the Reformation, and considering the enactments made and ordered by statute and otherwise for the due keeping of parish registers, we can scarcely form the conclusion that those at present extant are the first and only registers. Obviously a graveyard surrounded the old church, yea the oldest church, and the rights of sepulture early given and registers doubtless duly kept, the first legal institution of parish registers being in 1501, King Henry VII. King Henry VIII. made the first use of his spiritual functions by issuing an injunction relative to the due keeping of church registers, an injunction more especially enforced by his son, Edward VI., in 1547. Ecclesiastical visitors were appointed to enforce obedience to the due keeping of the said registers, the following injunction guiding them in the exercise of their duties:—"Also that the parson, vicar, curate, and parishioners of every parish within this realm, shall, in their churches and chappells, kepe one booke or regester wherein they shall write the daye and yere of everye wedding, christening, and burial made in their parishe for their tyme, and so every man succeeding them likewise, and also therein shall write every parsone's name that shall be wedded, Christened, or burial; and for the saufe keeping of the same booke, the parishe shall be bound to provide of their common charges, one sure coffer with two locks and keyes, whereof th' one to remain with the parson, vicar, or curate, and th' other with the wardeynes of every parishe, churche, or chappell wherein the said booke shall be laide up, whiche booke they shall every Sunday take furthe, and in the presence of the said wardeynes, or one of them, write and recorde in the same all the weddings, Christenynge, and burialles made the hole weeks before, and that done, to lay up the booke in the said coffer as afore; and for every tyme that the same shall be omitted, the partye that shall be in the fault thereof shall forfait to the said churche iijs. iiijd. (3s. 4d.), to be employed to the poor men's box of that parishe." Considering the provision which was thus

made for the due care and preserving of the parish
documents and register, we can scarcely conceive that
Horwich would be devoid of some such provision, or
rather a complete disregard of legal requirements. The
carelessness which mark the early registers, their present tattered, torn, and shredy appearance, the plain
and obvious mutilations, whole pages and parts having
disappeared, would give them the appearance of a kind
of salvage belonging to a more valuable, because to a
more ancient, wreck. At present they are guarded
and protected with that care which their worth
demands, but doubtless the copy which now we present
to our readers will be the only one that their rapidly
decaying pages will allow to be taken. There are two
small books, and judging from the dates given, it would
appear that both were in use at the same period, and
we shall give them exactly as they are, with their
defects and omissions :—

HORWICH CHURCH REGISTER.—Book No. 1).

Baptised in the year of our Lord 1660.

William Gorton, the son of Gyles Gorton, of Horwich
month obit

Robert Yeatts, the son Robert Yeatts, of Horwich, October
the 6th

— Hunt, the son of Nicolas Hunt, of Horwich, feb. the 27th

No baptism recorded in 1661.

Baptised Anno ye Dom 1662.

William Hart, ye sonne Richard Hart, month obit
(Three more on this page and date obliterated.)

Buried in the yeare 1662.

Esther Greenhalgh was buried ye 26th D o.
John Hodkinson was buried y* 5th day of April
William Turner was buried ye 4th day of January
James Makinson of Horwich, was buried ye 20th of March
Mary Greenhalgh, ye daugnte: of James Greenhalgh,
month obit
Annie Walkden, widdowe, was buried ye 5th, obit
Stillborne child of Benjamen Hunt, febar., obit

Buried in ye yeare 1664.

Ellen Longworth ye daughter of Joshua Longworth, month
obit
— Horrocks, of Horwich, was buried, daughter of Joshua
Longworth
Another, of Horwich, obit

Baptised in ye yeare 1

Anne Knowles, ye daughter of John Knowles, March ye 22
Oliver Greenhalgh, ye son of James Greenhalgh, Aprill ye 19th
Alice Walkden, ye daughter of John Walkden, July ye 9th
Jonathan Harte, ye son of Richard Harte, October ye 26th
Abigall Knowles, daughter of John Knowles, was baptised ye 12th day of the month of May, in the yeare of our Lord 16—

Baptised in the yeare of our Lord 1672.

John Hodkinson, son of Adam Hodkinson, of Horwich, July 28th
Ralphe Walkden, ye son of John Walkden, of Horwich, and ye daughter of William Hodson Lostock, September —
Peter Thornley, ye son of Richard Thornley, of Horwich, and Alice, daughter of Robert Heighe, of Horwich, was baptised November ye 17th
Ellen, ye daughter of William Makinson, ye Taylors, December ye 15th
Mary, ye daughter of William Cross, of Walker fould, ffebruary ye 23
Mary, daughter of Martin Greenhalgh, of Borwich, March ye 9th

Baptized in ye yeare 1673.

Elizabeth, ye daughter of William Greenhalgh, of Horwich, and
Elisabeth, daughter of William Bene, of And-ton, March ye 30
— daughter of James Hoodbin, of Rivington, April —th
— of Elizabeth Thornley, of Horwich, April —th
— of James Harte, of Lostock, Ju'y ye 6th

Buried in the yeare 1672.

Augustuse Greenhalghe, of Horwich, was buried April the 25th
William Harte, of Horwich, was buried August the 22
Regnaild Greenhalgh, of Aspull, was buried September ye 22
Thomas Grenhalgh, of Horwich, commenly called Tho. Roberts, April ye 3
Thomas Horrockes, of Horwich, November the 8th
Peter Boardman, of Horwich, December the 23rd
Katherine, the daughter of John Knowles, of Horwich, ffebuary ye 5th

Buried in the yeare 1673.

Mary, the wife of Myles Aspinall, of Horwich, Aprill the 7th
E'lzabeth, the daughter of Robert Yeatts, of Horwich, Aprill ye 18th

Robert Yeatts, of Horwich, was buried May the 23rd
—Wife of Thomas Horrocks, May the 23rd
— ,,   William Greenhalgh, of Horwich, August —th
— ,,   John Walkden, of Horwich, August the 9—
Another, obit

(In back of the above page in reg. is the following, and
obviously by a later hand.)

John Knowles, the son of John Knowles, of Horwich, was
   baptized October the 4th, 1678
Peter Knowle, the son of John Knowles, of Herwich, was
   borne July 29, Anno Domino 1681
Johnathan Knowles
Margaret Knowles, the daughter of John Knowles, was born
   January 2, 1675, and was baptized January 9, Anne
   Domino 1675
Peter Knowles, was baptized July 30, Anno Domino 1681
Johnathan Knowles was born September 28, and baptized
   October ye 4, 1678
                              JOHNATHAN KNOWLES, Hand.

Buried in the years 1674.

Katherine, daughter of John Walkden, of Horwich —
William Whittle, the son of Thurston Whittle, of Horwich
Ellen Thompson, of Horwich, July the 13th
Mary, the daughter of Thomas Thomason, of Horwich —
Marjery Greenhalgh, commonly called Madge of Horwich,
   who was both deafe and dumbe ——— about 70 yeares
   old, she was buried Aug. the 17th
William Cross, of Walker-fould, in Horwich —
Dorothy, ye wife of Doctor Harte, of Horwich, November
   ye —
John Harte, the son of Jane Harte, of Horwich, November —
Nicholas Hunts, of Horwich, January the 25th
(Two more on this page obliterated. A large number of
   leaves obviously cut away from this book.)

CHAPTER VIII.

REGISTER BOOK, No. 2.

Elizabeth Bromley was baptised November the 11th, 1663.
Ellen Knowles, ye daughter of John Knowles, September ye 28th, 1663.

BAPTIZED ANNO YE DOM., 1664.

Mary Sharples, ye daughter of Ralph Sharples, Aprill ye 3rd, 1664.

Abraham Gill, ye sonne of Robert Gill, March the 27th, 1664.

Mary Makinson, ye daughter of William Makinson, May ye 20th, 1664.

Ellen Hindley, ye daughter of Robert Hindley, of Westhoughton, May ye 22nd, 1664.

Elizabeth Meow, ye daughter of —— Meow, was baptised June ——, 1664.

Anne Walkden, ye daughter of Peter Walkden, September ye ——, 1664.

Anne Wetherby, ye daughter of John Wetherby, December ye five, 1664.

BURIALS.

Humphrey Walkden was buried April ye 19th, 1665.

Dorothy Hodgkinson, ye daughter of Henry Hodgkinson. —1665.

Elizabeth Greenhalgh, of Horwich, who was commonly called Bessie Roberts, was buried August the 24th, anno ye dom, 1667

Old Henry Hodgkinson, of Horwich, was buried ye 19th of ye month of ffebruary, anno ye d:m, 1667.

James Pendlebury, of Horwich, was buried April ye 30th.

Ellen, ye wife of Nicholas Hunt, of Horwich, was buried June ye ——.

Esther Pendlebury, of Horwich, was buried August ye 21st, 187—.

John Whittle, ye son of Thurstan Whittle, of Horwich was buried ——.

Old Robert Hunt, of Horwich, was buried May 15th.

Anne Morris, of Horwich, widdow, was buried ——

—— daughter of Martin Greenhalgh, ffebruary ye 6th, ——

Katherine Knowles, ye daughter of John Knowles, of Horwich, was baptized ye 21st day of May, 1671.

Thomas Dittonson, ye son of John Dittonson, of Horwich, was born and baptised ye 20 day of July, Anno ye Dom, 1671.

Mary, ye wife of Richard Pilkington, of Horwich, dyed of child beareing ffebruary ye 22nd, and buried ffebruary ye 23rd 167—.

Thomas Thompson, of Horwich, on Wednesday, March ye ——.

—— son of John Dittonson, of Horwich, on Wednesday, ——.

BAPTIZED IN YE YEARE 1674.

Elizabeth, ye daughter of Robert Pendlebury, of Horwich, on Wednesday, March ——.

William, ye son of Thomas Roscow, of Horwich, Aprill ye 5th ——.

Mary, ye daughter of Adam Hodgkinson, on Sunday, October ye 2nd ——.

Mary, ye daughter of Robert Highs, of Horwich, ffebruary ye 7th ——.

—— son of William Greenhalgh, of Horwich, March ——.

——, son of John Knowles of Horwich, March the 14th ——

BURIED 1673.

—— Hunt, of Horwich, the daughter of Nicholas Hunt, of Horwich, who was born in the month of June anno ye dom, shee was buried March ye 17th, 1673, beinge aged 68 yeare.

Elizabeth, the wife of Robert Pendlebury, of Horwich, daughter of Adam Schoulcroft, of Horwich, dyed of childbearing, Sunday, March the 22nd, and was buried on Tuesday, March ye 24th.

—— ye son of Nicholas Hunt, of Horwich, died ——

Robert Brown, in Hindley, on Monday, June ye 7th, was brought and buried att Horwich Chappell, June ye 8th ——.

Thomas Gorton, of Horwich, was buried June ye 17th ——.

Margaret Hindley, of Horwich, was buried December the 10th ——.

John Walkden, of Horwich, was buried December the 11th ——.

Ellen Longworth, of Horwich, was buried December the 16th ——

Robert Greenhalgh, of Horwich, was buried March the first, 1675.

Dorothy Greenhalgh, of Horwich, was buried Sept.——

William Greenhalgh was buried ye 29th June ——

Hen—Ainsworth was buried ye 25th July, 1677.

Hen—Thornley was buried the 3rd September, 1677.

Mary Lowe, ye wife of Thomas, was buried ye 13th October, 1677.

Dorothy Seddon buried ye 17th day of January, 1677.

Mary, the daughter of Samuel Hart, baptised January the 23rd, 1680.
—— the son of Thomas Simith —— baptised feb. the 6th, 1680.
David, the son of Nicholas —Baptised Feberary the 10th, 1680.
Robert Leigh, the sonne of Peter Leigh, baptised 12th date of December, 1681.
Margery, the daughter of Ralph Lalend, baptised the 12th date of December, 168L
——November 26th, Henry Scofield, son of Ellis Scofield, was baptised 1681.
Johnathan Wakdin, the son of Peeter Wakdin, babtised Feberary the 8th, 1681.
Robert, the sonne of Jonathan Markland, baptised on Tuesday, 17th October, 1681.
——Yate, the sonne of Richard Yate, baptised the 17th March ——
John Hodskinson, sonne of Henry Hodskinson, baptised April ——
Elisabeth, daughter of William Greenbalgh, att Hoome, baptised April —
Hannah, daughter of William Makinson, baptised August 5th, 1688.
Mary, the daughter of Hugh Whittle, baptised August 9th, 1688.
William Pendlebury, the son of John Pendlebury, baptised the 21st of April.
Elizabeth Bromelly was baptised April the 28th——
Nathenal, the son of Nathenal Knowles, in Horrigh, was baptised 1 day of May, 1670.
—— the daughter of William Makinson was baptised the 4th day of May, 1490.
Elizabeth, the daughter of James Aspeinall, in Horrigh was baptised the 6th day of July, 1680.

The parchment we have before us is the original faculty for taking down the first chapel and erecting the second, which, through the courtesy of Mr. John Longworth, "The Knowles," and chairman of the local board, we are permitted to give our readers. The parchment itself is a valuable relic, duly prized by Mr. Longworth, and is as follows :—

"Beilby, by Divine permission Lord Bishop of Chester, to all Christian people to whom these presents may come, or in anywise appertain, greeting. Whereas, we did by a certain instrument in writing, under the

seal of the office of our then Vicar General and Official
Principal, bearing date the eighteenth of June, in the
year of our Lord one thousand, seven hundred, and
seventy-nine, grant a commission of authority to the
Reverend Robert Latham, clerk, Vicar of Dean, in the
County of Lancaster and diocese of Chester; the
Reverend John Norcross, clerk, Curate of Horwich,
within the parish of Dean, aforesaid; Richard
Pilkington, the elder gentleman; Thomas Greenhalgh
(since deceased), Robert Etough, William Longworth,
and Robert Greenhalgh, yeomen; and Hugh Whittle,
husbandman, owners of estates within the chapelry of
Horwich aforesaid, who were thereby appointed commissioners to take down the old Chapel of Horwich
aforesaid, and the seats, stalls, and pews therein,
and in the room thereof, and on the part
of the yard belonging to the said chapel, to erect
and build a large and more handsome and convenient
chapel, to contain in length, from east to west, twenty-
two yards, and in breadth, from north to south, twelve
yards or thereabouts, and to erect galleries on the north
and south sides, and at the west end of the said new
and intended chapel, with seats or pews therein, and
to allot, appropriate, and dispose of the seats and pews
built on the ground below and in the gallery, in a fair
and equitable manner, first to such who were possessors
and proprietors of seats in the old chapel, in lieu and
full compensation of the seats they were possessed of
therein, and to dispose of all other additional seats
gained by reconstructing and enlarging of the said
chapel, and the uniformity of the seats therein as are on
the ground below, as in the gallery above, to such of the
inhabitants of the said chapelry and others frequenting
Divine service in the said chapel as stood in need thereof and would purchase the same at the best prices that
would be given for them. And also to enlarge the said
chapel-yard by taking in part of a field at the east end
thereof belonging to Henry Blundell, Esquire, and by
and with his approbation and consent, to contain in
length ten yards, and breadth eight yards or thereabouts. Willingly and requiring the said Commissioners, as soon as they should have fully executed
the said Commission, to return to us our Vicar General,

or other competent judge, a full certificate thereof together with a scheme or chart of the seats and pews built and set up in the said new erected chapel, and of their allotment, ordering, and disposition of the same, in order to our future appropriation and confirmation thereof. And whereas the aforesaid Reverend Robert Latham, clerk; the Rev. John Norcross, clerk; Robert Etough, William Longworth, Robert Greenhalgh, and Hugh Whittle, six of the survivors of the said commission, have by a certain writing under their hands bearing date in the year of our Lord one thousand seven hundred and eighty-two, duly certified to us that the said chapel hath been by them accordingly rebuilt with pews and seats therein, and that divine service is performed therein, and that they had according to the best of their skill and judgment, and to every information they could procure, allotted, appropriated, and disposed of the seats and pews in the said chapel to and amongst such persons as are mentioned in a certain schedule on their part, exhibited and deposited in our Consistory Court, who were legally entitled thereunto; and have also returned unto us a scheme or chart of the seats and pews built and set up in the said chapel, and also by the enlargement of the said chapel yard, agreeable to the dimensions aforesaid, and have certified to us that they had not as yet erected any galleries in the chapel, but have besought us to approve and confirm the allotment and disposition which they have already made. And whereas the Reverend and Worshipfull John Briggs, clerk, and Master of Arts, our vicar-general and official principal, lawfully constituted right lawfully and judicially proceeding, did enter a general citation or edict, and cause the same together with the schedule of disposition aforesaid, to be duly published in time of Divine Service in the Consecrated Chapel of Horwich aforesaid, upon Sunday, the first day of September last, thereby citing all manner of persons in general having or pretending to have any right or title to or interest in the said chapel, or the seats and pews therein, or in the said chapel yard as the same is now enclosed, to appear before our said Vicar General and official principal his surrogate, or other deputy judge in that behalf, in the Consistory Court within the Cathedral Church of Chester, upon Thursday, the fifth day of November aforesaid, at the hour of hearing causes there, and produce reasonable and lawful cause why the allotment, appropriation, and disposition of the said seats and pews in the said scheme or chart, and particularly described in the schedule aforesaid to the said estates annexed, should not be confirmed to the inhabitants of the said chapelry therein mentioned for the purpose of standing, sitting, preaching, or hearing Divine Service and sermons therein on Sundays and holidays, and shall at all opportune times, all others excluded without their leave has been obtained, at the instance and promotion of the said Reverend Robert Latham, Reverend John Norcross, Robert Clough, William Longworth, Robert Greenhalgh, and Hugh Whittle, intimating to all persons so cited as aforesaid, that if they did not appear at the time and place aforesaid, or appearing did not show a reasonable and lawful cause as aforesaid to the contrary to our vicar general, and official aforesaid, his lawful surrogate or other competent judge in their behalf, would proceed to approve of and confirm the allotment, appropriation, or disposition of the seats and pews to the several and respective persons mentioned in the said schedule for the purposes aforesaid, and likewise to conform the said chapel-yard, so enlarged, to the inhabitants of the said chapelry. And, whereas, upon return of the general citation or edict or prænonization of all persons there judicially made, no person appearing to show cause to the contrary, the Reverend Robert Vanburgh, clerk, and Master of Arts, lawful surrogate of vicar general, and official principal aforesaid, rightly, lawfully, and judicially proceeding at the petition of the proctor of the said Robert Latham, John Norcross, Robert Etough, William Longworth, Robert Greenhalgh, and Hugh Whittle, did approve of the allotment, appropriation, and disposition aforesaid therein alloted, appropriated, and disposed, and did also decree the aforesaid chapel-yard, as it is enlarged, inclosed, and described in the said scheme or chart now remaining in the public Episcopal registry of our diocese, to be confirmed to and for the use of the inhabitants of the said chapelry, as by the Act of

Court in their behalf, made on Thursday, the 5th of November last, reference thereunto being had may appear. Know ye, therefore, that we, the said Beilby, Lord Bishop of Chester, have approved of and confirmed, and by these presents do approve of and confirm, the aforesaid new erection, and the allotment, appropriation, and disposition of the seats, pews, and sitting places built and set up, and as they are numbered and described in the schedule hereunto annexed, and described in the scheme or chart aforesaid, unto and to the use of the inhabitants of the said chapel, viz, for the purpose of burying the dead therein, and do also (as far as in us lies), and by law we now confirm the respective seats, pews, and sitting places within the said chapel to the several persons mentioned in the schedule and scheme or chart aforesaid, to whom they thereby appear to have allotted, appropriated, and disposed of to and for uses of standing, sitting, kneeling or hearing divine service and sermons therein, on Sundays and holidays, and at all other opportune times by themselves, their families, and tenants, so long as they shall continue to resort to divine service in the said chapel, all others excluded without their leave first had and obtained, and the ordinary right and jurisdiction of us and all our successors in all the seats, pews, and sitting places within the said chapel, and also in the yard of the said chapel being always hereafter saved and reserved. In testimony whereof we have caused these letters testimonial to be made, and the seal of the office of our vicar general and official principal aforesaid, which we use in this behalf to be put hereto. Given at Chester, the eighth day of May, in the year of our Lord one thousand seven hundred (the remaining portion of the year has been cut from the parchment). This agrees with the decree of court.

     HUGH SPEED, Deputy Registrar.

CHAPTER IX.

Annexed to the faculty we have an account of the distribution of the seats, to what lands they belong, who the owners of the land are, and the names of the tenants or occupiers, with the number of seats belonging to each as allotted and appointed by the Commissioners under a faculty 1782.

No.	Lands.	Owners.	Tenants or Occupiers.	Sittings.
1	Roscoe's...... Greenough's	Hy. Blundell, Esq............ Mr.Greenough	Gabriel Pilkington................4 Wm.Butterw'rth	2 to the isle
2	Part of Mak-insons	Mr.Thos.Scott	Jas. Grandy	2 to the wall
3	Hodgkinsn's	Rev. H Offley Wright......	Jno. Hodgkinson..4 Jno. Hopwood...4	
4	Knowles's...	Mr. R. Pilking-ton	Jno. Turner	2 to the isle
5	Walker Fold	Miss Byrom...	James Scolfield	2 to the west
6	Wilson Fold	Hy. Blundell...	Wm. Kirkman, 4 P. Eause, and J Longworth...4	
7	Dakins's......	Robert Etough	Robt. Tong, &c..4	
8	Pendl'bury's	H. Blund'll, Esq	Robt. Pendl'bury4	
9	Whittle's ... Makinson's...	Rev. H. Offley Wright...... Evan Makins'n	Mr. Peter Gorton Robt. Pendl'bury	2 to the isle 2 to the wall
10 11	Boardman's	Mrs.Wright ...	Thos. Scolfield ...8	part by p'chase
12	Markland's..	Richard Mason	Richard Mason...4	
13	Gill's, Whit-tle's, and Stook's	Hy. Blundell...	Robert Etough...2 to isle and west Hugh Whittle ...2 to wall and west R. D. Pilkington, & Jno. Clough. 2 to isle and east H. Makinson......2 „ „	
14	Horrocks's, Peak's & Knuston Rev. H.	Jane Mersden Jno. Knowles & Jas. Lomax Offley Wright	Thos. Kershaw...2 to isle and west Jas. Turner and Jas. Smith......2 to wall & west Rd. Bromilow & J. Kershaw......4 to the east	
15	Makinson's. Markland's.	Boardman......... John Mason......	Wm. Longworth4 to the west John Mason......4 to the east	

No.	Lands.	Owners.	Tenants or Occupiers.	Sittings.
16	Lost'ok Hall	Hy. Blundell, Esq	J. Shaw & others	6
17	Wallsuch	Hy. Blundell, Esq	Mr. T. Ridgway.	4 west, by p'chase
		Mr. T. Ridgway	Mr. T. Ridgway.	4
18	Horwich Ch'ple l'nd	The Curate of Horwich	Rd. Worthingt'n	8
19		Mr. R. Greenhalgh		4, by p'chase
20		Wm. Longworth		4 "
21		Robt. Pendlebury		4 "
22		Hugh Whittle		4 "
23		Harry Stones		4 "
24		Jas. Scowcroft		4 "
25		Widow Worth'gton		4 "
26		Robt. Sharples		4 "
27		Mr. Thos. Ridgway		4 "
28 / 31		The Singers		1 "
32	Schol's B'nk	Rev. H. Offley Wright	Mary Stones	4 "
33	R. Bro'nlow			4, by p'chase
34	Jno. Clough			4 "
35	Greenhal'h's	Mr. T. Nuttall	Mr. Jas. Eckersley.	4
36	Part of late Bolton Peel Chapel Lands	Mr. R. Pilkin'ton Peel Chapel		1 isle 3 to wall
37	Walker F'ld	Wm. L'ngworth	Wm. Longworth.	4
38	Pilkington's and Knowles's	H. Blundell, Esq.	Mr. Rd. Pilkingt'n (the elder Wm. Thornley	2 to isle 2 to wall
39	Colman's	Mr. R. Gr'nhalgh	Mr. R. Gr'nhalgh.	4
40	Gorton's and Mather's		Mr. Peter Gorton R. Pendlebury, Hilton and P. Longworth	4 to west 4 to east
41	Old Lord's Hilton's	Rev. H. Offley Wright	Mr. Nightingale Mr. P. Gorton	4 to west 4 to east
42	Walton's Dr. And't'n's	Mr. H. Pilkin'ton	Mr. Charter Mr. H. Pilkington	4 to west 4 to east
43		James Stones		3, by p'chase

R. LATHAM, Vicar.
JOHN NORCROSS, Curate of Horwich.
ROBERT GREENHALGH.
ROBERT EATOCK.
WILLIAM LONGWORTH.
HUGH WHITTLE.

The position of the curate-in-charge at Horwich at this period may be gathered from the fact that the Rev. John Norcross, in addition to his spiritual duties, was also master of Rivington Grammar School; and it is only in bearing in mind his dual character that some of the references made to him in old prints can be understood, as the following :—Nov. 30th, 1784, Mr. Ralph Rothwell, of Brownlow Fold, Bolton, was married on Thursday to Miss Norcross, daughter of the Rev. Mr. Norcross, of Rivington." His death is thus referred to :—"July 1st, 1783, on Sunday last, died the Rev. Mr. Norcross, master of the Free Grammar School at Rivington, and curate of Horridge Church, in this county. We hear that the Rev. Robert Latham, vicar of Dean, has presented the Rev. Mr. Johnson, M.A., of Manchester, to the valuable curacy of Horridge, vacated by the death of Mr. Norcross." A tombstone in the churchyard reads as follows : "To the memory of Margret, wife of Rev. J. Norcross, curate of this chapel ; died Aug. 14th, 1779, aged 50. The remains of the Rev. John Norcross, husband of the above, and curate of this chapel, whose preaching and worthy conduct in the station which he filled entitled him to the esteem of the congregation. He died on the 21st of June, in the year of our Lord 1788, and in the 60th year of his age." The following is an abstract of the will of the above-named Rev. John Norcross :— "In the name of God, amen, I, John Norcross, of Rivington, in the parish of Bolton, and county of Lancaster, clerk, being, through the mercy of God, sound of body, &c., do., this 9th day of May, 1787, make this my last will and testament. First, I will that all my debts, funeral expenses, &c., be paid. That the vicar of Dean and the six governors of Rivington school be desired to attend my funeral, and but few others, if any wishing, that as little expense may be laid upon it as possible in the mourning, and that my body be laid in the same grave with my first wife at Horwich Chapel. After that, I order that my present wife—Jenet—receive from my executors, securities, such as shall please her, for the sum of £475, which I had with her, and which is now placed out in my name, and also for her kind, tender, and faithful care of me and my children the further sum of 10 guineas, and five guineas more for mourning, and that she has the liberty to take all the goods which belonged to her at my marriage with her; next, it is my will that the messuage in Withnell, with appurtenances, all my personality, cattle, household goods or furniture, books, ready money, &c., be equally divided between my five children, viz., Elizabeth, John, Thomas, Alice, and Margaret; and if Alice and Margaret should not be of age at the time of my decease, it is my desire that the interest of their respective shares be paid to 'them by my executors till they come to the age of 21 years, and then the principle be immediately paid to them. Lastly, I appoint my beloved wife, Jenet, my sons John and Thomas, and my son-in-law, Ralph Rothwell, executrix and executors of this my last will. In witness whereof I have herewith subscribed my name and set my seal this 9th May, 1787.

JOHN (seal) NORCROSS.

Signed, sealed, published, and declared, &c., in the presence of us, William Pilkington, John Hampson, Ralph Green." The above will was proved at Chester on the 29th December, 1788. It may not be out of place to give here the following statement of accounts. April 16th, 1755. Richard Pilkington being churchwarden and constable, his accounts are as follows:—

	s	d.
April 16—For going to Court-Light (Leet)	0 1	0
May 19.—For Viewing Windows	0 1	0
,, 23—For going to Bury with dublickets (duplicates)	0 1	0
,, ,, For singing (signing) the man 2 warrants	0 2	0
,, For Bread and wine.........................	0 1	0
July 10.—Peiad a Money Warrant.................	2 9	1(2)
,, For Bread and wine.........................	0 1	0
Peiad a Church Lay..........................	1 3	4
For going to Court Light	0 1	0
,, Court fees......................	0 3	0
For going to Boulton on Linsell (Licence) day	0 0	6
For going to Bury............................	0 1	0
For Bread and wine.........................	0 1	0
For prays (prayers) for the fast day ...	0 0	8
For mending Sleat on Chapel	0 0	8
Peiad Money Warrant.......................	0 8	1
,, ,, ,, ...	0 2	2
Peiad Thomas Knowles.....................	0 2	2
To make up Land Tax	0 10	11

		£	s.	d.
July 10.—For going to Boulton about fog and Sephton		0	1	0
Spent		0	0	10
For Bread and wine		0	1	9
Peiad Money Warrant		1	8	6
For going to pay it		0	1	0
Paied James Nightingale for viewing Windows		0	1	0
Paied Mathew fog		1	5	6
1755—For viewing windows		0	1	0
Paied a Church Lay		1	3	4
Paied John Sharples		0	14	0
Peied Myles Burey		0	0	8
Paied John Sharples		0	0	8
Peiad Will Longworth about fog		0	2	6
For Parchment		0	0	4
To Mr. Horrox		0	0	6
Court Fees		0	0	8
Collect Land Tax to make Salary 5 shilling		0	2	0
Paied James Pendlebury for Writing		0	5	0
Spent concerning fog		0	0	6
		11	10	2

"Sale of Tythe at Horwich. This Indenture made the twentieth day of December, in the twenty-seventh year of the reign of our Sovereign Lord King George the Third, and in the year of our Lord one thousand seven hundred and eighty-six, Between Henry Blundell, of Ince Blundell, in the County Palatine of Lancaster, Esquire, of the one part, and Richard Pilkington, of Horwich, in the said County, Gentleman, of the other part, Witnesseth that for and in consideration of the sum of sixteen pounds four shillings and sixpence of lawfull money of Great Britain by the said Richard Pilkington to the said Henry Blundell in hand at or immediately before the sealing and delivery of these presents well and truly paid in full of the consideration money agreed to be paid for the absolute purchase of the Inheritance of the Tythe, Hereditaments and premises with the appurtenances hereinafter described, the payment and receipt whereof he the said Henry Blundell doth hereby acknowledge and own and of and from the same and every part thereof doth hereby acquit, release, and discharge the said Richard Pilkington, his Heirs, Executors,

Administrators, and every of them for ever by these presents ; and for divers other good causes and valuable considerations he the said Henry Blundell Hath Granted, bargained, and sold, and by these presents Doth grant, bargain, and sell unto the said Richard Pilkington, and to his heirs and assigns, All and all manner of Tythe of Corn, Hay, and Grain, and all other Tythe, great and small, predial, personal, and mixt, and all other Tythe and Tythable matters, pensions, sum, and sums of money in lieu of Tythes, compositions, and all tenths, Tythe, and Hereditaments whatsoever, commonly growing, arising, and being renewing, increasing from and out of all and every or any of the Lands, Hereditaments, and premises of him the said Richard Pilkington, commonly called and known by the name of Knowles, situate, lying, and being in the township of Horwich, in the parish of Dean, in the county of Lancaster, and the reversion and reversions, remainder and remainders, yearly and other rents, issues, and profits of all and singular the said premises. . . . And, moreover, that he the said Henry Blundell, and his heirs, and all and every other person and persons having, or lawfully or equitably claiming, or who shall or may at any time or times hereafter have, or lawfully or equitably claim any estate, right, title, trust, or interest into or out of the said tythe, hereditaments, and premises herein before-mentioned, to be hereby granted, bargained, and sold, or any of them, or any part or parcel thereof, by, from, or under own trust for him or them, or any of his ancestors, or any other person or persons whatever, shall and will from time to time, and at all or any time or times hereafter, at and upon the reasonable request, and at the proper costs and charges of the said Richard Pilkington, his heirs or assigns, make, do, acknowledge, levy, suffer, and execute, or cause and procure to be made, done, acknowledged, levied, suffered, and executed all and every such further and other lawful and reasonable act and acts, thing and things, devices, conveyances, and assurances in the law whatsoever, for the further, better, more perfect, and absolute conveying and assuring the said tythe, hereditaments, and premises herein before conveyed with their and every of

their appurtenances unto and to the use of the said Richard Pilkington, his heirs, and assigns. . . . .
And further that he the said Henry Blundell, his heirs and assigns, shall, and will from time to time, and at all times forever hereafter, well and truly pay or cause to be paid unto the present vicar of the Church of Dean aforesaid, and his successors, vicars of the same church for the time being, forever the annual or yearly stipend or sum of ten pounds of lawful money of Great Britain. As, and when the same shall from time to time become due and payable, and also from time to time; and at all times hereafter at his and their costs and charges find and provide bread and wine to be yearly and every year forever hereafter used and spent in wine at the Holy Sacrament in the same church on Easter Sunday. And likewise from time to time and at all times hereafter well and sufficiently repair, uphold and keep all the chancel of or belonging to the same church in good and efficient order and repair, and of, and from, the said annuity or yearly stipend, or sum of ten pounds, and every part thereof, and the charges and expenses of finding and providing bread and wine for the Sacrament on Easter Monday at the church aforesaid. And also of and from the repair of the chancel of and belonging to the said church, he the said Henry Blundell, his heirs and assigns, shall and will save and keep harmless and indemnified the said Richard Pilkington, his heirs and assigns, and his and their land and tenements from the same. In witness whereof the said parties to these presents have hereunto set their hands and seals and the day and year first above written.

CHAPTER X.

The Rev. Samuel Johnson, whose name appears as perpetual curate in succession to the Rev. John Norcross, was buried March 19th, 1826, aged 74, the Rev. Henry Hey Sutcliffe being the officiating minister, the first funeral at which he officiated being that of "Peggy Farington, of Horwich, aged 22 years." At the beginning of this century, Horwich and neighbourhood were not behind in making martial preparations in view of the threatened invasion. Not only was the beacon on the "Pike" kept over ready to belch forth its warning fire, but the inhabitants of the district enrolled themselves as volunteers, and a sermon was preached in 1809 by the Rev. S. Johnson, M.A., "before the volunteers of Horwich, Heaton, and Halliwell." At this period the inhabitants of Lancashire did not possess, nor yet did they know, anything of many of the common articles which are now in daily consumption. In the "Philosophical Transactions of the Royal Society for 1775," we have the following :— "The lower classes of the people in this County (Lancashire) formerly lived upon the coarsest food; wheat a hundred years ago was almost unknown to them, and so lately has it been cultivated in Lancashire that it has scarcely yet acquired the name of corn, which in general is applied only to barley, oats, and rye." The earthquake which visited Manchester and neighbourhood on Sunday morning, Sept. 14, 1777, was deeply riveted on Mr. Johnson's mind. Being a curate at one of the churches in Salford, he was officiating, when the trembling of the earth set the bells in motion. To this Mr. Johnson, one of the legends of Horwich has a direct reference ; and many perhaps may have heard the story which we venture to give, "How Parson Johnson laid the Horwich Ghost." In almost every hamlet and village there are traditions peculiar to that hamlet or village. Ghosts and hobgoblins generally form the principal

legends of the district, and even with the improved
education around us, there are not wanting those who
have a timid regard, or a hesitating, half-hearted
belief in the supernatural stories handed down from
a distant period, stories of crime, around which ghosts
delight to hover. Such stories in unbroken chain are
"bequeathed from sire to son," and clothed, despite
our efforts, with a ghastly significance. The writer can
remember his old grandfather dilating upon the title of
M.A., as affixed to ministers' names, as indicating that
they alone had the power to lay spirits, and as further
indicating that their intelligence was such as to enable
them to answer any question which the disentombed
might put. Failing to answer aright meant instant
death. Not only did the title assume a more than
ordinary force of intellect, but by some occult influence
it enabled the titled minister to see spirits that were
invisible to other eyes. When on a mission of "spirit
hunting" the fleetest horse was brought into requisition,
and to be interrogated by a chance passer-by was to
break the spell, and the spirit-hunter having thus held
converse with things carnal, had to leave things
spiritual for a time. Let us give the old man's story.
A spirit was said to have visited the immediate neighbourhood of Moorgate, and a feeling of uneasiness and
dread rested on the villages. What did it portend?
Some dire calamity, pestilence, murrain amongst the
cattle, some terrible local visitation, a dead visitor
to some family circle. At night the children sat in the
corner afraid to play; nor was the sire less fearful than
the son. What could be done? Only one in the village
could be of service, and he was from home. The old
chapel was visited by day, and in many a rural cottage
the shadow of a prayer was offered for the advent of
their deliverer. At length the curate—the M.A.—the
spirit-layer of the village returned, and at once set to
work to allay the fears of his parishioners. Mounted
on the swiftest horse the village could afford, he went
in search of the unwelcome visitant. But here arose a
difficulty, as the spirit was invisible to the parishioners;
none could guide him in his search, if any had been
willing. Through thicket and plantation, through moss
and bog, over hill and dale, the spirit-hunter sought,

but in vain. The vigilant spirit eluded his pursuer. At night a meeting of the villagers was improvised, and "Owd farmer Yetton" was the Aaron of the occasion. "Well, Pa'son Johnson, have you rid us of our foe?" "No, farmer Heaton; as yet my search has been fruitless, but by the blessing of God I will yet succeed." "Amen," was the hearty response of the listeners, and into the adjoining hostelry parson and people wended, and over many a tankard of ale, amidst the smoke of the fuming weed, did they talk over the apparition. Ere they departed Hopwood, the village constable, ventured to express the hope "that before to 'morn neet Pa'son you'll ha laid id gradely, for God doat it, it has caused o deal o unyessinies omung us." With early morning, having fortified the inner man with a bowl of oatmeal porridge, supplemented with his usual tankard of ale, Parson Johnson sprang into the saddle, and, taking a zigzag course, found himself riding at a smart trot over the route of the present Chorley New Road. From Lostock Hall the bugle of less spiritual Nimrods could be heard, the howling of the dogs somewhat disturbing the cogitations of the worthy parson. Still on and on he rode, and ere the sun had sunk far in the western sky, Parson Johnson found himself close to the Old Hall, Heaton. Sticking spurs into his horse, as a real or imaginary object struck his vision, the village curate proved a veritable Jehu and rode furiously. As he neared Horwich Moor in hot pursuit, a noted villager named "Owd Adam o'th Heyes," with wallet slung over his shoulder, was on his way to Bolton, and though Adam, like the rest of the village, had heard of the mysterious but perverse visitor, and had had his share of fear, yet, like many under less trying circumstances, was a little absent-minded. Seeing Parson Johnson riding so furiously and forgetting the cause, Adam with respectful deference saluted the parson and bade him good morning. The spell was broken, the charm dispelled, and the labours of a day lost. "Dog," cried the enraged spirit-hunter, "were it not for the sake of the spiritual office I hold and the peaceable requirements thereof, I would descend this saddle and fell thee as I would an ox, or whip thee as I would a dog. Thou knewest, fool, the mission I was on, and yet could not restrain that ever-wagging member of thine for a season." The day following being Sunday, Parson Johnson had other duties, and, at the "Bull," when the day's devotion was over, the village worthies gathered as was their wont. The wonder this Sunday was that Parson Johnson had made no reference to the "ghost" in his sermon. Monday morning came, and with the rising sun Parson Johnson was again in the saddle, and ere the orb of day had reached its meridian journey a solitary horseman might have been seen galloping up the ascending slope, through devious and lonely paths, skirting precipices, and leaping swollen rivulets, over boulders, and shaly surface. Reaching the base of the famous "Pike," he suddenly stopped and dismounted, and it may interest the visitors to this famous spot to remember, ere they ascend, that in an old legend of the village below they are passing over the spot where good Parson Johnson laid the spirit.

The Rev. Samuel Johnson was succeeded by the Rev D. Hewit, and from the Registers we gather that the first funeral at which he officiated was on July 13th, 1826, being that of "William Parr, of Wigan, aged 11 months." Horwich had obviously increased in population, for almost on the advent of his ministry an agitation was set on foot for a larger and more commodious "house of prayer." From the preceding chapters our readers will have determined the capabilities of the old chapel, but even the crippled dimensions of the ancient chapel—considering that at this period three other places of public worship existed—would seem to be capable of meeting the spiritual requirements of the church portion of the population, though the increase was somewhat great. In an article in the "Philosophical Transactions of the Royal Society," referring to a Survey of Manchester and Neighbourhood in 1774, the population of Horwich is given as, males 149, females 156 ; the population in 1801 was 1,565 ; in 1811, 2,507. The annual value of property in 1815 is returned at £5,706 ; parish rates £355. In 1821 population 2,873 ; 1831, 3,562. In the preceding year the corner stone of the present noble structure was laid. We extract the following from the *Manchester Courier* May 29th, 1830 :

"On Friday, May 21st, 1830, the ceremony of laying the first stone of a new church, to be dedicated to the Blessed Trinity, took place at Horwich, amidst an immense concourse of spectators of whom there could not be less than six or seven thousand present. The circumstances attending this ceremony are at once so nove and interesting that we are induced to give them at greater length than we might otherwise have done. At an early hour in the morning, in accordance with previous arrangement, the men employed by Mr. Thomas Ridgway, of Horwich, at his Lever Bank Bleachworks, marched through Bolton, accompanied by a band of music, and were met by their fellow-workmen of Horwich at the Jolly Crofters' public-house at the commencement of the Horwich-road. They then walked in procession and halted upon the lawn fronting the residence of Mr. Ridgway Brideon, nephew and partner of Mr. Thomas Ridgway, where they were supplied with refreshments. After which they marched to Ridgmount, headed by a sturdy veteran on horseback, who was otherwise distinguished by a badge of honour, on which was inscribed 'Forty-two years' service.' They were altogether a very fine body of men, in number about eight hundred, and were divided into companies, at the head of each of which a banner was carried exhibiting a representation of their several branches of labour in bleachworks, coal miners, &c. The gates leading to the grounds of Mr. Joseph Ridgway were thrown open for their reception, and they halted some time before the residence of that gentleman, they then proceeded down to the village, and joined the main body, as it may be termed, of the procession, which was forming opposite the Black Bull. About ten o'clock the procession left the Bull Inn, and proceeded to the house of Mr. Thomas Ridgway, where it was joined by the clergy, magistrates, and gentry, and from thence they moved in the following order to the ground :—Special constables, constables of Horwich and Heaton, overseers of the poor, Sunday school children, band, the committee; architect, with plans; clerk of work, with coins and inscribed plate; contractor, with silver trowel borne in a case of red morocco; foreman of masons, with mallet and level; the churchwardens, the clergy, Mr. Ridgway, magistrates, gentry, Freemasons, band, Orangemen, band, Oddfellows, friendly societies, band, inhabitants, workmen. The procession for the most part walked four abreast, and consisted of at least 2,000. By the time they reached the spot where the ceremony was to take place (which is close to the old chapel), an immense concourse of people had collected. A platform had been raised for the accommodation of the ladies, to whom tickets had been presented, and also for the Sunday school children. The proceedings commenced with the singing of the Old Hundredth Psalm by the children, after which the Rev. David Hewitt, M.A., incumbent of the chapelry, read the inscription upon the brass plate intended to be placed upon the stone, which was as follows:—"The foundation of this church, dedicated to the Blessed Trinity, was laid May 21st, 1830, by Joseph Ridgway, Esq., one of his Majesty's justices of the peace for the County Palatine of Lancaster. Francis Bedford, architect, and the site was given by Francis Stoner, Esq., and the expense of the erection jointly contributed by his Majesty's Commissioners for Building New Churches and the principal inhabitants of the township." The rev. gentleman then handed the plate, together with a bottle containing the coins, to Mr. Ridgway, who placed them in the cavity prepared for their reception. After which Mr. Hewitt presented to that gentleman, in the name of the township, a massive silver trowel, accompanied by an address forcibly expressive of the high sense entertained of his services in furtherance of the object which was now so near its accomplishment, to which Mr. Ridgway made the following reply—'I am much obliged by this mark of kindness on the part of my fellow-townsmen. I feel flattered in having been selected, and have great pleasure in attending to lay the corner stone of this church, which I hope will not only prove an ornament to the township, but promote that pure and reformed religion to which we have the happiness to belong. The want of sufficient accommodation for divine worship has been long and extensively felt by the lower classes of this chapelry, but the gratifying ceremony of the present day warrants the

hope that it will soon cease to exist, and I trust that at
no distant period a numerous congregation will have
the satisfaction of hearing within these sacred walls
those sound doctrines which it is our duty to transmit
to posterity.' Mr. Ridgway then went through the
usual formality of spreading the mortar, after which the
stone was lowered, and he completed his part of the
ceremony. The children then sang a hymn written for
the occasion, at the conclusion of which a most impressive and appropriate prayer was offered up by Mr.
Hewitt. 'God save the King' was then sung, accompanied by the various bands, and Mr. Ridgway Bridson
proposed a closing hurrah, which was heartily complied
with. The Freemasons then advanced, and performed
the ceremony of pouring oil, corn, and wine upon the
stone, invoking at the same time the blessing of God in
prayer. The procession then formed in the same order
as before, and after marching up the road some distance
began to separate. Great credit is due to Mr. Bridson
and the rest of the committee for the excellence of their
arrangements; not the slightest disturbance took place.
The men belonging to Messrs. Ridgway and nephew
were regaled at their masters' cost with an excellent
dinner at the Bull, at which house the committee also
dined. The Orangemen, Freemasons, Oddfellows, and
Druids distributed themselves at the Bull, Brown Cow,
the Squirrel, the Crown, and the Millstone. A large
party of gentlemen were entertained at the house of
Mr. Thomas Ridgway, and a handsome dinner was provided by Mr. Lambert, Horwich Moor Gate, to which
about thirty gentlemen sat down. After the cloth was
removed Mr. Kellie, of Bolton, was called to the chair,
and the following toasts were given amongst others:—
'The King, God bless him, and may he soon recover;'
'Joseph Ridgway, Esq.;' 'Lancashire Witches;'
'His Majesty's Ministers;' 'Rev. Mr. Hewitt,
incumbent of Horwich, and clergy of the neighbourhood;' 'W. Hulton, Esq., of Hulton Park;' and 'The
magistrates present at that day's ceremonial, William
Garnet Taylor, Esq., T. Ridgway, Esq., T. R. Bridson,
Esq.,' &c. The new church when completed will contain
sittings for 1,500 persons. It is a light and elegant Gothic
structure, and reflects great credit on the architect."

CHAPTER XI.

The Rev. Samuel Johnson on his instalment as curate-in-charge of Horwich found the position surrounded with difficulties. His predecessor, more perhaps from necessity than choice, was much of an absentee, his clerical duties were only secondary to his scholastic, but the position of the church at this period was not such as to inspire confidence, or lead to energy; the more influential inhabitants, if not entirely estranged, were painfully apathetic, and the church was merely a representative of a certain ecclesiastical fraternity, instead of the centre, the leader of religious opinions and religious actions. Perhaps no organization possesses in so complete a form the necessary elements of progress as is manifested in the English Church in its ramifications and policy; its ecclesiastical arrangements and its innate influence, worked by mental and social superiority, give a power which none other can exercise. Mr. Johnson, we may gather from the traditionary history of the village, was a clergyman who believed in the vital power of religion; to him his position was a trust; he recognised the peculiarities of his position, and laboured to success. The advent of the Ridgways and their social influence was doubtless of secondary advantage to the zealous curate—(but of the Ridgways we shall have more to say as we proceed in connection with the general history of the village). A Sunday school was established, and though differing much from the modern Sunday school, its introduction into the village was a power for good, for at this period means of secular education were few, and almost entirely denied the working classes. We are not averring that Mr. Johnson first introduced the Sunday school system into the village, because we shall find that he was only imitating what had already been introduced in connection with another of the Christian Churches at Horwich; but we may venture to say that the countenance and encouragement given to the movement by Mr. Johnson tended much to their early firm establishment. With surprising progress the movement sprang into popularity, and in 1793 the present "Old School" at the east end of the church was built by voluntary contributions for the "encouragement of useful learning, and the promotion of true religion and virtue." For a time at least these schools were directly self supporting, or aided by voluntary contributions of an unsystematic character, till "Charity Sermons" gave a more regular and more extended income. A "Charity Sermon" preached by the Rev. Edward Hill, B.A., of Wigan, in 1821, realised £30. As before remarked, Mr. Johnson was succeeded by the Rev. D. Hewitt, and during the early portion of his incumbency the present noble edifice, the pride of the village, was erected, chiefly from Parliamentary grants, largely supplemented by private subscriptions. Its position is bold and commanding, and from the lower part of the villlage—apart from architectural distinction—seems suggestive of those proud and towering structures which in bye-gone ages were the strength and hope of a district. To perhaps no individual family does Horwich Church owe so much as to the Ridgway family; a history of Horwich, in its more modern connection, is to a large extent the history of this family; and the impetus given to the village, and its increased population, is a paraphrase of the energy shown by this family. It cannot be denied that much of what would otherwise have given an undying name to the best known member thereof is somewhat sullied by the insatiable ambition which marks the gift, and the spirit far from true "Charity" which limited its operation. That Joseph Ridgway, Esq., J.P., D.L., of Ridgmount, was benevolently disposed to Horwich and its church none will care to question, and we venture to give our readers such portions of his last will and testament as relate more directly to charity for the inhabitants and endowments for the church. "I desire to be buried in my vault at the church in Horwich, and I direct my executors to erect a monument in the same church to my memory, to be executed by a London artist, at such expense as they, my executors, may think proper, but not less than £1,000; also a tablet recording the benefactions which I have made by this my will or otherwise, to the said church, and the officers thereof, so that the said benefactions may not be lost for want of due notice of their proper application. I direct my executors to procure and set up a clock face on each of the east, west, and north sides of the tower of the church in Horwich aforesaid, corresponding in appearance with the clock face already set up on the south side thereof, with proper works for showing the time at each of the said faces, and for striking and telling the quarters of the hour. I direct my executors to set apart and invest in Three Per Centum Consolidated or Reduced Bank Annuities a sum producing the clear yarly income of £132, free from legacy duty, commencing from the end of one year, from the time when the Reverend David Hewitt, now Incumbent Minister of the Church at Horwich aforesaid, shall have ceased to be such Incumbent Minister; but if such one year shall expire during my life, then commencing from the time of my decease. And I direct the said yearly income of £132 to be paid and applied to and at the direction of the minister and wardens of the church of Horwich aforesaid for the time being, and my trustees and executors hereinafter named or the trustees acting in their place, under this my will for the time being, or such of the said several persons as may from time to time attend and be present as follow, *videlicit*. Forty pounds a year, part thereof, as a salary for the organist of the same church for ever. Thirty pounds a year, further part thereof, to pay the singers or choir of the same church for ever. Twenty-four pounds a year, further part thereof, to pay the ringers of the bells of the same church for ever. Sixteen pounds a year, further part thereof, to provide and furnish the clerk of the same church for ever with a gown and habiliments, like those worn by the clerk for the church for the blind at Liverpool, and the remainder of the said £16 as a perpetual salary for the same clerk of the church at Horwich, but for which he is to clean and take care of the tablet and monument hereinafter directed. Twelve pounds a year, further part thereof, to provide and furnish the beadle of the same church for ever with a gown and habiliments like those worn by the beadle of the church for the blind at Liverpool aforesaid, and the remainder of the said £12 a year as a perpetual salary for the beadle of the same church at Horwich aforesaid. And ten pounds a year, residue thereof, as salary for the organ-blower for the same church at Horwich for ever. I further direct my executors to invest, as aforesaid, a sum producing a yearly income of £10, free from legacy duty, commencing from the time of my decease, to be paid and applied by my trustees and executors herein afternamed, or the trustees acting in their place, under this my will for the time being, during the incumbency of the said David Hewitt, as a salary for the person who shall wind up and regulate the clock of the same church at Horwich, and who shall also ring one of the bells in the tower at the hour of six in the morning and eight in the evening for the space of fifteen minutes, and after the determination of such incumbency of the said David Hewitt, then I direct the said income of £10 a year to be paid by and at the discretion of the said minister and wardens for the time being, and my trustees acting in their place under this my will for the time being, or such of the several persons as may from time to time attend and be present, as a salary for such clock winder and regulator and ringer for ever. And I request that Mr. Rollinson, who is now employed as ringer of the said bell at six and eight o'clock, may continue to be so employed, and hold that situation during his life. And from and after the determination of the said incumbency of the said David Hewitt, I direct my executors to provide, at the expense of my estate a service of Communion plate for the use of Horwich Church aforesaid, the same to be massive and embossed with, an inscription, and my armorial bearings thereon, also a verge, or sceptre, of silver, to be carried before the minister of the same church from the vestry to the reading desk and pulpit; and a full suit of canonicals for the first and next incumbent of Horwich aforesaid other than the said David Hewitt. And from and after the decease or marriage again of my said wife, I direct my executors to set apart and invest in three per centums consolidated or reduced bank annuities a sum producing a yearly income of £100, free from legacy tax, and commencing from the death or marriage again of my said wife (unless I survive her, and then from my decease). And I direct the said income of £100 a year to be applied as part of the annual produce of my residuary personal estate until the said David Hewitt shall have ceased to be the incumbent minister of Horwich Church, and from and after the death or marriage again of my wife, and the said David Hewitt ceasing to be such incumbent minister, then the said yearly income of £100 to be added unto and become part of the salary, stipend, or living of the incumbent minister of the same church at Horwich. Provided that in case the present or any future Vicar of Deane shall take or hold the said curacy, living, or incumbency of Horwich, or if the said David Hewitt shall ever hereafter take or hold the same, then during all such tenure or holding the said payment and application of the said yearly income of £100 to the purpose aforesaid shall be suspended, and the same income during all such time be applied as part of the yearly produce of my residuary personal estate. And from and after the decease or marriage again of my wife I direct my executors to set apart and invest in three per centum consolidated or reduced bank annuities a sum producing a clear income of £150 a year, free from legacy duty, and commencing from the death or marriage again of my said wife, unless I survive her, and then from the time of my own decease, to be paid and applied as follows, that is to say: Fifty pounds, part thereof, to be paid and applied at the discretion of the minister and wardens of the same church at Horwich for the time being, and of my trustees and executors hereinafter named, or the trustees acting in their place, all for the time being, or such of the said several persons as may from time to time attend and be present, as a salary for the master of the school at the east end of the same church, which master shall be a member of the Established Church of England, and for which salary he shall instruct in reading and writing 40 poor children of the township of Horwich, the same children to be nominated by and at the discretion of the said minister and churchwardens of the township of Horwich aforesaid, all for the time being, and of my executors and trustees hereinafter named, or the trustees acting in their place under this my will for the time being, or such of the said several persons as may from time to time attend and be present. One hundred pounds a year, being the residue thereof, to be applied by and at the discretion of the said ministers and wardens for the time being, and my trustees and executors hereinafter named, or the trustees acting in their place under this my will for the time being, or such of the said several persons as may from time to time attend and be present in the purchase of clothing and bedding for poor inhabitants of Horwich, to be distributed at or soon after Old Michaelmas Day in each year, and in such distribution I wish the oldest and poorest inhabitants of Horwich who have been most regular in their attendance at church on Sundays to be preferred, regard nevertheless being had to such as from sickness or old age are unable to attend. I further direct that if the sum of £400 can be raised by subscription or otherwise within one year of my decease and the death or marriage again of my said wife to build or provide a parsonage house for the residence of the incumbent minister of Horwich, then my executors do and shall, after the death or marriage again of my said wife, whichever shall happen first, subscribe and pay from such part of my estate as may be legally bequeathed, or given by will for that purpose, the sum of £800 free from legacy duty with interest from the time of my death and the death or marriage again of my said wife until actual payment; but unless £400 can be so raised by subscription or otherwise this legacy of £800 is to lapse and sink into the residue of my estate." The original trustees were Messrs. John Woodhouse and John Mangnall, of Bolton. The will was proved at Chester on the 25th January, 1843. Not only was Horwich benefited by the benefactions of Mr. Ridgway, but as will be gathered from the following list his charity was of no meagre character :—

	£
For building, enlarging, or improving a school in Bolton	2000
Bolton Infirmary	1000

To schoolmaster of intended new school (yearly)...	100
To the Society for Building Churches, Diocese of Chester	1000
To Widows and Orphans of Clergy, Diocese of Chester	500
Society for Propagation of the Gospel	500
Society for Promoting Christian Knowledge	500
Society for Promoting Education of the Poor	200
Manchester School for the Blind	200
Manchester School for the Deaf and Dumb	200
Manchester Infirmary	200
School for the Blind, Liverpool	500
Blue Coat School, Liverpool	200
Deaf and Dumb School, Liverpool	200
Collegiate Institution, Liverpool	200
Additional Curates' Society	200
Sons of Clergy	200

In accordance with the provision of this will, a neat board at the entrance of the church gives the amount available yearly to the church officers. For ten years the more important and directly beneficial clauses of the "will" were inoperative, as only in 1852 did the Rev. David Hewitt resign the incumbency. The why and wherefore of Mr. Ridgway's obvious antipathy to the rev. gentleman is not to our purpose to inquire, sufficient is it to say that Horwich Church is perhaps somewhat incongruously made to be more or less a heraldic monument of the Ridgway family, and perhaps an inquiry might lead to the conclusion that the proscribed clergyman suffered through an unavoidable clash in defence of ecclesiastical rights and privileges. In 1852, however, Mr. Hewitt resigned, and on Wednesday, December 1st, 1852, the upper room was crowded by those who delighted to do the venerable clergyman honour. The gathering was for the purpose of presenting him with a token of regard and esteem, by his late parishioners at Horwich. The presentation took the form of a massive silver salver, of circular form, 20 inches in diameter, and chased in the Louis Quatorze style, its value being £58. In the centre of the salver was the following inscription: "Presented to the Rev. David Hewitt, M.A., by the congregation of Trinity Church, Horwich, on his resignation of the incumbency after a faithful and effective ministry of more than twenty years.—Horwich, November 30, 1853." Amongst those present at the presentations were the following :—Revs. D. Hewitt, H. S. Pigott (Incumbent designate), J. H. Johnson, Mr. Joseph Ridgway, who presided and made the presentation ; Mr. W. Hulton, and Messrs. Charles and Christopher Howarth Mr. W. Bennett, Mrs. Longworth, Miss Sharples, Miss Brownlow, &c.—The Chairman, in eulogistic terms, referred to Mr. Hewitt's long connection with Horwich, concluding by reading a beautifully prepared address, which was signed by Joseph Ridgway, Anna Maria Ridgway, &c.—The Rev. David Hewitt, on rising to receive the emblems of esteem, spoke under visible affection. He said his regret at leaving them was lessened by the happiness of knowing that he would be succeeded by an active and zealous clergyman.—On this occasion the present highly respected vicar (Rev. H. S. Pigott) addressed a meeting of his parishioners for the first time.

The present church is equally attractive in its inner arrangements, lofty and commodious, many of the seats attached, and the difficulty of getting a pew acts as a deterrent to many who would worship within its walls. The most striking object in the interior of the church is the monument erected under the above will to the memory of the said Joseph Ridgway, and said to be the last work of the celebrated Westmacott. The figure is that of a lady (Mrs. Ridgway) in the posture of prayer, the expression of the features being life-like and striking. The monument is of white marble and bears the following inscription :—" Sacred to the memory of Joseph Ridgway, Esq., late of Ridgmont in this parish, for many years a Justice of the Peace and a Deputy Lieutenant of the County of Lancaster. He was firmly attached to the Protestant Church, a liberal contributor to its institutions, and he zealously supported the laws and constitution of his country." Immediately over this monument is the following tablet to the memory of his parents :—"Sacred to the memory of Thomas Ridgway, Esq., of Wallsuches, who died 30 of August, 1816, aged 77. Also Mary his wife, who died 23 April, 1803, aged 63. They were both interred at the Parish Church of Bolton. 'Blessed are the dead which die in the Lord.'" On the opposite side is a tablet of black and white marble, with protruding figure, under a cornice, supported by black marble pillars. The design is both beautiful and complete, and is to the memory of one of the "village worthies," Mr. Wm. Longworth, better known as "Squire Longworth," a gentleman who by his active interest in all things appertaining to the village, his genial and frank disposition, and by a display of those characteristics which always distinguish the true gentleman, "morality with dignity," has given his name an undying association with the village. Above the figure, which represents the Angel of Judgment, are the words in gilt letters, "The trumpet shall sound and the dead shall be raised," and the following : "In memory of William Longworth, The Knowles, who died Sept. 18, 1861, aged 63 years. And of Jane his wife, who died April 11, 1877, aged 65 years. Erected by their sons John and Nathaniel." In close proximity is one to Mr. Charles Howarth, late of Moor Platt, and bearing the following inscription :— "Sacred to the memory of Charles Howarth, of Moor Platt, Horwich, whose strict integrity, uprightness, and warm hearted friendly qualities endeared him in life to all who knew him. Born Aug. 19th, 1805 ; died May 29th, 1860." Tablets to the "Memory of Editha, wife of the Rev. H. S. Pigott, erected by the teachers in Horwich Church Sunday School," and to the "Rev. Samuel Johnson," a son of the Rev. Samuel Johnson referred to in these pages. He was vicar of Atherton for a period of 34 years. Between the pulpit and reading desk is a beautiful Lectern, the gift of the present vicar. The most conspicuous object in the churchyard is a large stone cross erected over the vault of Thomas Ridgway Bridson. In immediate contiguity is one to the memory of Joseph E. Greenhalgh, son of Mr. Wm. Greenhalgh, of Wilderwood Mills. Perhaps the most interesting are those of the Willoughby family, and the Greenhalghs of Colemans, the latter family having resided at that ancient residence for over 200 years. The Peak family claim the oldest grave so far as adducible evidence can warrant, but this perchance is open to question. On the grave stone of George Southern, of Aspull, who died June 3rd, 1774, we have the following lines :—

Go home, dear wife, and cease your tears,
I must lie here till Christ appears;
My debt is paid, my grave your fee,
Wait patiently, you'll follow me.

The silver service in connection with the church was presented by the late Joseph Ridgway, Esq., but the old service is still preserved. Upon the chalice of the old service is engraved the words, "From an oratorio, 1781," doubtless referring to the fact that the purchase money was the proceeds of an oratorio. Upon the tankard or wine cup is engraved, "The gift of the Rev. H. Olley Wright to Horwich chapel, 1782;" the alms dish bearing the following inscription:—"The gift of the Rev. John Parker, Breightmet, to Horwich chapel, 1782." The first christening in the new church was on Sunday, November 6th, 1831, the Rev. D. Hewitt, M.A., officiating, the name of the child being "John, son of Adam and Elizabeth Kay, of Horwich, mill-wright." The first funeral at which the Rev. H. S. Pigott, M.A., officiated was that of Ellen Valantine, of Horwich, January 2nd, 1853, there being during that month the extraordinary number of 21 funerals.

CHAPTER XII.

As we have already seen, Dissent or Nonconformity early made its appearance in the village, and possessed a power at once threatening to the Episcopal Church, and a vitality that was the soul of the religious effort of the village. At a period when Dissent was an organisation in the village, Milton wrote of "Giving Cæsar his own and no more, and to render the Divine Being His own and no less." When and how Dissent first appeared it would be bootless to inquire, but of this fact we have authority, apart from the coincident evidence we have submitted in our retrospect of Church history in the village, that in this part of Lancashire Dissent received legal sanction first at "Horridge," licences being granted in 1672 under James 2nd "for a preaching place at Horridge in the house of Thomas Willesbi." In a sermon preached by Mr. Walker, at Rivington, September 7th, 1698, in relation to the death of Samuel Crane, reference is made to the Church Societies at "Horridge" and Rivington. The position of "New Chapel" is both suggestive and instructive; its name carries us back to a period when another chapel existed in the immediate neighbourhood. To speak of "New Chapel" in relation to the antiquated structure now under consideration sounds like an anachronism, and it is only in considering its modern name as having a somewhat ancient association and meaning, that we can realise the adaption of name. The name is architecturally suggestive, and it may interest our readers that the "Old (church) Chapel" in architectural features may be taken as phototyped in the then and now "New Chapel."

We have said the position is both instructive and suggestive. At the period of its erection the worshippers within its walls could glance around at a landscape beautiful in its extensive swoop, and attractive in its rugged grandeur; as a back ground, in brown and frowning aspect, stood "the everlasting hills," before them was the gold-tipped clouds, which mark the "everlasting bed" of the Great Monarch of Day, and within the bold and beacon-like synagogue, in winter's shortened day, as the benedictions rose to heaven, he, too, would give his cheering "good night" as he sunk to rest in golden state. "New Chapel" speaks of the period when in the name of "religious concord" and for the "good of the commonwealth" governments and capricious monarchs attempted the impossible. The "Fires of Smithfield" lit Latimer's prophetic candle, "Acts of Uniformity" and "Five Mile Acts," supplemented with "Test Acts" and others of "Disability," moulded into shape the tiny atoms of crude and ill-digested religious thought, and gave organisation and vitality to a premature uplifting of the religious system. Religious progress is marked and progressive in proportion to the character and virulence of the opposition; Christianity was "born in trouble," and flourishes most in adversity. Monarchs, in their eagerness for a system, forgot its free, unchallenged, and unchallenging character. Milton more graphically puts it in the following form :—"I doubt not if some great and worthy stranger should come amongst us, wise to discern the mould and temper of a people, and how to govern it, observing the high hopes and aims, the diligent alacrity of our extended thought and reasonings in the pursuance of truth and freedom, but that he would cry out, as Pyrrhus did, admiring the Roman docility and courage, 'If such were my Epirots, I would not despair the greatest design that could be attempted.' Yet these are the men cried out against for schismatics and sectaries, as if when the temple of the Lord was building—some cutting, some squaring the marble, others using the cedars—there should be irrational men who could not consider there must be many schisms and many dissections made in the quarry, as well as in the timber, ere the House of God can be built, and when every stone is artfully laid together it cannot be united into a continuity: it can but be contiguous in this world, neither can every part of the building be in one form. Nay, rather the perfection consists in this; let us then be more wise in spiritual architecture when great reformation is expected." The history of "New Chapel" is said to be synonymous with the passing of the "Five Mile Act," and its linear position would seem to favour the suggestion. In the traditionary history of the village it is recorded that in the passing of the "Uniformity Act" in 1662 many who "for conscience's sake" despised the Act, and refused to subscribe to its declaration, made the Winter Hill their temple, and under the overhanging rocks of Horwich Moor assembled to worship, and in the bi-centenary celebration of 1862, the congregation of this place, led by their pastor, the Rev. William Wilsden, assembled on this time-hallowed spot, where in more troublesome times their fathers had gathered to worship. There is evidence to prove that a place of worship adorned the present spot as early as 1690, and the original trust deeds bear date of 1716. The first minister of whom record is given was the Rev. J. Walker, who was said to be "evangelical both in his principles and in his preaching." After him came the Rev. John Wood, who preached his last sermon there on July 17th, 1743, his text being Philippians iv. 6, "Be careful for nothing, but in everything by prayer and supplication, with thanksgiving, let your requests be made known unto God." He died at Atherton, March 10th, 1744, being interred at Chowbent, his funeral sermon being preached by Mr. Valentine, from Psalm xxxiv. 4. After Mr. Wood's departure the ministry was vacant for a period of four years, when in 1747 the Rev. John Hardy succeeded to the pastorate, his first sermon being from the text "Mary has chosen that good part which shall not be taken away from her;" he ceased his connection with "New Chapel" in 1754. About this period doctrinal troubles invaded "New Chapel," Arianism became more widely preached, and the pastor of "New Chapel" was not free from the taint. In the church books, opposite Mr. Hardy's name, is the following significant sentence, "Probably an Arian, then said to be orthodox." And at this period doubtless the views of the pastor found in the congregation active sympathisers. The Rev. Thomas Bispham was the successor to Mr. Hardy, and his somewhat tragic death is thus quaintly referred to : "A Socinian died between morning and afternoon services." It is said that unaware "The Angel of Death" had called their pastor away. The congregation, who had assembled to worship at the call of the bell, waited when its sound was hushed for the appearance of their pastor, but a messenger found him with his hands folded "sleeping the sleep of the just" in his chair at home. The present Mrs. Martin, relict of Mr. Peter Martin, J.P., of Rivington, is the grand-daughter to this Mr. Bispham; his death, however, is said to have happened in the vestry. The Rev. John Hughes was the next pastor, and his ministerial career at Horwich is passed over in the statement "he removed to Bury." Rev. Mr. Evans is the next pastor, and of him three items of information are given, (1), "he was a thorough Unitarian"; (2), "he stayed a very short time"; (3), "went to America." The Rev. George Watson became minister in 1779, and under his ministry the Unitarian heresy was considerably mitigated. "One fact," says the Rev. F. G. Collier, "untold by any church book, I am able to add, that is, that he took to himself a wife in the person of Mrs. Martin's grandmother, who lived at the Parsonage." Mr. Watson left Horwich in 1797 to undertake the pastorate of Carter-lane Chapel, London, from thence removed to Daventry, and finally died in Birmingham. In 1797 the Rev. James Kenworthy settled at New Chapel. It was said that he had trained with a view to taking "holy orders," but conscience made him a Dissenter; his learning and his scholarly sermons gave to the church at New Chapel quite a name in the village, and amongst the congregations often might be seen prominent and leading Churchmen, Mr. Thomas Ridgway being notably one of the attracted. Like the Rev. John Norcross, at the Old Chapel, he found his income to be too small for his needs, and not having an endowed school at Rivington at which to become "head master," he opened a scholastic institution at Moor Platt, on the spot where the mansion of the late Mr. Thomas Lever Rushton now stands. The Rev. John Crossley was the successor to Mr. Kenworthy, whose ministry lasted 28 years, and it was only through ill health and old age that he resigned the pastorate in 1825, and after living three years in Manchester with his son, he was brought to his last rest at New Chapel. During his ministry the chapel was enlarged and a Sunday school originated. In October, 1825, Mr. Crossley assumed the ministerial duties, and, says the Rev. F. G. Collier, "from the Informal Church Book I gather two facts, (1) that there were only three persons who could be said to be Church members—Thomas Vause, Mary Vause, and Richard Pilkington ; (2) that the first church meeting ever held at New Chapel was on the first Sabbath of March, 1828." The Richard Pilkington referred to was a benefactor to New Chapel, and held important public offices in the township. Mr. Crossley undertook no other pastorate, though he resigned his position here in 1844, and died at Farnworth in 1864. Another vacancy of four years, and in November, 1848, the Rev. William Wilsden began his pastorate, resigning in 1864. The Rev. H. H. Scullard, of Belper, accepted the pastorate iu October, 1865, leaving Horwich in 1873, to undertake ministerial duties in Bolton. In April, 1875, the Rev. F. G. Collier accepted the ministry. During his pastorate the chapel was greatly improved in aspect; but perhaps the extent of the improvement was more determined by accident than design. While alterations were proceeding in 1877 a violent gale arose, and on Thursday morning, September 6th, it was found that the north wall of the chapel had been blown down, and an additional sum of £300 imposed on the congregation. £800 was now required, and a Christmas tree and sale of work was opened on December 27th, 1877, by the Mayor of Bolton (Alderman Greenhalgh), the Rev. Philip Hains, vicar of St. George's, Wigan, being one of the speakers. From the Charity Commissioners' report we gather the following :—" Pilkington and Morris endowment ; house yielding a rental of £4, former income £5 10s. The £4 is distributed in charity. R. Pilkington, Horwich, endowment, £91 4s. 4d. in consols ; yearly £2 14s. 8d. for minister of Presbyterian Chapel ; charity founded by will of 1832. New Chapel, Horwich, endowment ; three houses, two acres, one rood, 22 perches of land, yielding a rental of £25 3s., which is to go to minister of Presbyterian Chapel."

The endowment fund in connection with the New Chapel is worth about £40 per year, about one-seventh of which is distributed annually in wearing apparel amongst the industrious poor of Horwich, preference being given to such as shall attend divine worship in the New Chapel; the remainder is paid to the minister officiating in the chapel for the time being. Mr. A. Mason (to whom we are indebted for much of the above information) is the present acting trustee and senior deacon of the church, as well as superintendent of the Sunday School; the latter position he has held for 30 years.

CHAPTER XIII.

Referring to the Rev. F. G. Collier, late minister at New Chapel, the "Congregational Year Book" for 1883 says:—"Collier, F. G., late of Horwich, near Bolton, son of the Rev. James Collier, of Manchester, was born at Hartlepool, February 6th, 1847. Endowed largely with natural gifts, Mr. Collier was a diligent student from youth. His quick perception, retentive memory, and natural aptitude for clothing his thoughts in well-chosen and vigorous language, clearly indicated that his vocation was public speaking. His educational advantages were uninterrupted up to the time of entering the ministry. After a few years of private tuition he was admitted to the Northern Congregational School, Silcoates, of which Dr. Bewglass was the principal, and afterwards became a junior teacher under Dr. Brewer, of Leeds. It was at this period he expressed his long-cherished wish to devote himself to the work of the ministry. When eighteen years of age he entered Lancashire Independent College, where he spent six years, an additional year being allowed for matriculation at the London University, which he passed in the first division. On the termination of his student-life, he was ordained pastor of St. Paul's Congregational Church, Wigan, in the year 1871, as the immediate successor to the late Rev. W. Roaf. His ordination service will be long remembered by many who were present. The usual statement was read by Mr. Collier with deep emotion, indicating that he entered upon his work with deep convictions of its magnitude and importance. The charge given by the Rev. Professor Scott added not a little to the impressiveness of the service. Mr. Collier's preaching was pre-eminently practical. He brought the principles of the Gospel to bear upon current topics and all the relationships of life. Without slavishly adhering to old modes of theological expression, he intelligently expounded and ably defended the fundamental truths of the Christian faith. Mr. Collier also showed great ability as a lecturer and platform speaker, and was frequently employed by the Liberation Society as an advocate of its principles. The subjects of two of his general lectures were 'Sidney Smith' and 'George Eliot.' After resigning his pastorate at Wigan, he accepted a call to New Chapel, Horwich, where his ministry, as in his former charge, was highly appreciated, and his character much respected. During the fourth year of his ministry at Horwich, his work, to which he was earnestly devoted, became a strain too great for his weak frame, in which the insidious disease of consumption was making perceptible progress. His health failing, he went to reside at West Kirby, Cheshire, with the hope that rest and change would re-establish his health, occasionally accepting engagements to preach. His last sermon was preached at Hoylake from the words, 1 Kings xx., 40: 'And as thy servant was busy here and there, he was gone.' After this all other engagements to preach were cancelled, and in the sick chamber he lay until reduced to a mere shadow, affectionately remembered by friends connected with his two charges and by many others who had cherished the hope that a successful career was before him. Prostrated as he was for several months by increasing weakness and exhaustion, he still took the keenest interest in all that was going on in the church and the world. As the end was approaching he was heard to whisper, 'Lord, now lettest Thou Thy servant depart in peace.' He died on March 30th, 1881, after a ministry extending over ten years."

In dealing with the history of Lee Congregational Church we are beset with difficulties of no ordinary character, difficulties arising from the imperfect records that chronicle its history. Lee Chapel, however, has a history, a history though obscured and chronologically imperfect, yet suggestive of its claim to be considered the oldest Nonconformist place of worship in Horwich. Two facts stand in bold relief in the consideration of its history. 1st, that it has a prior history than that to

which present church documents or church records
refer; 2nd, that the traditionary unwritten history of
Lee Chapel gives collateral evidence of its extended
lineage. As to the first, the evidence adduced in chap.
12 suggests an affinity existing betwixt the churches at
"Rivington" and "Horridge." Who was Thomas
Wellesbie ? Where did he reside ? We have a clearness
of date, but a confusion of position; but even this confusion of position is brought within narrow geographical
limits in the fact that the two churches at Rivington
and Horwich respectively, were closely allied and
connected.

New Chapel, as we have seen, bears a first date of 1690,
but a church existed in "Horridge in the house of
Thomas Wellesbie, and was duly licensed as a preaching place in 1672." In this historic fact are embraced
others of significance. We have evidence of a prior
church; the church was not created for the "act of
licence," but the licence was issued for a then existing
church. How long had such church existed ? A church,
or rather an affinity of churches, limited to a small area,
embracing in such affinity two churches geographically
rural, alike insignificant in population or historic
associations, that yet stood so prominent as to demand
Royal attention, and be the first Lancashire churches
that could seek and find favour for their Nonconformity
in the protection of a capricious monarch, and not
over-enlightened or liberal legislature, must have possessed some attributes, some power, and some influence
which juxtapossibly commanded attention. We shall
find that "Lee" Church was closely allied, that doctrinal
differences led to schism, in which the church at
"Horridge" and at "Rivington" was "rent in twain,"
and in this fact we gather the proof that "the house of
Thomas Wellesbie" was the birth-place, or rather the
spot where Lee Chapel received its legal or civil baptism.
For a time at least it would seem that the church at
Horwich was so closely allied with that of Rivington
that its separate existence was lost, or rather so interwoven as the two districts possessed only one place of
meeting or chapel, and that at Rivington, for upon the
"Socinian heresy" being pointedly preached at
Rivington, and their allegiance denied, we find them

destitute of a place "to assemble and meet together." If we accept traditionary evidence, one of the low, antiquated looking structures that adjoin the chapel, apologies for cottages, and part of the "glebe" is the spot which primarily was dignified into a chapel. However this may be, the cottage evidently was, either from structural alterations or other causes, denied them on their separation from the church at Rivington.

About 1754 the doctrinal troubles which, like a mysterious earthquake, shook the very foundations of Nonconformity, gathered within its mighty occult wave the peaceful Church at Rivington, and so terrific was the shock that the temple was indeed rent in twain; and many, trembling for their soul's salvation, seceded. These were the "Pilgrim Fathers" of Lee Chapel. For a time they met for prayer and worship in a dingle or stone quarry at the base of Rivington Pike, and there the Gospel was preached to the faithful few. One Sunday morning they assembled, as was their wont, when the dark overhanging clouds portending the storm brought graphically to their minds the vicissitudes of their position. To worship the God of their fathers only in a clear sky was an alternative to men of their calibre suggestive of action. One of their number, addressing his companions in adversity, thus spoke; his words were few, but like the "Peace, be still," of old, they were pregnant with meaning:" "Brethren, something must be done." That something was done, and a small cottage was obtained, and in this cottage, Lee Chapel in embryo, the Church was gathered. In this cottage the first day school was held, and in part of that cottage the first Sunday school assembled. The history of the church at Lee Chapel is set forth as follows in the "Church Records": "About the year 1760 four pious men, whose history deserves a record, deploring the introduction of Socinianism at Rivington Chapel — Hugh Makinson, Moses Cocker, Thomas Anderton, and John Ashworth — procured occasionally the ministerial labours of the Rev. Messrs. Ralth, late of Bolton; Harrison, late of Bury; Goburn, of Lymm; Hurst, of Bacup; Lord and Pendlebury, who, like men moved by the Holy Ghost, preached with simplicity and energy the doctrine of the Cross.

Like the missionaries to the South Sea Islands, they laboured long, few believing their report, for it was not till about 1770 that a small church was formed in Rivington by the Rev. John Goburn. In 1774 they contemplated a new chapel, and in the same year was the foundation of Horwich Lee Chapel laid. The Rev. Messrs. Pendlebury, Harrison, and Priestley, of Manchester, were their first preachers. Soon after they gave Mr. Harrison a call, which he declined. Introduced by some friends at Lancaster the Rev. L. Redmayne supplied them occasionally. He and the Rev. J. Pendlebury were proposed to the people, a majority of whom prefered the former, and Mr. Redmayne accepted the call about 1777. In the year 1778 he formed a Church, which was composed of about nine members. During the course of his ministry there were about 104 members admitted, and when he resigned office their number was about 20." Such is the brief history of Lee Chapel, as chronicled in the "Church Records."

But these "records," though undoubtedly reliable and for historic reference authentic, yet bear evidence of some prior church records of which they are but an imperfect reflex. As a separate and distinct church its early formation was surrounded with difficulties. The Rev. Leonard Redmayne began his ministry 1777, and in 1778 the church consisted of nine members; his ministry was progressive, and in June, 1787, a Sunday School was opened in connection with the chapel. This being a step in advance, and surrounded with difficulties of no mean order, he called to his assistance five men, who in that age of imperfect education were so far able to be "helps" by virtue of their superior mental attainments, that the school so far proved successful that upwards of 100 children attended. These pioneer Sunday School teachers were dignified by the title of "Masters." A modern Sunday School is but a faint reflex of these primary institutions, and the peculiar instruction, with the entire absence of collateral aids, made the position of "Master" both trying and difficult. In 1822 the venerable servant of Christ resigned his ministry after a pastorate of 45 years. A tombstone in the older portion of the burial ground attached thus records: "Also all that was mortal of the Rev. Leonard Redmayne, who was Minister of the Congregation of Protestant Dissenters assembling at Lee Chapel, Horwich, 45 years. He ceased from his labours and was called to receive his reward, May 26, 1829, aged 82." In 1723 the Rev. Robert Harris succeeded to the ministry, when death severed the connection on May 19, 1840, after a ministry of 18 years. The Rev. John Jones succeeded him in 1841, but his connection with Lee Chapel was brief, he resigning in 1842. In 1843 the Rev. A. Bateson began his ministry, and after a pastorate of five years resigned. During his ministry, in 1846, the Horwich Vale Print Works closed, owing to Mr. Chippendale resigning his connection therewith. The stoppage of these extensive works is always attended with direful results to Lee Chapel. From this and other causes may be attributed the fact that the pastorate was vacant till 1854, when the Rev. Mark Hardaker accepted the pastorate, with the concomitants of a flourishing church around him, for in 1849 Mr. Buckley, as representing the Deepdale Printing Company, took over the printworks. During the ministry of Mr. Hardaker the present beautiful structure that adorns Lee Lane was erected, viz., in 1856. In 1854, upon the very advent of Mr. Hardaker, arrangements were entered into for erecting a new chapel, Mr. George Woodhouse being appointed architect, the style being that known as early English. The following particulars will doubtless be read with interest:—Inside dimensions: length, 62 feet; width, 35 feet 6 inches; vestry, 12 feet square, with the heating apparatus underneath; height of side walls from floor, 23 feet; to apex of roof, 45 feet; to ceiling, 35 feet 6 inches; space above used for ventilation. The roof is an open span, the crossed principals opening from moulded stone corbels; inside walls are wainscoted 4 feet 6 inches, the accommodation being for 600, its cost being £1,500, of which sum the Lancashire Congregational Building Society contributed £500; the builder was Mr. W. Pickersgill, the joiner work by Mr. Joseph Clarkson, now of Brisbane, Australia,—the other portion being entrusted to Mr. Sharples, of Chorley. The following were the building committee:—John Turner (Rivington), chairman; James Clarkson, treasurer; Jabez Waterhouse Devonport, sec.; Rev. M. Hardaker, P. Martin, A. Peak, W. and J. Clarkson, Jesse Hood (Adlington). The chapel was opened for Divine worship on Wednesday, June 11th, 1856, the first sermon being preached by the Rev. Thomas Raffles, D.D., LL.D., of Liverpool, who preached from Matthew xvi. 18, that in the evening being preached by the Rev. Enoch Mellor, M.A., of Halifax, from John iii. 3. On the following Sunday the Rev. Robert Vaughan, president of the Lancashire Independent College, preached from John xiv. 6, in the morning, in the evening from 2 Timothy iii. 14, the Rev. William Roaf, of Wigan, preaching in the afternoon from Rev. xxi. 22. The collections at the opening services realised £100 14s. 0d. In 1867 Mr. Hardaker resigned the pastorate, and the chapel had "supplies" till 1869, when the Rev. R. Nicholls began his ministry, but resigned the year following. The Rev. D. Williams, then of Adlington, and now of Bolton, had the oversight of the church for six months, and in 1871 the Rev. I. Watkins began his ministry, which continued till 1878. In 1832, Sunday, May 7th, the present pastor, the Rev. W. J. Houlgate, began his ministry. The day school in connection with Lee Chapel possesses quite an interesting history, but it will perhaps be sufficient for our purpose to give only a brief sketch. So far as reliable data determines, James Rothwell was schoolmaster in 1814, and held his position for six years. Mr. John Hood succeeded, and taught for a period of 19 years. At this period schools were in that state which is supposed to first indicate a change. The cane and other instruments of corporal punishment were looked upon as necessary adjuncts of education, and the scholars of the period viewed the school much in the light which a garrotter looks upon the "triangular" apartment where Justice has decreed his more excruciating punishment. The schools, too, were a reflex of the condition of the population. Money was verily an article of value then. Labour then was in abundance, but the intrinsic value of that labour, or in what degree it was represented by the current coin of the realm, was an enigma which they thought not of unravelling. One word explains the position—the "truck system" in its most tyrannical form abounded, and even schoolmasters were remunerated in "kind." The schoolmaster's desk was transformed into a grocer's counter when "school-pence" (!) were brought, and the best rule, and the most practical to the village schoolmaster, was the "rule of exchange," for the piles of groceries, sometimes too great for private needs, or a superabundance of one article, with the absence of another, rendered a study of barter profitable. Mr. Mark Allatt followed Mr. Hood, and notwithstanding the many difficulties that have surrounded this school, Lee Chapel can now boast of its schools, not only architecturally, but from the success which gathers around them.

CHAPTER XIV.

To write even a summary of the history of Methodism in Horwich is to write a history of the village, and though the progress of the latter may have been more conspicuous than that of the former, we cannot separate the one from the other, they being bound together by a kind of natural affinity. The exact time when Methodism took root in Horwich is not been given with chronological exactitude; but that it dates from the cradle of Methodism cannot be doubted. Methodism was first introduced into Horwich by one of the ancestors of Mr. William Thornley, of Bolton, or Astley Bridge. This worthy pioneer walked from his residence in Bolton every Sunday morning, to stimulate, encourage, and teach his charge, the bleak, dismal, cheerless surroundings of Wilderswood being enlivened with the song of praise and thanksgiving. The mill of Mr. Joseph Crowther, at Wilderswood, was consecrated to this purpose. This mill is situate at the back of Messrs. W. Greenhalgh and Son's, at present known as Wilderswood Mill, and here, too, is said to be the birthplace of that vast industry which Lancashire claims as peculiarly her own. Some there are who place the birthplace of the cotton industry at a spot called, even to this day, "The Bobbin Shop," while some give Gorton Fold the honour; but judging from traditionary history, and the surroundings of Crowther Mill, we are certainly inclined to favour the belief that the spot where Methodism first saw light in Horwich is also the honoured birthplace of the cotton trade. To this spot, then, Mr. Thornley each Sunday morning walked from Bolton in the Moors to Horwich in the Wilderness, to propagate youthful Methodism. Mr. Crowther then worked the mills, if such a structure can be so called. The supply of water being plentiful, a water wheel provided the motive power. Every Monday morning the wheelgate was carefully swept, and Mrs. Ormston, who is now 85 years of age, and a daughter of the said Mr. Crowther, often refers to the time when, in childhood, she had heard speak of the great preparation made for the Sunday school in her father's mill. The first charity sermon was preached in Lee Chapel, Mr. Crowther inducing the Rev. Mr. Redmayne, pastor, to grant the loan of the school. On this occasion Mr. Crowther came in for more than an ordinary share of notoriety. It became known that he had given a "guinea"—sovereigns were not in vogue then—and from mouth to month this singular display of liberality was communicated, and on all hands it was allowed that "Mr. Crowther had gon none rest, for he'd pud o guinea into t' box." Mr. Crowther never lost an opportunity of telling this characteristic story. At that time Horwich did not present the same lively appearance it does now, though its growth has been comparatively slow. Then Lee-lane did not present an unbroken chain of houses, but some five or six, standing in green fields, alone marked this now the busiest thoroughfare in the village, the present residence of Mr. A. Peak, and one occupied by Mr. Richard Bond, in Silverwell-street, being relievers to the monotony of space in Lee-lane. Speaking of Silverwell-street, it is now known in popular phraseology as "Nail Rock," and at the time of which we are speaking, under the spreading boughs of a giant ash, "the village smithy stood;" yes, we say that under the spreading boughs of the ash tree the village day school stood, for while the good blacksmith's anvil rang with the sound of his heavy strokes, the voice of his good dame could be heard implanting with measured voice, and sometimes we fear in accents fierce and loud, the foundation of the rude education of the day. From this fact it is not hard to discover the origin of the name "Nail Rock." "Nail Rock" is also associated with one whom "Wigan ever delighteth to honour," and few, perhaps, may know that, ancestrally, Mr. Nathaniel Eckersley is connected with this spot; we have had no means of determining by documents, or collateral evidence, the exact date of the connection of the Eckersley's with "Nail Rock," but

In conversation with one of the "ancients" of Horwich, we were informed that the father to the present Mr. N. Eckersley carried on the trade or business of a weaver in that locality, and that one of the now cottages was the "weaving shed" which alone gave Mr. Eckersley a standing as a manufacturer, and during the French war, when recruiting was by ballot, and each town and village had to send its quota, one of the Eckersleys was drawn for Horwich.

Speaking of the Rev. Mr. Redmayne, it may perhaps not be out of place to refer to a story which is often spoken of by the ancients of the district. At the time that Mr. Redmayne held the pastorate of Lee Chapel, a Rev. Mr. Hibbert held the pastorate of Rivington Chapel, the two being very intimate, not so much, perhaps, because of the similarity of taste which marked their more secular history, both being passionately devoted to a small farm, which was at once their pride and pleasure. On one occasion the vagaries of trade brought them into direct collision. He of Lee Chapel wanting an increase of stock, his brother divine of Rivington determined to supply the needful. Having in his stock a cow "not quite so young as she used to be," he sent for Mr. Redmayne. Previous to his arrival he had got an occasional employé of his to file up the cow's horns; and having anointed them with a colouring which gave quite a natural tint, when Mr. Redmayne had viewed the cow he bought it for a much younger animal. On the day of its arrival at its new home rain fell in copious showers, and the pintment not being impervious to rain, the deception was discovered. Seeing that he had been sold by his brother of the cloth, Mr. Redmayne philosophically exclaimed, "Friend Hibbert, thou hast done me, but I will be square with thee yet." How far he kept the threat the "wise saws" say not. But to our subject. From Wilderswood the school was removed for convenience down Gorton-fold, and took up its abode in Gorton-fold Mill, then worked by Mr. William Hatton. The cause had so far flourished that a superintendent was found in Horwich, a man named James Bolton acting in that capacity. At this period, about 1806 or 1807, a bleach croft belonging to Mr. Ridgway was situate not far from the spot where Mr. Mason's tuyere works now stand. The superintendent of the Sunday school (James Bolton) was also overseer, or "gaffer" of the bleaching croft; and perhaps this dual capacity brought with it a more than ordinary degree of responsibility. On a hot Sunday the clear, pellucid stream which meanders past this croft, and formed its necessary supply (not the black, fetid, and dirty stream as now), was an attraction to the parched lips of the children; and the "sour tubs" which lay exposed proving an additional attraction. The care of Bolton was divided between the school and the croft. Great preparations were then made for the "charity sermons," and almost all the little girls in the schools were merged in choristers for such occasions—Mrs. Ormston (to whom we have before referred) having a lively recollection of the time when she thus appeared. To-day it would seem a strange spectacle to hear the "song of praise," and listen to the "glad tidings of grace," with cards and rovings forming a picture for the background. About this time such success had attended them that it was thought advisable to have a school specially for the object, and about the year 1810 the present chapel was opened. At this time the surroundings of the Methodist Chapel were quite the reverse of what it is now—standing in a conspicuous position, around which green fields clustered, it was considered an architectural feature and an ornament to the straggling village. Shortly after its erection, the street which now leads to the chapel began to be formed, Mr. Conner taking the initiative, closely followed by Mr. Longworth. At this time reading and writing were taught in Sunday schools, Mr. Leach, cashier at Wallsuches, acting as writing master; the *modus operandi* of communicating writing lessons being as follow :—The boys were provided with copy books, which were deposited in a box and conveyed to the residence of the writing master, who set the copies, this being a task which few could undertake. Mr. Pennington, at this time, was the "trust steward," who made a practice of presenting a new cap on the occasion of the Charity Sermon to each of the female singers. The first superintendent in the new place was Mr. John Carrothers. The new chapel was devoid of galleries, Mr. Plumpton putting in the first. The chapel was built in "faith" in the widest sense of the word, the pioneers of the movement, having no means at their disposal, they could only trust and hope for the result. Up to within a very recent period the incubus of debt hung like a millstone on their efforts, the interest crippling the efforts of the society; but by energetic action, aided by their Bolton friends, this incubus was removed after a lapse of time, which had caused the remark to partake of the character of an aphorism, "That every stone had cost a sovereign." At the time to which we have just referred, a radical change was adopted at the Old School in connection with the church. The crossman and writing was the chief aim of instruction imparted at this school, but owing to day schools and night schools being brought more to the front, writing was discontinued. This innovation was the cause of a good number who felt a desire to improve their writing leaving the Old School and going to the Methodist, where the practice was continued, Mr. John Wallwork being the writing master. Amongst the number who thus migrated we find the name of one who has done so much to improve and stimulate his native village, we refer to Mr. Andrew Peak. To bring its history to a later date is unnecessary. The memory of its Rushtons, its Dickinsons, and its Wallworks are fresh to the memory of the present generation. Its chequered history and its powerful influence, coupled with the results, has left its mark on the present history of Horwich. Perchance to few places a greater sanctity and a holier remembrance is more keenly associated, and though for its past services in the cause its crumbling walls and propped up structure would plead eloquently, for the good of the Church and the honour of Methodism we hope that ere long the time-honoured "light of Methodism" which has cast its pure ray around, may be focussed in a temple worthy to be associated with its past history, and a living memorial of happy memories which are not lost but gone before. In addition, the Independent Methodists have a plain but substantial chapel also in Lee-lane, and its vigour and usefulness cannot be over estimated. It was first originated in a gathering of teetotalers, amongst whom were Mr. Thomas Hopkins and Mr. W. Crumblehulme, now of Great Lever, iron founder, then of Horwich. Two cottages were joined together for temperance meetings, at a spot now enclosed and part of Mr. A. Peak's tuyere works, Crown-street, and on the 7th Sept. 1862, in this low back cottage Independent Methodism was born in Horwich. In March, 1867, the foundation stone of the present chapel was laid by Mr. James Lomax, of Farnworth. In the Sunday School are over 160 scholars, whilst the Band of Hope connected therewith numbers some 400 members. The Primitive Methodists have also a neat stone chapel at Horwich Moor, and so far as the avenues of "religion" are concerned they are in "full supply." How far their influence is exercised the following remarks by the present Sergeant of Police— Sergeant Ryder—to the writer of these pages may perhaps be testimony, "That in 13 years' service in the police force he had never been located in a place so distinguished for its quietness and general respectability of its inhabitants."

CHAPTER XV.

In taking a retrospect of the history of Horwich in its general aspect, we draw an exemplification of the history of the country, and view those rude chaotic efforts which have culminated in our boasted civilisation. The manners and customs of our forefathers are the dark outline of a brilliant picture; the laws and polity are the hidden foundation of the constitutional structure. We gaze back upon the fact; with the resuscitated feeling of one escaped from danger, unmindful of the fact, that we copy and imitate much that we abstractly condemn, and find ourselves obeying laws and following customs which we brand as of a "barbarous age." Few of us care to inquire how many laws are yet upon the Statute Book and verily the laws of the realm, that were promulgated at a period when society was but a name, and the *vox populi* only the voice of the privileged few, and those not distinguished by any characteristics of mental superority—the living idol—to which man in all ages have been willing to bow the knee. Civilization is a veritable "adverb of degree," and can only be judged in a comparative form, its highest altitude, and its lowest depth, are but the "staves" that mark the relative position; and perhaps n no more special manner is this demonstrated than by the provision made and the laws relating to the treatment of the recipient poor. - "Freedom is our birthright," but that freedom is more or less shackled by moral or legal enactments, that dims that spontaneity of action which constitutes perfect freedom. At an early period in our history it was imperative "That the stranger when travelling, should he have cause to leave the high road, to shout out or blow a horn," otherwise he was liable to be taken as a thief; and would have to pay for his redemption. To harbour an outlaw, flema or fugitive, subjected his receiver to a fine equal to his own weregild. This interference with free intercourse, and a denial of the rights of prospective improvement, was perchance a requirement more of the age, than the result of an effort to destroy individual freedom. The head of the house was responsible for himself, for his family, and for his servants. The lord was held responsible for his retainers, bond or free. Such laws were defined to compel every man to some definite and permanent locality, where he might claim affinity and have his dwelling. In this chapter we shall lay before our readers copies of "permits" and "local habitation" orders which will have direct reference to the "law of settlement." And as our object is not to trace in chronological order the various "Acts" and "statutes" relative thereto, but merely to give our readers such aid as may tend to their enlightenment in the perusal thereof, we shall simply refer to the more cogent and direct Statutory Acts.

The law of "settlement" was necessary at a time when a rude, turbulent, unsettled and almost lawless people had to be dealt with ; to bring such a people within the power and influence of civilisation could only be brought about by compulsory measures. The habits and customs of the people were more of an itinerant character, and in both Saxon and Norman periods laws were promulgated for the purpose of compelling the inhabitants to content themselves with some profitable occupation of the land, to engage in some handicraft in defined localities. In the 12th Richard 2nd, cap. 7, 1388, we have a law "prohibiting any labourer from departing from the hundred, or town, where he may dwell without a testimonial ;" and in the 22nd Henry 8th, cap. 12, 1531, we find the justices commanded to assign to the impotent poor the limits within which they are to beg. By statute of 1 Edward 6th, cap. 3, 1547, "the officers are directed to convey the impotent poor, on horseback, cart, or chariot to the next constable, and so from constable to constable, till they were brought to the place where they were born, or most conversant with for the space of three years, there to be nourished of alms." In the second year of Charles 2nd, 1662, a system of settlement and removal was introduced in Parliament that might at another period have caused a revolution. The nation

was as yet suffering from that desperate but successful
effort which had cost England a King, and taught them
the mistakes and abuses of a Commonwealth, yet even
the paralytic nation might have been spared the stigma
of receiving as a reward for efforts which even the gods
favoured such an insult as under : "That any Individual upon the warrant of two justices, on the sug-
tion of the overseer or overseers, were liable to be
placed under control, and forcibly carried, driven by
the cartwhip—if needed—to the place of his birth," and
yet in this 19th century we might be astonished to find
that this and the following laws are not the obsolete rules
of our forefathers, but the *de facto* laws of our own
time, in a much wider sense than we should care to see
exercised. "Be it therefore enacted by the authority
aforesaid, that it shall and may be lawful upon complaint made by the churchwardens and overseers of the
poor of any parish to any Justice of the Peace within
40 days after such person or persons coming so to
settle as aforesaid in any parish, in any tenement under the yearly value of £10, for any
two Justices of the Peace whereof one to be
of the Quorum of the Division, where any person
or persons are likely to become chargeable to the parish
where they should come to inhabit, by their warrant to
remove and convey such person or persons to such
parish where he or they were last legally, either as a
native, householder, sojourner, apprentice, or servant,
for the space of forty days at least, unless he or they
give such sufficient security for the discharge of the
said parish, to be assisted by the said parish. Provided also that (this Act notwithstanding) it shall be
lawful for any person or persons to go into any county,
parish, or place to work in time of harvest, or at any
time to any other worke so that hee or they carry with
him or them a certificate from the minister of the
parish and one churchwarden, and one of the overseers
of the poore for the said yeare, that hee or they have a
dwelling-house, or place in which hee or they inhabit.
And hath left wife and child or some of them there.
If the person, or persons, shall not return to the place
aforesaid when his or their worke is finished, or shall
fall sick or impotent whilst he or they are in the same

works, it shall not be accounted as a settlement in the cases aforesaid. But it shall and may be lawfull for two Justices of the Peace to convey the said person or persons to the place of his or their habitation, as aforesaid, under the pains and penalties in this Act prescribed." The vagrants and mendicants were left to the tender mercies of the constable or beadle, who was generally kept from showing any sympathy by being denied any restitution of costs which charity or sympathy with the unfortunate had led him to incur. Such cost coming from the rates imposed, any charge therein for such purpose was invariably disallowed. The constable or beadle was considered to have rendered only efficient service, and conformed to the requirements of his office, when he had driven the vagrant, by threats, or by the application of the whip, into the next parish. "Nobody's child" was a human football, to be kicked from village to village until his final settlement had been determined. To give our readers some guide by which they may determine the position and responsibilities of the constable, which was an office often conjoined to that of churchwarden, and which, in lieu of voluntary service, could be impressed upon any parishioner possessed of certain legal requirements, we give the following "Requisitions to Constables," bearing date 1703:—"To make your presentments, fairly written on parchment, with answers to the following questions:

1st. What treasons, petty treasons, felonies, or burglaries have been committed in your township?

2nd. What vagabonds or wandering rouges have been apprehended?

3rd. What Popish recusants, or others, have you that wilfully absent themselves from Divine worship?

4th. Have you any unlicensed alehouse keepers?

5th. Have you any common drunkards, or profane cursers or swearers.

6th. Is there any decay of houses, or husbandry contrary to law?

7th. Have you any ingressors, regrators, or forestallers?

8th. Has Winchester watch been duly kept?

9th. Are your poore well provided for?

10. Are your highways in good order?

The answer returned being generally conventional in form as under :—"We have no treason, felonies, or like misdemeanours committed within our liberties to present to the best of our knowledge, we have permitted no vagabonds or suspected persons to pass through our town unpunished that we know of; Winchester watch has been duly observed; we have no drunkards, swearers, or cursers to present." On one of the pages in an old town record we have the following notice, which may throw some light upon the mode and manner of the election to the office of churchwarden and constable in 1700 :—

"Take notice that these names that has not the yeare of our Lord fixt to them, must when they serve, and have served be entered on the first page, and when they all done so, they will be for ever void in this place. Witness my hand, Samuel Hodkinson."

"Fore Die Junis, Ano. yr Dom., 1694.

Wee the churchwarden and overseers of the poore of Halliwell and others the inhabitants whyse names are hereunto subscribed do hereby certify that all p'sons whom it may concerne and specially ye churchwarden and overseer of the poor of Horwich and the rest of ye inhabitants thereof that John Cunliffe is acknowledged to be a settled inhabitant with us in Halliwell aforesaid. And it is his abode or dwelling in Horwich all aforead shall not bee accounted any settlement there; And wee do hereby covenant and pramise y upon notice given to us or any of us; By the churchwarden and overseer of the poor of Horwich for the time then being to remove or cause to be removed the said John Cunliffe at any year's end, soe as hee shall not at any tyme thereafter challenge or clayme to have any settlemt in Horwich aforesaid. Nor be chargeable or burdensome to the inhabitants thereof in any wise. In testimony whereof we have put or hands the day and year above written. Noah Heaton churchwarden William Morris overseer for the poore."

"Jany 19, 1741.

This is to sartifie that Adam Pendlebury widdow and children may dwell in our town of Westhoughton while they behave themselves sivelly and do no damadg towards our town, William Hodgson, overseer."

"County Lancashire.—These may certify whom it may concern, whereas I Elizabeth Lee of Westhoughton do promise and engage that my mother Mary Lee shall not become chargeable to the Hamlett of Horridge in the county aforesaid whilst that I am able to maintain her. In wittness hereof I set my hand Elizabeth Lee her mark, dated April the 7th 1719. In witness John Dootson his mark, James Hilton 19th of January 1729."

"Alexander Lomax saith that in or aboute the year 1729, he farmed eight pounds and 10d. In Hallewell, and the same year he farmed five pounds and fifteen shillings in Little Bolton and the same year he farmed the aforesaid Lands he and his family in Hallewell and the reason why this was committed to writing was to satisfie both the towns how the farming was. Notice being given by Hallewell to Horwith touching the settlement of the said Lomax and the above written as here witness my hand, Alex. F. Lomax his mark, witness John Brandwood, William Turner."

"County Lancashire.—I James Lomax overseer of the poor of Sharples the churchwarden being now dead, doe hereby certify to the churchwarden and th' overseer of the poor of Horridge in the said county That I doe nowe acknowledge Peter Thornley his wife and family to be inhabitants of and legally settled in Sharples aforesaid and who for his better way of living are now lately removed into ye towne of Horridge, I doe therefore promise and undertake for myself and successors and the rest of the inhabitants of Sharples aforesaid that wee will remove care and provide for the said Peter Thornley his wife and ffamily as our settled Inhabitants when on soe soone as they or any of them shall become indigent, or liablesome, or found to aske reliefe of you or any of the inhabitants of Horridge aforesaid, as witness my hand and seal the 3rd day of ffeburary Anno Dom 1700, James Lomax overseer."

To the Churchwardens and Overseers of the Poore of the Townshipp or Hamell of Horwich in the County of Lancaster Wee the Major parte of the Churchwrrdens and Overseers of the Poore of the Townshipp or Hamell of Sharples in the said County of Lancaster send greeting Whereas John Horrockes and Samuel Horrockes, two children of Timothy Horrockes of Sharples aforesaid are desirous for their more convenient and better way of living to reside and dwell for some time within Horwich aforesaid and to that end have requested to give such certificate for indemnifieing the said Townshipp of Horwich aforesaid as by law is required. Know ye therefore that wee the said Major parte of ye Churchwardens and Overseers of the Poore of Sharples aforesaid whose hands and seals are hereunder putt Do hereby certifie that we do owne and acknowledge the said John Horrockes and Samuel Horrockes to be inhabitants legally settled in Sharples aforesaid and we do hereby promise and engage for ourselves and successors in the said several offices and the rest of the inhabitants of Sharples aforesaid that we will remove and receive back again into Sharples aforesaid the said John Horrockes and Samuel Horrockes whensoever they or either of them shall become any way chargeable or burdensome to Horwich aforesaid. In witness whereof we have hereunto set our hands and seals this fifteenth day of ffebruary Anno R Rs George's Seconds Anno gr Dom 1730, Churchwarden John (seal) Brooke Daniel (seal) overseer."

CHAPTER XVI.

November the 27, 1740.

I, Joseph Cooper, of Halliwell, do own to have received the sum of eighteen shillings from William Hart and John Hodskinson, overseer of the Poor of Horwich, for the said sum of 18s. I do deliver Thomas Entwistle goods, and do aquit Thomas Entwistle and own to have received all claims and Demands due from the Town from the begining of the world to this day.

In presence of William Pendlebury,

I say Received by

JOS. COOPER.

The Examination of William Gellie, of Karesbrough, in the County of York, *Wiggmaker*, taken upon oath before me, Samuel Hallows, Esqr., one of His Maj^{tes} Justices of the Peace and Quorum in and for the said County of Lanc., the Thirtieth Day of June, Anno yr Georgii Secundi Regis, Anno yr Dom, 1722.

This Examinat upon his oath deposeth and saith that he was born and first settled at a Place called Firth, in the Kingdom of Scotland, and was afterwards bound apprentice and served for the space of Three Years with one Thomas Roughhead, a *Wiggmaker* at the town of Newcastle-upon-Tine, and after that worked abroad in several parts of England for about ten years, but never was apprentice nor stayed as a servant for a whole year with any Person whatsoever during that time, nor did any other act or deed to gaine a settlement. But this Exam^t upon his oath saith, That about the end of the said Ten Years he was hired as a servant for a whole year with one Martin Hawkridge, of Knaresbrough afore^{sd}, Wiggmaker, and that he stayed with and served him the s^d Martin Hawkridge a whole year according to the said Hireing, without any intermission, and rec^d Ten Pounds, wages, meat, drink, washing, and lodgings from him. And further this Examt saith, That he never was hired and stayed as a servant for a year, nor did any act or deed to gaine a settlement since his said service at Knaresbrough.

       Signed WILLIAM GILLIE.
S. Hallows.

"To the Chairman and Overseer of the Poore of Horridge in the Parish of Dean in the County of Lancaster. Wee the Churchwarden and Overseer of the Poore of Westhaughton in the said county send greeting. Whereas one William Turner together with Hanna, John, William, James, and Ellin his children are desirous for their more convenient and better way of living to reside and dwell for some time within Horridge aforesaid, and to that end have requested me to give such certificate for indemnifieing the Inhabitants of Horridge aforesaid as by law is required. Know yee therefore that wee the said Churchwarden and Overseer of the Parish of Westhaughton aforesaid whose hands and seals are hereunder putt, Doe hereby certify that wee doe owne and acknowledge the said William Turner, Hanna, John, William, James, and Ellin his saide children to bee Inhabitants legally settled in Westhaughton aforesaid, And wee doe hereby promise and engage for ourselves and successors and the rest of the inhabitants of Westhaughton aforesaid, That wee will receive back again into Westhaughton the said William Turner, Hanna, John, William, James, and Ellin his said children, whensoever they or any of them shall become any way chargeable or burdensome to the inhabitants of Horrigde aforesaid. In witness whereof wee have hereunto putt our hands and seals the Sixth Day of July Anno gr Dom 1711.

Attested by us who were present att the signing and sealing of the above written certifiate.
 Henr. Mundey
 Richd. Lightbourne

PETER LOBKER (seal)
 Churchwarden
GYLES MARSH (seal)
   Overseer

 Allowed by us two of her Mag'ty Justices of the Peace and Quorum for the sd. County Court.

      THOS. MARSDEN
      THOS. SMITH."

" To the Churchwarden and Overseer of the poore of Horridge. Whereas John Isherwood of Harwood, ffrancis his wife and James, William, and Ann Isherwood their sons and daughter for their better imployment and more convenient way of living are desireous to reside for some time w^{th}in Horridge in the said County and to that end have requested of us whose hands and seals are hereunto putt being the major part of the Churchwardens and Overseers for the Poore of Harwood afore^{sd} to give such surety for the Indemfinfiseing of ye said townshippe of Horridge as by law is required, Tuerefore know ye that we the said Churchwarden and Overseer of the Poore of Harwood aforesaid, Doe hereby certifie unto you the Churchwardens and Overseers of the Poore of Horridge afore^{sd}. That we doe owne and acknowledge the said John Isherwood, ffrancis his wife, James, William, and Ann Harwood their sons and daughter to the inhabitants legally settled in Harwood afore^{sd}, In testimony whereof wee have hereunto put o' hands (Seals the 11th Day March Anno Dom 1704.

Allowed by us who now witness the signing and sealing of the certificate.
    William Parkinson
    Lambert Heaton

{ JOHN   WELCH (seal)
           Churchwarden
  JOHN DEVENPORT (seal)
           Overseer

    Allowed by us two of her Maj. Justices of ye Peace for the County.
        CHA. HULTON
        JONA. BLACKBURNE."

Forasmuch as comp^{lt} hath been made unto us whose names are subscribed, her Maties Justices of the Peace and Quor^m in and ffor the said County of Lancaster, by the Churchwardens and Overseers of the Poor of Horridge in the s^d County, that one Charles Boardman, Hope, his wife, Philip, James, Robert, Dorothy, Elizabeth, and Hope Boardman, theirs sons and daughters, are now lately come to reside and dwell in Horridge aforesaid, endeavouring to settle themselves their, and having no legal title soe to doe, but being Poor are already become Chargeable to the Inhabitants of Horridge, as appeares unto us upon oath. And whereas also it appears unto us by a certificate dated the fourth day of May last past, under the hands and Seals of the Churchwardens and Overseers of the Poor of the Parish of Carswall in the County of Stafford, That the said Charles Boardman, his wife, and six children afore^{sd} are owned and acknowledged to be legally Inhabitants settled Carswall afore^{sd}, therefore we, her Maj^{ties} Justices of the Peace of and for the said County of Lancaster, doe hereby declare and adjudge the s^d Charles Boardman, his wife, and six children, before named, to be poor and chargeable to the Inhabitants of Horridge afore^{sd}, and their last legal settlement to be in Carswall, in the County of Stafford afore^{sd}, and doe hereby order the Overseer of the Poor of Horridge afore^{sd} to remove and convey them to Carswall afore^{sd}, and them deliver to the Churchwardens and Overseers of the Poor there, or to some one of them, who are hereby required them to receive and provide for according to Law.

Given under o^r hands and Seals at Bolton, the fifteenth Day of ffebruary, Anno Regina Anne, Reg. Anno gr. Dom. 1706.

Tho. Smith.
Tho. Marsden.

By Vertue of An Act of Parlim^t made in the eighth and ninth Yeares of the Raigne of o^r most gracious Soveraigne Lord Willm. the third, Intituled an Act for the reliefe of the poore of this Kingdome,

Wee, William Waringe, Churchwarden for Adlington in the pish of Standish, and Thomas Makenson, overseer of the poore of the said Towne, Doe hereby certifie to the Churchwardens and Overseers of the poore of Horwich, That Thomas Smithells and Ann, his wife, or any child or children by them begotten are Inhabitants and legally settled in the Town of Adlington aforesaid. In witness whereof we have hereunto putt o^r hands and Seales, the Third Day of December, Anno Dom. 1701.

Seen and allowed by us, his Maj^{ty} Justices of the Peace for this County,

C. L. Stanley.
Robt. Mawdesley.

"To the Churchwardens and Overseers of the Poor of the Townshippe of Horwith, in the Parish of Dean, in the sd. Cunty. We the major part of the Churchwardens and Overseers of the Poore of Blackrod, in the sd. County, Send Greeting. Whereas, one Mary Seddon, widow, and Regnald, Ann and ffrances, her children, are desirous for their more convenient and better way of liveing to reside and dwell for some time within Horwith aforesd., as by law required. Know ye therefore that we the said major part of the Churchwardens and Overseers of the Poore of Blackrod aforesd., whose hands and seals are hereunder put, Do hereby certifie that we doe owne and acknowledge the sd. Mary Seddon, Regnald, Ann, and ffrances, her children, to be inhabitants legally settled in Blackrod aforesd., and we doe hereby promise and engage for our selfs and successors and the rest of the inhabitants of Blackrod aforesd., that we will receive back again into Blackrod them, the sd. Mary Seddon, Regnald, Ann, and ffrances, her children, whenever they or any of them shall become any ways chargeable or burdensome to Horwith aforesaid. In witness whereof we have sett our hands and seals the 26th Day of April, in the year of our Lord, 1720.

Allowed by us
Bertie Entwistle,
Jo. Walmesley.

      Churchwarden
    MICHAEL (seal) RAWLINSON.
    JAMES his (seal) mark ENTWISTLE.
    RICHARD his (seal) mark DOOTSON.
        Overseer of the Poors.

"To the Overseers of the Poor of the Township of Horwich. Whereas you have made complaint to us whose names are hereunto set and seals affixed, being two of his Majesty's Justices of the Peace and Quorum, in and for the said County, That Richard Fairclough and Betty his wife, Peter aged seven years, Molly aged five years, and Nancy aged two years—their children have come to inhabit in your said Township, not having gained a legal settlement there, nor having produced a certificate owning them to be settled elsewhere, and the said Richard Fairclough, Betty his wife, Peter, Molly, and Nancy their children having become actually chargeable to your said Township. We the said Justices upon due proof made thereof upon oath, and likewise upon due consideration had of the premises do adjust ye the same to be true, And we do likewise adjudge that the lawful settlement of them is in the Township of Thornley in the County of Lancaster. We therefore require you the said Overseers of the Poor, or some one of you to convey the said Richard Fairclough, Betty his wife, Peter, Molly, and Nancy their children from and out of your said Township, to the said Township of Thornley, and them together with this our order, or a true copy thereof to deliver to the Overseers of the Poor there, who are also hereby required to receive and provide for them according to law. Given under our hands and seals the fifteenth day of September in the year of our Lord 1780.

AD. FLETCHER.
RA. FLETCHER."

The "law of settlement" was not only a grievous hardship to the poor, but oft its determination was a costly undertaking to the township. Litigation was a frequent necessity, and costly arbitrations arose. We place before our readers the following as some proof of our assertion; others we have now before us :—" County Lane Memd. That there has this day been an bearing before us whose names are subscribed His Mag^{ty's} Justices of the Peace and Quorum in and for the said county concerning the settlement of Richard Leigh his wife and children which is this day in dispute between the Townshipps of Horwich and Westhaughton. And upon a full Hearing of both the said Towns and Examination of the said Richard Leigh and of several other persons touching the premisses. We the said Justices do hereby declare that we are of opinion and it is our judgement that the settlement of the said Richard Leigh his wife and children now is in the said Township of Westhaughton. Given under our hands at Bury in the said County this Third Day of January Anno R R's Dom George's Mag Britt Decimo Anno yr Dom 1723.

J. L. EGERTON.
S. HALLOWS.
A. LOWDNES."

"To John Hodgekinson, Overseer of the Poor of the Townshipp of Horwich.

This is to give you notice, That the Churchwardens, Overseers of the Poor of the Township of Harwood, intend to make their Appeal at the next General Quarter Sessions of the Peace, to be held by adjournment at Manchester, against the order you lately obtained for Removal of John Haslewood Owen his wife, James their child, out of your said Town of Horwich into our said Town of Harwood.

     I am y' friend,
       JAMES HETON, Overseer.
Harwood, 30th March, 1741."

To be legally entitled to "aid" from some Friendly Society was considered a sufficient discharge of the liability of the town in which the ." stranger" might be located without "order of settlement," and to this period many of the friendly societies of to-day date their beginning. Doubtless churchwardens and overseers saw in their creation an adaptation to the requirements of the period, and every effort to stimulate and encourage the growth of such societies was but an expenditure of moral power tending to lessen pecuniary obligation, and a means of avoidance to legal squabbles and official disagreements; hence we find that churchwardens and others officially connected with the town not only gave their sympathy but their support, led up their processions, became treasurers to their funds and honorary subscribers; this active sympathy leading to their development and their rapid extension. The reason for their co-operation may perhaps be implied in the following :—

" To the Churchwardens and Overseers of the Poor of the Township of Horwich, in the Parish of Dean and County of Lancaster. We, whose names are hereunto subscribed, being Two of the Trustees of the Friendly Society called the 'Females Society,' holden at the house of John Robinson, in Blackrod, in the Parish of Bolton and in the said County of Lancaster, established in pursuance of the Act made in the Thirty-third year of his present Majesty's Reign, intitled 'An Act for the Encouragement and Relief of Friendly Societies,' Do hereby certify and acknowledge Betty Porter is a member duly admitted into our Society as aforesaid, and that the Rules and Articles of the said Society are duly enrolled. In witness whereof we have hereunto set our respective hands and places of abode the 12th day of December, in the year of our Lord 1800.

    The mark of JENNY DARBYSHIRE.
    The mark of CATHERINE GRUNDY.

Attested by William Porter.
 ,, ,, John Green.

      Magisterial Signature,
      ROBT. NORRIS."

The following has reference to a lunatic case, which we purpose giving our readers free from comment:—

Know all men by these presents that we Thomas Kershaw and Robert Pendlebury, both of Horwich, near Bolton, in the County of Lancaster, are held and firmly bound to Josiah Birch, of Manchester, in the County of Lancaster, esquire, treasurer for the time being of the Lunatic Hospital, in Manchester aforesaid, in the sum of fifty pounds of lawful money of Great Britain, to be paid to the said Josiah Birch, or his certain Attorney, Executor, Administrator, or Assigns. For the true payment whereof we bind ourselves, our Heirs, Executors, and Administrators jointly, severally, and firmly by these presents. Sealed with our Seals. Dated this 21st day of March, 1785. Whereas Betty Hilton, of Horwich aforesaid, aged about 24 years, has for six weeks last-past been unhappily disordered in her senses, who at the speacial instance and request of the above bounden Thomas Kershaw and Robert Pendlebury, has been this day admitted a patient of and taken into the Lunatic Hospital, in Manchester, there to remain until it shall please God she shall recover her former senses, or until four or more of the Managers of the said Hospital together with the Physician shall order her to be from thence discharged. Therefore the conditions of the above written obligation is such, that of the above bounden Thomas Kershaw and Robert Pendlebury, or either of them, shall at their own proper charge and expense find and supply the said Betty Hilton with all proper and necessary wearing apparel, and do, and shall well and truly pay or cause to be paid to the said Josiah Birch the sum of seven shillings weekly and every week for the board and maintainance of the said Betty Hilton during her continuance in the said Hospital. And in case of the death of the said Betty Hilton shall pay and discharge all the expenses of her burial, or if after the said Betty Hilton shall be duly discharged by four of the Managers of the said Hospital and the Physician the said Robert Pendlebury and Thomas Kershaw shall receive again the said Betty Hilton, or otherwise pay or cause to be paid to the said Josiah Birch the sum of twenty shillings of good and lawful money weekly and every week.

Signed in the presence of
James Hilton, secretary.
{ THOMAS KERSHAW (seal)
ROBT. PENDLEBURY (seal). }

CHAPTER XVII.

The manners and customs of our forefathers, when viewed in relation to the more advanced customs, and perchance more refined manners of the present day, possess many peculiarities inexplicable to ourselves. Overseers and churchwardens with village constables were burdened with duties that their successors would scorn to perform. Now the duties appertaining to these offices are more of the lavender-glove kind; they contain and impart a certain social dignity with few cares and little work. In this chapter we shall lay before our readers copies of old documents which will enable them to form some opinion of the doings of our forefathers, and give them an insight into their somewhat laborious duties.

"KNOW ALL men by these presents that I, William Johnson of Horwich, in the County of Lancaster, *Weaver*, for and in consideration of the sum of Too Pounds and five Shillings paid or secured to be paid by Robert Hart, churchwarden, and Thomas Knowles, overseer of the Poor of Horwich, in the County of Lancaster, or one of them at or before the execution of these presents and for other Good Considerations, we hereunto moving have Granted, Bargained, and Sold and by these Presents Do grant, bargain, and sell unto the said Robert Hart and Thomas Knowles their Executors, Administrators and Assigns, the several goods, Chattles and Househould Stuffe herein after mentioned and particularly specified. That is to say a Chimney Cro and tongs, one Brass Watch, one felled Christ, one plank, ark churn, two pigins, one feigh, two Half headed Beds and Beding, three Chears and Cuishons, six Stooles and too Littel Chears, one pair of Loomes, fall Bord and too Shelves, one littel Table and one Spade, a Cradle, and three Wheels, one Stand and one Deshen, one Iron Girdle, And all my right, title,

benefit claims and demands to the same, To have and
to hould the said goods, chattles, household stufe, and
all other the promises hereby bargined and sold, or
intended to be bargined and sold unto the said Robert
Hart and Thomas Knowles, there Executors, Administrators and Assigns to and for the use Benefit and behoof
of all the Inhabitants and owners of Land within the
township of Horwich. And I the said William Johnson do for myself my Executors, Adminst., Covenant
and grant to and with the said Robert Hart and
Thomas Knowles and there Assigns shall and may
quietly hold and enjoy or expose to Sale, all and
every of the said bargined goods, chattles, and
household stufe, to and for the use aforesaid, without any interuption or molestation of or by the said
William Johnson, or any other person; or persons, By
or through my means, privy act, or procurement in
anywise, And I have delivered one putur spoon unto
them before the ensealing hereof in the name of the
whole. In witness whereof I have enterchangably set
my hand and seal the 7th day of May, in the year of
our Lord, 1741.

Signed, sealed, and delivered, ⎰ WILLIAM (seal) JOHNSON
(the triple Sixpenny|Stamps
being visible). In presence of
us,
    Thomas Dalton,
    John Seddon.
Feby the 28, 1755."

"An Inventory of the goods which the town bought
and sent to Thomas Entwistle, Done by me, James
Pilkington, Overseer of the Poor of Horwich :—

    A fire greete, tongs, and crow,
    One pear of bedstocks and beding,
    Three chears and two stools,
    Three wheels, one brass pan,
    One iron pot and back stone.

Horwich, Decemb 15th, 1778."

An account of Goods of Jn°. Tornlys sold by Robt
Pendlebury, his Landlord, to Hugh Whittle, ye Overseer of ye Poor of Horwich, as follows :—

	£	s.	d.
Chimney crow and tongs................................	0	5	0
Iron pot 1s., a tin kan 4d.............................	0	1	4
A tin toaster 4d., a tin dish 4d...................	0	0	8
Muggs and pots in ye Nook........................	0	0	6
A frying pan 6d...	0	0	6
A three footed table 6d., a child's chair 6d. ...	0	1	0
Three stools, an old chair..........................	0	0	6
A cubbard and two boxes............................	0	1	6
Cards and stock	0	2	0
A hand pair of cards..................................	0	5	0
Three spinning wheels, an old chair	0	1	6
A pewter dish	0	1	0
IN YE SHOP.			
Looms, a steel reed and gears, brushes, and drying iron...	2	2	0
Weys, a lead peand, a basket	0	0	6
Bed stocks and goods	0	4	0
Chaff bed and two b.ankets	0	4	6
Chaff bed and a blanket	0	2	0
Two feather pillows	0	1	6
Chaff and a blanket	0	3	0
Dough deation...	0	0	8
Smoothing iron and heaters	0	3	6
	5	18	1

As witness our Hands
Robert Pendlebury,

I John Thornley, of Horwich, Promise to pea to the Township of Horwich, the sum of 1d. p. week for the Hire of the goods within menchoned.

As witness my hand.

Witness, Thomas Peak.   JOHN THORNLEY.

	£	s.	d.
Paid Robert Pendlebury for rint	3	0	0
„ William Johnson for writing	0	2	0
„ For Criing..	0	0	8
„ John Halton	0	1	0
„ John Sharples....................................	0	1	0
„ The Bells	0	5	0
„ Mason his fee...................................	0	3	6
„ Spent at boulton	0	1	0

Feby. 12th, 1779. I have sold the within mensbond goods to Hugh Whittle, ye Overseers of the Poor of Horwhich, at the above sum af £5 10s. 7d. by mee,

JOHN ENTWISTLE,
Sworn Auctioneers,

	£	s.	d.
Little Bed	1	3	0
Large Bed	1	4	6
Large Bed Stocks	0	16	0
Parlor Bed and Stocks	1	6	0
Two Stools	0	0	4
Relsh Cheairs	0	2	6
Tongs	0	1	6
Iron Crow	0	0	8
Ole Board	0	2	6
Seven Batery Cans	0	2	0
Five Brass Spoons	0	1	0
Four Puter Spoons	0	0	4
Three Knives with Forks	0	0	4
Oula Brush and Spade	0	0	3
Frieying Pan	0	1	4
Large Chouir	0	0	6
Brass Pan	0	1	0
Iron Pot	0	0	4
Two Tin Kans	0	0	10
One Wash Tub	0	1	8
All the Arthen Wares	0	1	0
One Candle Stick	0	0	2

And its fairder covenaned and agreed by Ralph Pendlebury to pay to the Ooverseer of the Poor of Horwich one penny a month for the use of the within (above) named goods. As witness my hand,

RALPH PENDLEBURY.

Witness, Wm. Thornley.
Herwich, March 4th, 1783.

An Inventory of the goods of Cornelius Yates sold by John Whitehead to Thomas Karshaw, the Overseer of Horwich, as follows:—

IN THE HOUSE.

	£	s.	d.
Chimney Crow and Tongs	0	6	0
Clothes Chist	0	10	0
A Oak Table	0	2	0
Clock, Cubert, and Snap Table	1	15	0
Eight Chears	0	6	0
Fall Table	0	2	0
A Mop and too Pictures	0	0	0
Smoothing Iron and Heaters	0	1	0

ROOM OVER HOUSE.

	£	s.	d.
One Bed and Bedding	1	0	0
A Fire Iron	0	1	0
Too Chears	0	6	0

	£	s.	d.
ROOM OVER SHOP.			
One Bed and Beding	0	15	0
A Pair of Bedstocks	0	1	6
A Pair of Stocks for Cards	0	2	0
BUTTRY.			
A Iron Pot	0	1	0
A Brass Pan	0	1	0
A Iron Pan	0	1	6
Two Tubs and Dough Eshon	0	3	0
Cups and Dishes and Spoons	0	1	0
IN THE SHOP.			
One Pare of Loomes	1	10	0
Heald Reeds and Brushes and Drying Iron	0	10	0
One Spining Wheel	1	0	0
Riddle and Spade	0	3	0

4th day of June, 1739.

This day is agreed between William Hart and James Pendlebury overseers of the poor of Horwich of the one part, and Thomas Entwistle a poor man belonging to Horwich aforesaid of the other part as followeth :—The said overseers by and with the privity and consent of the inhabitants of Horwich aforesaid hath this day lent unto the said Thomas Entwistle one pair of fustian looms, healds and reed excepted, and the same looms being purchased by the inhabitants of Horwich aforesaid ; and the said Thomas Entwistle doth hereby promise and engage that the same looms with all materials (healds and reed only excepted) in as good order as they now are, shall, on the demands of the present overseers or any of their successors in the said office, be peaceably and quietly delivered up to them on their order, as witness my hand

                                    THOMAS (x) ENTWISTLE,
Witnesses   his (x) mark.
    Andrew Taylor,
    James Brandwood.

One June 30, 1742, we find an inventory taken of the above Thomas Entwistle's goods by William Hart, churchwarden, and Peter Longworth, overseer, as follows :—"One little chimne or grate tongs and gib, a brass pan, little caldron, 4 cheers, 7 little stools, 2 tresses, one feild chist, one piggin, 6 muges and pots, 3 wheels, one littel box, 2 beds and beding, 2 bucks and one great wisket, one pair of looms that the town bought, drying pan, and 2 pair of brushes, weys and weights, bread Beak and back spittle.

Witness JOHN SEDDON.

Know all men by these presents, That we Margret Vause and Elizabeth Vause, of Horridge, in the County of Lancaster, for In consideration of the sum of thirty-one shillings and four pence to us in hand and paid by John Etock, churchwarden, and James Aspinall, overseer of the Poor of Horridge, In the County of Lancaster, or one of them at or before the execution of these presents, and for other good considerations to us hereunto moving. Have granted, bargained, sold, and by these presents do grant, bargain, and sell unto the said John Etock and James Aspinall, their Exors., Adminst, and Assigns, the several goods, chattles, and household stuffs, hereinafter particularly specified and mentioned. That is to say, a chimney and tongs, two spinning wheels, one plank ark, two boxes, one trunk, three chairs, two plates, two spoons, a treat, one Iron pot, two pans, a smoothing iron and heaters, three shelves, three pictures, three spoons and pot-hooks, pots, three books and a bible, a table, a bed and bedding, and all our right, title, interest, benefit, claim, and demand to the same. To have and to hold the said goods, chattles, household stuffe, and all other the premises hereby bargained and sold, or intended to be hereby bargained and sold unto the said John Etock and James Aspinall, their Exors., Adm^n., and Assigns, to and for the use, benefit, behoof of all the inhabitants and owners of land within the said township of Horridg. That the said John Etock and James Aspinall and their Assigns, shall and may quietly hold and enjoy, or expose to sale all and every the said bargained goods, without any interuption or molestation of or by the said Mary and Eliz. Vause, or either of them, or any other person or persons by or through their mean privity act, or preventive in anywise. In witness whereof we have set our hands and seals, the Second Day of December, in the year of our Lord 1735.

Signed, sealed, and delivered MARGRET (seal) VAUSE, being duly stamped in the her x mark.
presence of us ELIZABETH (seal) VAUSE, her x mark.

Jeremiah Pendlebury   Lawrence Bromiley.

CHAPTER XVIII.

We purpose in this chapter to give extracts from the constable and overseer's accounts. Such being very voluminous, we shall content ourselves with just an extract here and there, sufficient to guide our readers in their investigations relative to a period to which many manners and customs only recently abolished, or yet continued, have pointed and direct reference. Previous to the "Local Health Act," which give such ample powers to local authorities, villages and rural districts were governed by an authority almost irresponsible, and yet was given vitality by the action of the inhabitants in "vestry meeting" assembled. Opposing forces sometimes fought their civil battles within the precincts of the parish church, or beneath its shadow. A vestry meeting was the signal which heralded a night's debauch, and many, careless alike of civil duties or responsibilities, always remembered that at the Black Bull and Brown Cow a town's meeting would be held. The former was more patronised, for as a writer in "The Temperance Magazine," signed "W. S.," remarked in 1837:—"At a place not six miles from Bolton part of the minister's salary comes from the wounds and bruises of a *Bull*," this being a pointed reference to the fact that the Black Bull was church property. This anomaly, we are happy to say, no longer exists, as some few years ago it was bought by Mr. John Sumner, of Haigh Brewery. Speaking of the Black Bull, we have before us the following reference:—"29th September, 1775. This original lease (Black Bull) was granted by the late Robert Blundell, Esq., of Ince, the parties to it are they said Robert Blundell and his son the late Henry Blundell, Esq., later Peter Hart, late William Longworth, late Robert Eatock, late Rev. John Norcross. Form of the lease 999 years. When the trustees are reduced to two fresh trustees are to be elected, not to exceed five. At a meeting held in Horwich, Sept. 9th, 1781, it was agreed between the trustees and the curate that the curate should receive two-thirds of the rent of the house, paying two-thirds of the repairs, and two-thirds of the chief rent of the house, which is ten shillings, to be paid annually on the 25th of March." The parlour of the Black Bull was the *sanctum sanctorum* of village politicians. Within it Mr. Ridway held his court; within it churchwarden and constable broke the law while looking for law breakers. The landlord of the Black Bull was an important personage; he was the repository of many secrets, and knew the outcome of village councils. Its connection with the church gave it a status that overshadowed its licensed authority, and made it the rendezvous of all sections of the community. The local aristocrats drank at its bar, and the village crofter gathered in its tap room. We might refer to darker connections; but why revive the ghosts of the past? The link is severed, and why should we weep over the dissolution? To these "town's meetings" and the sum spent, which refers to the expenditure in drink at the Black Bull, &c., we find many references.

1779.	£	s.	d.
Paid for this book	0	2	0
Ballance to Hugh Whittle	0	4	0
May 3.—Necessity money to Sam Thornley's son Richard	0	15	0
July 25.—Funeral expenses for Mary Green	0	15	0
Aug. 14.—Bedgown and hose for Nightingale's daughter	0	3	1
Aug. 21.—Shifts for Schofield's wench	0	6	3
Aug. 23.—Cloth for Widow Young's little wench, coats	0	5	0
Sept. 3.—Two brats for Schofield's wench	0	1	3
" Hugh Whittle's expenses, together with time and the horses at the quarter sessions	1	3	5
Oct. 18.—To Cornelius Yates for child's coffin, &c.	0	5	0
Oct. 21.—Going to Blackrod with summons and gave David 2s	0	2	6
Lawyer Peter's fee	0	10	6
Going to retain him	0	1	0
Spent at town's meeting	0	5	0
Dec. 21.—Enlisting money to James Vause	0	2	6

1780.   £ s. d.
Jan. 1.—To Bill Brown for relief................   0 2 6
Jan. 24.—Rent to Brindle Poorhouse 0 8 6
Feb. 7.—For making Schofield's wenchcoat,
  caps, and handkerchiefs........................   0 0 11
Spent at sessions on account of the Militia   0 8 4
Mar. 21—Spent at town's meeting.............   0 8 0

Two references in the above may require a word of explanation. "Going to Blackrod with summonses," and the liability of Horwich in regard to "Brindle Poorhouse." At this period the prisoners from Horwich were conveyed to Blackrod, and only recently has the strong stone building which had all the appearance of a prison been pulled down. "The Bolton Union" either judicially or in regard to the poor, had little or any power in the village. We have before us many receipts for the quota of Horwich towards the rent of Brindle poorhouse, and many references which plainly indicates that Blackrod dungeon answered the requirements of the district. It would be easy to show that Horwich, as well as districts similarly situated, were then almost free from taxation, and if any extraordinary aid was required such aid was met by a small voluntary subscription, as the following may be evidence:—

May 2 1734.
An account what hath been given in the Hamlet of Horwich towards the poore Stock of the Pariah:—
                                                        £ s. d.
Nathaniell Longworth 0 0 6
Ms. Boardman 0 2 0
Jonathan Knowls 0 1 0
Widow Pendlebury 0 0 2
Ann Longworth..................................... 0 0 1
Rob. Greenhalgh 0 1 0
John Pilkington..................................... 0 1 0
Wm. Hart.. 0 0 6
Giles Gorton 0 1 0
James Nightingall.................................. 0 0 3
James Peake 0 0 3
John Hodkinson 0 0 6
Thomas Knowls..................................... 0 0 6
Hugh Whittle.. 0 0 6
Richd. Pilkington 0 0 6
Henry Tornley 0 0 2
James Longworth.................................. 0 0 6
Wm. Boulton 0 1 0

	£	s.	d.
John Mason	0	1	0
John Norcross	0	1	0
James Marsh	0	2	0
Rebecah Nightingale	0	0	6
Robert Pendlebury	0	0	6
Robt. Hart	0	0	4
Robt. Greenhalgh	0	1	0
James Greenhalgh	0	1	0
Christopher Horrox	0	0	6

From the following, direct proof of the liability of Horwich, and the extent of such liability in reference to Brindle poorhouse, may be gathered:—"Received, Jany. 2nd, 1750, from the overseer of the poor of Horwich, the sum of eight shillings in full for one year's rent last past, due this day to Brindle workhouse from that township. I say received by me,

THOS. CALVERT."

In some of the old town's records before us we find minutes of detail and a completeness of description, that betokens a lively interest in the public duties they were called upon to perform. In more modern times the term "incidental expenses" would embrace such details as the following:—"Paid Hugh Whittle for taking a notice to the overseers of Anderton, 6d." "For going to Thos. Worsley, 6d." A number of other details of a similar nature, causes the "overseer" to write as follows upon one of the pages of the book:—
"As there are several journeys charged at 8d. and 1s., I hope the town will not think the charge too much, as I can reckon up several times to Bolton and other places which I have not charged at all.

ROBT. GREENHALGH."

The village had its "relieving officer," but not as at present, a highly salaried official. Inquiries were made and the position and surroundings of the applicant carefully considered ere relief was granted; to have paid more than half of the sum collected for relief for the distribution of the lesser half would have been unpardonable extravagance. The following extracts may give some light upon the mode of proceeding ere relief was granted, and the cost thereof:—"Hugh Whittle for examining Thos. Turner, 1s." "Do. for viewing

William Fallows, 1s." The amount of relief was much similar to the present rate :—"April 29, 1780, to Jane Young for two week, 4s." "Paid Henry Pendlebury for having Betty Hilton twelve weeks, £1 4s." The duties appertaining to the office of constable may be gathered from the following :—"My accounts for serving a long year of the constableship is as followeth. James Turner, June, 1760 :—

	£	s.	d.
For going to Salford court	0	1	4
For Samuel Sandsford and Mee, viewing windows	0	2	0
For putting on acoers at Bolton	0	1	0
For livoring assessments at Bury	0	2	0
For signing of dublicates	0	5	0
For one money warent	1	15	9
For second money warrant	0	13	5
For the third money warrant	0	3	2
For the fourth money warrant	0	1	5
For presenting ye alehousekeepers at Bury	0	1	0
For paying a money warrant at Manchester	0	1	0
Paid to James Stones for churchwarding use	2	2	0
For livoring in ye militia man at Manchester	0	1	0
For assice presentments and livering them	0	1	6
For paying money warrant at Ashton-under-line	0	0	9
For ye town clerk's wages	0	5	0
For relieving a wounded soldier	0	0	6
For ye fifth money warrant	0	1	9
For going to Salford court out of time	0	1	0
For a new town's box	0	2	0
For signing Edward Vause dublicates	0	2	0
For what ye land tax falls short	1	1	0

	£	s.	d.
Collected	8	13	11
Disburst	7	8	2
Deter to town	1	5	9

James Turner's accounts in serving the office of churchwarding for the year 1761 are as followeth :—

	£	s.	d.
Paid for too new bears	1	1	0
For bread and wine	0	1	11
For one new bellroap	0	1	9

	s	s.	d.
For one thanksgiving peaper (prayer)	0	0	8
For one peaper concerning the sopression of vice	0	0	8
For bread and wine	0	1	11
For athoring (altering) the prayers a peaper	0	0	6
For ringing on the cronation (coronation) day	0	0	6
For John Sharples lad going to Blackrod	0	0	2
For making the presentment	0	0	6
For parish use at church first half-year	1	6	8
For court fees, first visitation	0	3	6
For bread and wine	0	1	11
For one peaper concerning the fast	0	0	8
For bread and wine	0	1	11
For bands for window sheets	0	0	4
For the clark's wages	0	11	0
For Thomas Knowles keeping ye bear cloath two yeare	0	2	0
For prayers and thanksgiving concerning Martinsor	0	0	8
For making the presentment	0	0	6
For parish use second half-year	1	0	0
For court fees, second visitation	0	3	0
Besides going to Bolton twice, and spending sixpence one time and ninepence another, about paying for the bear, which I reckon at	0	3	3
	£5	12	8

		£	s.	d.
Collected 1 Ley		4	6	11	2
Received from Games Stones	0	5	7	2
	4	12	7	0
Disburst	5	12	2	0
Out of purse	1	0	5	0

CHAPTER XIX.

There are certain peculiarities in the performance of official duties that would seem to imply that our forefathers, even in the lesser government of villages, looked upon their position as paternal in character and responsibility. While singularly jealous of bearing any burden other than that which civil obligation or legal necessity demanded, equally were they zealous in the performance of any civil or moral obligation which the poverty or needs of the necessitous might impose upon them. To be a poor person in the past did not necessarily imply that they were paupers, or that they were receiving any money payment or aid from public funds or local organisations. We have already seen that a person unable to sit upon a £10 rentality was in the view of the local authorities sufficient to place him in the category of poor persons. His every movement was diligently watched, an improvement of his position by a removal into the adjacent or other village or place was denied him, unless he carried with him a kind of civil pass. The passport system was in vogue with more than foreign vigour, and society was edge-bound with conditions and requirements which interfered with that full development of national character more recently exhibited. In the death of these singular customs we fail to find any action which would bespeak any credit to the Legislature. It would be astonishing were a compilation made of the laws, which are now virtually the law of the realm, to be found on the statute book, possessing the elements of authority, and the machinery of legality, which no power could stay in operation, and which have sunk into disuse, but not destroyed, possessing a vitality easily resuscitated. The strange laws of our forefathers are our own, and society has merely taken a power which is not its own, and forgets a law which is inconvenient to its needs. To provide and make due provision for the duties which in their station of life they might be called upon to fulfil, was an obligation which rested upon the local authorities in respect to these so-called poor persons. A girl taken to perform the merest drudgery of house work, must needs be protected with all the formula which to-day is only called into requisition in case of the more exalted callings. Seal, stamps, parchment, witnesses, signatures, and co-signatures with all the obscurity of legal phraseology was called into action, as much so for the due washing-up of a dinner pot as to-day would be required for the conveying of an estate. We give our readers two from a large number now before us.

"This Indenture, made the seventh day of September, in the year of our Lord 1734, and in the 8th year of the reign of our Sovereign Lord George the Second, over Great Britain king, Defender of the Faith, and between Hugh Whittle, churchwarden, and James Longworth, overseer of the poor of Horwich, in the county of Lancaster, of the one part, and Ralph Entwistle, of Edgworth, in the said county, ffustian weaver, of the other part. Witnesseth that the said churchwarden and overseer of the poor by and with the consent and allowance of two of His Majesties justices of the peace and quorum in and for the said county, according to the forms of the statutes in that case made and provided, have putt, placed, and bound, and hereby do putt, place, and bind William Entwistle, son of Thomas Entwistle, of Herwich aforesaid, a poor child of Horwich aforesaid, an apprentice to the said Ralph Entwistle to the art, trade, or occupation of a ffustian weaver ffor the terme of seven years from the day of the date of these presents, during all which time and term the said apprentice his said master well and faithfully shall serve, his secrets keep, his commands lawfull, and honest everywhere, and at all times shall obey and do, hurt and damage to his said master he shall not do, or suffer to be done of others, but to his power shall lett or hinder the same or forthwith give notice to his said master. The goods of his said master he shall not inordinately waste, purloyn, or steal,

nor them lend to any without his said master's
consent. Taverns, Inns, or alehouses he shall not of
custom frequent. Unlawful games, or dishonest company he shall in no wise use, ffornication he shall not
committ. Matrimony he shall not contract, at cards,
dice, or other unlawfull games he shall not play, nor by
night or day absent himself from his said master's service, but everywhere and at all times, shall behave
himself towards his said Master and his family as a
good, and faithfull apprentice, and covenant servant
during the said terme. And the said Ralph Entwistle
the master in consideration thereof, and of the sum of
forty shillings to him in hand paid, or secured to be
paid by him the said James Longworth at, and before
the execution of these presents, the receipt whereof is
hereby acknowledged. Doth hereby for himself, his
executors, administrators, and assigns, covenant, and
grant to, and with the said churchwarden and overseer
of the poor, and their executors, administrators, and
successors in the said offices respectively for the time
being. That he the said Ralph Entwistle the master,
his executors, administrators, and assigns, shall do his
and their best endeavours to inform, teach, and instruct, or cause to be informed, taught, and instructed,
him the said William Entwistle the apprentice, in the
art, trade, mystery, or occupation of a ffustian weaver
during all the said term. And also, that he the said
Ralph Entwistle, his executors, administrators, and
assigns, shall, and will at all times during the said
term, find, allow, provide, and give to his said appretice, sufficient wholesome, and convenient meat, drink,
and lodging, washing, and also all manner of apparell,
both linnen, wollen, hatts, shoes, and stockings, fitt
and convenient for such an apprentice to have and
wear during the said term. And at the end thereof
shall discharge and deliver up to the said apprentice
with two good suits of apparel of all sorts, both linnen,
wollen, hatts, shoes, and stockings, one of them fitt to
wear on holy days, and the other on other days of the
week. And lastly shall yearly pay to his said apprentice the sum of sixpence each Christmas day, during
the said term, for and as his hyre and wages. In
witness whereof the parties aforesaid to these

~~presents, they hand and seal interchangeably have
set, the day and year first above written.~~

11 September, 1734.   Hugh (seal) Whittle.
Seen and allowed by us.   James (seal) Longworth.
S. Fallows } Magisterial.   Ralph (seal) Entwistle.
J. Sharples   his—R—mark.
                              William (seal) Entwistle-
                                  his   mark."

The following we give as a sample of others relating to female apprentices:—

"This Indenture made the twelth day of April in the fourteenth year of the Reign of our Sovereign Lord George the Second, by the grace of God, of Great Britain, France, and Ireland, King, Defender of the faith, and in the year of our Lord 1732. Between Robert Hart Churchwarden, and Thomas Knowles and Peter Longworth, Being the Major part of the Churchwardens, and Overseers of the Poor of Horwich in the County of Lancaster of the one part, And Thomas Ormerod living in Elton, but belonging to Tottington in the same County, weaver, of the other part. Witnesseth that the said Robert Hart, Thomas Knowles and Peter Longworth by and with the consent and allowance of Two of his Majesty's Justices of the Peace in and for the said County, Have, putt, placed, and bound, and by these Presents, Do put, place, and bind Ellen Aldred, a poor fatherless child belonging now to Horwich, apprentice to the said Thomas Ormerod to cohabit, and dwell from the day of the Date hereof for, and during the full time and term of 10 years, During which said term, the said apprentice her said Master sho shall serve, his secrets keep, his lawfull commands obey, observe and do hurt to her said Master She shall not do, nor consent to the doing thereof, She shall not waste the goods of her said Master, nor lend the same to any person, or persons without her Master's consent, At Cards, Dice, or any other unlawfull game She shall not play, whereby her Master shall sustain damage, fornication she shall not commit, nor matrimony contract during the said Term, nor from her said Master's service absent, or depart night or day, but in all things as a dutifull, faithfull, and obedient servant shall behave herself towards her master, his wife, and family during her apprenticeship. And he, the said Thomas Ormerod, in consideration of the said service, and of the sum of three pounds of lawfull British money to be paid by the aforesaid Robert Hart, Thomas Knowles, and Peter Longworth, as churchwarden and overseers of the town, that is to say forty shillings in hand, at or before the sealing and delivering of these presents, the receipt whereof is hereby acknowledged, and twenty shillings the remainder to be paid when Thomas Ormerod hath lived one whole year in the town where his settlement is, and his apprentice hath lived and served him one whole year in the town where his settlement is, that is Tottington, if his apprentice be then living. And the said Thomas Ormerod doth hereby for himself, his heirs, executors, admst, and assigns, covenant, promise, and agree to and with the said Robert Hart, Thomas Knowles, and Peter Longworth, and either of them, there, or either of there executors, administrators, that he, the said Thomas Ormerod, his executors, admst, or assigns, shall and will from time to time, and at all times during the said term of 10 years, as well in sickness, as in health, find and provide for the said apprentice sufficient and convenient meat, drink, washing, lodging and apparel of all sorts of clothes fit and convenient for such an apprentice, and at the end of the term shall deliver the said apprentice up in good and decent apparel. And further that the said Thomas Ormerod, his executors, admst, or assigns, shall and will from time to time, and at all times during the said term well, and sufficiently, educate, instruct, and inform the said Ellen Aldred in the trade, art, or occupation of housewifery, or cause her to be taught the best way he can fitting for such an apprentice. In witness whereof the parties above said to these presents, their hands and seals interchangeably have set.

Magisterial signatories,
  John Bradshaw,
  Rob. Booth.

ROBERT (seal) HART.
  his   mark.
THO. (seal) KNOWLES.
PETER (seal) LONGWORTH.
THOS. (seal) ORMEROD.
ELLEN (seal) ALDRED.
  her   mark.

We have before us the following Indentures, as under :—

Date	Name of Apprentice.	To whom Apprenticed.	Trade or Occupation.	Premium paid.	Magisterial Signatories.
1729	John Entwistle	Robert Abrem	Taylor, L'pool	0 16 (	W. Marsden R. Gildart
1733	Robert Yate	Thomas Brimelow, Lostock	Fustian weaver	1 0 0	S. Dunstow. S. Hallows
1734	James Worsley	James Kersley	Weaver	0 15 0	Robert Leigh Wm. Riley
1800	Betty Greenhalgh	John Pilkington		4 5 0	R. Fletcher A. Fletcher
1749	John Vause	Daniel Lawson	Linnen weaver	3 5 0	Alex. Leigh Holt Leigh
1776	Esther Nightingale	Richard Mason			R. Dewhurst D. Rasbotham
1776	John Greenbalgh	John Hall	Small ware weaver	4 13 6	D. Rastotham R. Andrews
1794	William Holt	Peter Thornley	Weaver	4 0 0	R. Prescot Thos Holme
1746	Mary Vause	Thos. Parr	Servant	4 0 0	As above
1737	Hosseley Anderton	Thos. Bromilow	Spining	3 10 0	Robert Duckinfield Robert Booth
1732	John Pendlebury	Thos. Grime	Weaver	3 0 0	James Bradshaw E. Whitehead
1735	James Yate	James Kersley, W-Houghton	Nailer	1 10 (	R. Bradshaigh J. Blackburn
1801	James Greenbalgh	W. Butterworth	Weaver	4 4 1	A. Fletcher R. Fletcher
1776	Robert Nightingale	Solomon Brownlow	Stonemason	8 0 0	R. Dewhurst D. Rasbotham
1796	Will'm. Bamford	Thos. Dickinson, Wigan	Blacksmith	4 12 6	Thomas Holme Thos. Barton
1801	Alice Greenhulgh	Thos. Bolton	Weaver	"sum of six pence"	A. Fletcher R. Fletcher
1781	Betty Nightingale	Peter Blackley	Servant	1 10 (	R. Dewhurst D. Rasbotham
1749	Joseph Vause	John Dalton, Abram		2 15 0	Ralph Assheton Will. Norton
1757	James Pendlebury	James Turner	Weaver	3 0 (	as above
1732	Will. Green	John Blacklow	Fustian weaver	3 0 0	Walmsley John Owen
1778	Willm. Young	W. Greenhalgh	Weaver	3 10 0	D. Rasbotham R. Dewhurst

Date	Name of Apprentice.	To whom Apprenticed.	Trade or Occupation.	Premium paid.	Magisterial Signatories.
1736	Thos. Green	Francis Crook	Fustian weaver	0 15 0	R. Booth J. Chetham
1762	A. Pendlebury	John Bromilow, Lostock	Weaver	4 5 0	J. Bradshaw E. Whitehead
1794	Joseph Adamson	Thos. Bromilow	Weaver	2 2 C	Thos. Prescot Rich. Barton
1774	Humphrey Nigutingale	John Scowcroft	Weaver	2 0 0	R. Dewhurst D. Rasbotham
1779	Robert Pilkington	John Magnall	Weaver	6 10 0	J. Bradshaw K. Fletcher
174	Mary Vause	Thos. Parr	Housewifery	4 0 0	Robert Booth Jas. Chetham
1746	James Thornley	N. Nickinson, Blackrod	Fustian weaver	3 3 C	Jas. Chetham Robt. Dukinfield
1761	Betty Pendlebury	James Brindle	Housewifery	0 15 0	J. Bradshaw E. Whitehead
1762	Will. Fallow	Thomas Lee	Mason	4 15 0	As above
1776	John Wareing	James Cowpe, Brindle	Linnen and cotton whitster	4 0 0	W. Cunliffe Shaw R. Shuttleworth
1731	Thos. Worsley	John Molyneux, Ince-upon-Mackerfield			J. Walmsley John Owen
178!	Richard Miller	Thomas Grime, Penworthham	Crofter	0 5 0	W. Hough W. Whittle
1734	Thos. Entwistle	Ralph Entwistle, Edgworth	Fustian weaver	2 0 0	S. Hallows T. Sharples
1739	John Yate	Andrew Taylor, Hindley	Fustian weaver	3 0 0	S. Hallows R. Entwistle
1773	Eddy Vause	Thos. Haslam, L. Bolton	Weaver	2 2 0	R. Dewhurst R. Andrews
1778	Henry Young	John Grundy, Little Lever	Papermaker	2 0 0	R. Dewhurst D. Rasbotham
1729	John Green	Mary Heaton, Aspull	Weaver	3 0 1	Robert Booth Willm. Leigh
1755	George Longworth	Thos. Markland, Lostock	Fustian weaver	1 0 0	None
1750	Patience Vose	John Borrobin, Blackrod	Weaving and housewifery	1 10 0	R. Assheton Thos. Percival
1775	Rich. Entwistle	John Thornley	Weaver	5 0 0	R. Dewhurst D. Rasbotham

CHAPTER XX.

We have pleasure in laying before our readers two documents that will doubtless tend to illustrate the respective periods to which they refer. For this privilege we are indebted to Mr. Richard Whittle, of Ashton House, Crewe, the lineal descendant of that very ancient village family bearing his name to which in these pages we have frequently referred. The document is quaint in phraseology, but we present it now in modernised form as follows: "This indenture made the last day of February in the six and twentieth year of the reign of our Sovereign Lady Elizabeth, by the grace of God, Queen of England, France, and Ireland, Defender of the faith, &c. Between Thurstan Whittle, of Horwich, within the County of Lancaster, husbandman, Elizabeth, his wife, and William Whittle, son of the said Thurstan, upon the one part, and Giles Morris, of Rumworth, within the said County of Lancaster, husbandman, upon the other part. Witnesseth that the said Thurstan Whittle, Elizabeth, his wife, and William, their son, for, and in consideration of the sum of fifty pounds of usual English money unto them the said Thurstan, Elizabeth, and William Whittle, by the said Giles Morris, at and before the using and delivery of these present indentures well and truely contented and paid, whereof and wherewith the said Thurstan, Elizabeth, and William, and every of them do hold and acknowledge themselves by these presents fully contented and satisfied, and the said Giles Morris, his executors, administrators, and assigns, and every of them thereof and of every part thereof clearly discharged, used, and for ever acquited by these presents, Have, given, granted allowed, appointed, relinquished, assigned, and set over, and by these presents, do fully, freely, and absolutely from them, and every of them, give, grant, appoint, relinquish, assign, and set over, unto the said Giles Morris and his assigns all that the moiety, and one half of all that messuage, tenement, with the appurtenances now in the holding of the said Thurstan, Elizabeth, and William, or any of them, or their assign, or assigns, situate and being in Horwich aforesaid, and the moiety, and one half of all buildings, orchards, gardens, folds, and certain parcels of land, meadow and pasture hereafter mentioned and expressed. That is to say all that portion of the dwellinghouse, beneath, or from the doors downward, two bays or bindings of and in the barn, that is to say, the west end thereof. All that building called the old shippon, with all the orchard and garden at the west end of the said dwelling house; the moiety and one-half of the meadow, that is to wit, that moiety next adjoining to the lane, one closure or parcel of ground called the 'Old Marled Earth'; one other parcel or closure of ground called the 'Round Croft,' one other parcel called the 'bottom,' one other parcel called 'The Long Marled Earth,' one other parcel called 'The Rye Croft,' one other parcel called 'The Rammock Hill, one other parcel called 'The Back-house Field,' one other parcel called 'The Barley Croft,' with the moiety and half of a certain ground called 'The Moor,' with the moiety and one of the Turbari, or turf room, with the moiety and one half of the folds, with all and all the (main ways), liberties, passages, and easements whatsoever to the same before recited premises, and every or any of them belonging or in any wise pertaining, or to the same used and accustomed. All the said premises before mentioned are parcel of the said messuages and tenement, and are appointed unto him, the said Giles, for the moiety of the said tenement, *to have* and to hold the said moiety of the said dwelling-house, with the said two bays in the barn, the said shippon, the orchard and garden aforesaid, with the said parcels and closures of land, meadow, and pasture aforesaid, and other the premises with all and (singular) their appurtenances, commodities, and profits; and all their right, title, and interest in and to the same, unto the said Giles Morris and his assigns, for the day of the date hereof, as tenants to the Lord for ever, and to his, and their own use and uses, as tenants unto the Lord as aforesaid, in as ample mind and form to every intent, purpose, and construction as they, the said Thurstan, Elizabeth, and William, or any of them should, as, might have enjoyed the same, yielding and paying therefrom yearly, unto the Lord and owner thereof, at the days and feasts usual and accustomed, twelve shillings and one half-penny of usual English money by even portions, if it be lawfully demanded, and also yielding, paying, and doing the moiety, and one-half of all such bonds, average duties and services as are or shall be yearly due and payable for the same tenement, and the said Thurstan, Elizabeth, and William Whittle, and every of them, for themselves, their executors, administrators, and assigns, and every of them, do covenant, promise, and grant by these presents to and with the said Giles Morris, his executors, and assigns, that he the said Giles Morris and his assigns, by force of these presents, shall and may well and quietly have, hold, and enjoy the same before recited premises and every part and parcel thereof, in manner and form aforesaid, without any manner, lawful, let, stop, trouble, denial, or contradiction of the said Thurstan, Elizabeth, and William, or any of them, or any other person or persons by them, or any of their movements, procurements, consents, or assents in anywise, and that the same before recited premises, or any part thereof, at any time hereafter shall not be in any wise chargeable with any more rents, settlements or services, but only with the moiety of the rents, settlements, and services due for the whole tenement, as aforesaid. And also it is agreed by and between the said parties and the said Thurstan, Elizabeth, and William Whittle, for them and every of them, their executors, administrators, and assigns, and every of them, do covenant, promise, and grant by these presents, to and with the said Giles Morris, his executors, administrators, and assigns, and every of them, that he the said Giles and his assigns, by force of these presents, shall and may well and quitely have, hold, and enjoy to his and their own uses all such tithes of corn and grain as shall yearly arise, renew, increase, and come in and upon the before recited premises and closures of ground, and every parcel thereof, during such term as he the said Thurstan Whittle, his

executors, or assigns, have or ought to have any
interest, title, or demand, in bond to the said tithes,
paying the moiety of the rents due for the same yearly,
without any manner, lawful, let, stop, or denial of any
person or persons. In witness whereof to these present
indentures the parties before named interchangeably
have set their hands and seals, the day and year first
above written, 1583." On the back of the parchment is
inscribed the following:—"Sealed, signed, and peaceable possession within the said two bays of the dwelling-house within mentioned, in nanme of all the lands
within specified, was delivered with these presents by
the within-named Thurstan unto the within named
Giles, in presence of

  James Jhonnes (Jones)
  — Grinhalgh (Greenhalgh)
  Ralfe Sedonne (Seddon)
  Andrew Seddonne."

"To all to whom these presents shall come. I, John
Whittle, of Manchester, in the county of Lancaster,
cotton manufacturer, send greeting, whereas my father,
Hugh Whittle, late of Horwich, in the said county,
yeoman, deceased, duly made and executed his last will
and testament dated the 29th January, 1788. Whereby,
after giving, devising, and bequeathing as therein
mentioned, he gave all the rest, residue, and remainer
of his personal estate and effects, together with twenty
five pounds therein mentioned to be paid by his son,
Robert Whittle, and charged upon the messuage or
dwelling-house and parcel of land given to him by the
said will, and then in the occupation of his the testator's
son-in-law, John Grundy, and directed to be added to
his the testator's other personal estate and applied
accordingly unto and amongst all his children, being
seven in number, share and share alike. And if any of
them should happen to die before they received their
respective shares of his estate and effects, then he gave
the part or share of him, her, or them so dying unto
and amongst the children or issue of him, her, or them,
who should be so dead equally if more than one child,
and, if no more than one, the whole thereof to such
only child. And he did thereby appoint his son,

Robert Whittle, and his brother, Richard Whittle, since deceased, executors thereof, and the said Robert Whittle duly proved the same in the Consistory Court at Chester and took upon himself the executors thereof. And whereas the said Robert Whittle hath settled an account with me and my brothers and sisters respecting his executorship, and the residue and remainder of the said testator's personal estate and effects, including the said sum of twenty-five pounds so as aforesaid directed to be added to his other personal estate, and applied accordingly after the payment of the said testator's general expenses and the charge of the probate of the said will, amounted to the sum of eight hundred and ten pounds and nineteen shillings, being the sum of £115 17s. a piece for me and the said *** ******. Now know ye that I the said John Whittle do hereby own and acknowledge to have had and received of and from the said Robert Whittle the sum of £115 17s., being my full part and share of the said residue and remainder of the said personal estate and effects, and of the said sum of £25 so charged as aforesaid, and thereof, and of, and from the same, and every part thereof, do fully, clearly, and absolutely acquit, release, and for ever discharge the said Robert Whittle, his heirs, administrators, and assigns, and the executors, administrators, and assigns of the said Richard Whittle, deceased, and also the said messuages or dwelling-house and parcel of land and all other in real and personal estate and effects of the said testator, and in consideration thereof, and being fully satisfied in the premises, I, the said John Whittle, for myself, my executors, administrators and assigns, remise and release unto the said Robert Whittle his heirs, executors, administrators, and assigns, and the executors, administrators, and assigns of the said Richard Whittle, deceased, all and all manner of action and actions, cause and causes of action, suits, legacies, reckonings, accounts, sum and sums of money, claims and demands whatsoever, both at law and in equity which against the said Robert Whittle, his heirs, executors, administrators, or assigns, or the executors, administrators, or assigns of the said Richard Whittle, or the real or personal estate and effects of the said

Hugh Whittle, deceased. I, the said John Whittle, ever had or which I, my executors, administrators, or assigns, can or may have claim, challenge, or demand, for or by reason or means or on account of the said parts, shares, sum and sums of money so given and bequeathed, ordered and directed to be paid to me, the said John Whittle, in and by the said last will and testament of the said Hugh Whittle as aforesaid, or by reason, or means or on account of the real and personal estate of the said Hugh Whittle in an will. In witness whereof I, the said John Whittle, have hereunto subscribed my name this 12th April, 1806.

Signed the paper, being first duty,

JOHN WHITTLE.

Stamped in presence of
Geo. Taylor."

The following refers to certain lands, &c., now in the possession of Mr. A. Peak, for which we are indebted to Mr. J. D. Greenhalgh, Bolton :—

" To all persons to whom these presents shall come; I, John Hampson, of Horwich, in the county of Lancaster, husbandman, send greeting. Whereas, I am now possessed, interested in, and intitled unto all that messuage, or dwelling, or farm, with the lands and premises thereunto belonging, situate and being in Horwich aforesaid, by virtue of a lease thereof, made to me by   , for the residue of a term therein mentioned, and now unexpired; under the yearly rent and covenants therein mentioned and reserved, and am possessed of and entitled unto divers household and other goods, stock-in-trade, cattle, and other husbandry, utensils, ready money, and money out at interest, all which I am desirous to dispose of as hereafter. Now, know ye that the said John Hampson for and in consideration of the natural love and affection which I have and bear towards my son, John Hampson, and my daughters, Mary and Margaret Hampson, and for their advancement and preferment, and also for and in consideration of the sum of ten shillings of lawful money of Great Britain, to me in hand, paid by the said John Hampson, Mary and Margaret Hampson, and for divers other good and valuable causes and considerations me thereunto moving, have given, granted, bargained, sold, assigned, let over, and by these presents do give, grant, bargain, sell, assign, and let over unto the said John Hampson, my son, and the said Mary Hampson and Margaret Hampson, my daughters, their executors, administrators, and assigns, all and singular, the said messuage, dwelling-house, farm, land, and premises, situate in Horwich aforesaid, and now in my possession or occupation, with all the liberties, advantages, and appurtenances thereunto belonging. To have and hold the said messuage, or dwelling-house, farm, land, and premises, and every part thereof, with the appurtenances unto John Hampson, my son, daughters Mary Hampson and Margaret Hampson, their executors, administrators, and assigns, for, and during all the residue and remainder of the said term, granted in and by the said lease made to me thereof, under and upon payment of the yearly rent and covenants mentioned and referred to in the said lease, subject nevertheless to the payment of the sum of forty pounds, and to the trust hereafter mentioned. And I, the said John Hampson, for the consideration aforesaid, have given, granted, bargained, sold, assigned, and let over unto the said John Hampson, my son, daughter Mary Hampson, and Margaret Hampson, all and every my household and other goods, horses, cows, cattle, ready money, and money out at interest, implements, stock, and all other my personal estate whatsoever now in my possession, or in the hands, custody, or possession of any other person or persons whatsoever, to have and to hold all, and singular, my household and other goods, horses, cows, cattle, ready money, and money out at interest, implements, stock, and all other my personal estate whatsoever, unto the said John Hampson, my son, daughter Mary and Margaret Hampson, their executors, administrators, and assigns, as their own proper goods and chattels for ever, in trust nevertheless, that they, the said John Hampson, my son, daughter Mary Hampson, and Margaret Hampson, and the survivor of them, his or her executors, administrators, shall and will permit and suffer me to hold and enjoy the said farm and premises for, and during the term of my natural life, and also to hold and enjoy all and singular, my said personal estate for and during the said term of my natural life. And also that he, the said John Hampson, daughter Mary Hampson, and Margaret Hampson shall and will well and truly pay, or cause to be paid unto other sons, James Hampson, Peter Hampson, and Thomas Hampson, the sum of forty pounds, equal to be divided amongst them, share and share alike, at the end of twelve months next after my decease, and to which sum of forty pounds I do hereby make all and singular my said personal estate charged and chargeable. In witness whereof I hereunto put my hand and seal, this twenty-fifth day of October, in the year of our Lord, One Thousand Seven Hundred and Seventy. Sealed and delivered on duly stamped paper, in presence of

[Names wanting.]

CHAPTER XXX.

In the latter part of the last century, many articles now of common domestic use were indeed articles of luxury. The lower classes were contented with their surroundings, though in these they were denied many—now considered—essentials, and robbed of privileges that were justly and rightfully their own. Society presented that calm, but withal that dangerous quietude that ever heralds a great change. Work was in abundance, but was denied system. Regulated labour was unknown, and a day's work was but a term applied to an irregular period. Wages bore no relation to the hours employed, and 16 or 20 hours labour was often embraced in the term "day." As to the value of such labour we present our readers with such aids as will enable them to determine. In the surveyor's account for 1791 we have the following:—

For work done on the highway.

	£	s.	d.
To 3 days one horse and cart	0	7	6
To 16 days work of a man with pick and spade	1	4	0
To 28 loads of broken stones	0	14	0
	2	5	6

From the suveyor's account for 1789 we extract the following items of iterest:—

Spent at viewing the road.

	£	s.	d.
Paid Wm. Sharples for repairing the wheelbarrow	0	2	6
John Hodkinson, 10 days work	0	13	4
James Kershaw, 9 "	0	12	0
Paid to James Mayson, 6 days	0	8	0
Paid James Hampson for getting stones	1	4	4
Spent at public meeting	0	16	0
Wm. Peak for half a day	0	0	8
To a cart 2 days	0	4	0

	s.	d.
Paid a cart with 2 horses	0	5	0
Paid for 8 load of sand	0	4	0
Paid for sell (ale) at sundery times	0	4	8
To the sallery (for salary)	4	4	0
Out of pocket	98	9	8½

In the following year 1790 we have the following amongst other entries :—

	£	s.	d.
James Marsden, for 2 days and ½	0	5	0
James Kershaw, for 1 day and ¼	0	2	3
Spent at a public meeting	0	5	0
To Calip Hilton (paving) 60 rood at 1s. 4d. per rood	4	0	0
Paid for 10 rood at 2s 4d.	1	3	4
Paid for sell (ale)	0	6	0
" "	0	3	0
John Hart for a load of stones	0	0	6
(This year) collected	81	12	2½
Desburst (disburst)	151	3	3

The surveyor noted that he was £34 9s. 2d. "out of hand." In the surveyor's accounts for 1792 we find several items that more prominently display the characteristics of the period. We have several sums for "sell"—ale—probably given to the men employed on the public roads, and as these items refer to the aggregate for a given period we may presume that such "allowance" was systematic. Another prominent item is that relative to the expenditure at "town's meeting." We have in one page "Spent at the town's meet, 5s. 0d.," and "Spent at a publick meeting, 4s. 6d." This is collateral evidence to a kind of traditionary testimony, which speaks of "these meetings as being the harbingers of a good spree," and they, and they only, were the "great men" of the village who liberally supplemented this public donation by allowing such of the "free" (?) and good villagers to get "as drunk as a lord" at their expense as they pleased. Change, however, we expect to find, only, we may say, in a lawyer's bill of costs. The conventional 6s. 8d. of 1883 was equally a regulated price of "advice given" in 1792, for on the page before us we find one, "Mr. Taylor, 6s. 8d." The other accounts on this page are as follows :—

	£	s.	d.
Going to Bolton	0	2	0
Paid for the order	(	(	(
Thos. Kenaw, 1 day	0	1	6
Paid Rlod. Pilkington for hommer homes	0	1	0
Going to Leigh	0	1	6
John Etock, for do.	0	1	6
To expenses	0	2	0
Thos. Kershaw, for 3 days	0	4	6
Paid Robert Hooff (Hough) for work	0	1	0
„ for aell (ale)	0	1	0

In this year we have the first mention of the name "Ridgway" in any of the public records, and we may assume, considering the active part one and each of the family took in town's affairs, that with their very advent such activity commenced. In reference to a public meeting held October 11th, 1792, we have the following minute :—"At a Publick Meeting of Inhabitants of Horwico It was aggreed that the following Persons are properly qualified to serve as Surveyors of Highways, viz., James Turner, Timothy Etock, Thomas Ridgway, Adam Howarth, Henry Pilkington, Richard Mason, Richard Pilkington, John Mason, John Etock, John Kershaw." We have also the following reference to certain taxes, which, however, in their naked condition may, perhaps, be of little importance :—Taxes, £3 3s. 10½d and £0 2s. 6d. ; land tax, £0 8s. 4d.; window taxes, £0 6s. 2d.; highway tax (two items), £0 12s. 0d., £0 15s. 0d. We have also reference to the following taxable articles (?) :—Male servants, their number and quality; female servants, do. ; carriages with four wheels, carriages with two wheels, number of horses, waggons, and carts, with the following instructions :— "That if any master or mistress means to pay for any of his or her servants, horses, carriages, waggons, or carts in another parish, he or she must annex a list of the same hereto, expressing their number, and specifying the county and parish wherein they mean to pay for them." There is also the following significant note :— "Bachelors are desired to make the same known by placing a B at the end of their signatures." Printed in the first page of the book is the following :—"In pursuance of the Act of the 25th of His present Majesty, for granting a duty upon all male and female servants retained or employed in the several capacities following, viz., maître d'hotel, house servant, master of the horse, groom of the chamber, valet de chambre, butler, under-butler, clerk of the kitchen, confectioner, cook, house porter, footman, running footman, coachman, groom, postillion, stable boy, helpers in the stables, gardener, not being a day labourer, park keeper, game keeper, huntsman or whipper-in, waiters in taverns, coffee houses, inns, alehouses, or any other houses licensed to sell wine, ale, or other liquors by retail (other than occasional waiters) or by whatever name or names male servants really acting in any of the said capacities shall be called, whether such servants have been employed in one or more of the said capacities of a servant. And also by another Act of the 25th of the present King, for transferring the receipt and management of certain duties on horses, carriages, waggons, and carts from the Commissioners of Excise and Stamps to the Commissioners for the Affairs of Taxes, you are required to make out, within fourteen days of the date hereof, a list of the greatest number of male and female servants, horses, carriages, waggons, and carts that have been kept, retained, used, or employed by you at any one time, or by any lodger or inmate living in your house between the 5th April, 17—— and the 5th of April last, which list must be signed by yourself, expressing the Christian and surnames of the servants, together with the capacities in which they severally served. And in pursuance of the beforementioned Acts you are further desired to deliver to me at the same time a declaration signed by yourself of the number of male and female servants, horses, carriages, waggons, and carts you mean to pay for in any other parish or place under pain of incurring the penalties recited in the said Acts.

—— Assessor."

"Note.—The assessors or surveyors are required to surcharge all masters or mistresses double the duty for every male or female servant, horse, carriage, waggon, or cart omitted to be returned by them to the assessors. And the inhabitant householder of any house in which there shall be lodger, or inmate, keeping any male or female servant, horse, carriage, waggon, or cart who shall fail to deliver a list thereof within a week after the receipt of this notice containing the Christian and surname of such lodger or inmate, and also of every servant retained by the said lodger or inmate will incur by the said Act a penalty of ten pounds."

We have before referred to the peculiar system by which the poor of any village or hamlet was assisted or aided, and how watchfully they provided against "aiding" or "relieving" any but *de facto* their own poor. To what extent such poor might be a burden perhaps may be gathered from the following for the year 1792:—

	£	s.	d.
Jany. 20—To relief	0	3	0
To 2 paire of loomes	1	9	0
Feb. 10—To relief	0	5	0

To gather any reliable information as to the full extent of such liability from the books before us we find impossible, as each separate individual, though having an account set apart, is intermixed with others, but this we may adduce that not only in the current coin of the realm was such "aid" given, but articles of need and domestic requirements were provided, and in these extracts our readers will perchance glean some information:—

	£	s.	d.
1791—July 7, to a load of coales	0	4	0
" to a paire of stays	0	6	0
" to 3 yards of lin cloath	0	2	9
" Dec. 3, to 2 load of coales	0	11	0
to shifts	0	3	8
to clogs and stockings	0	2	0
Rent for 1 year, at 6d. per week	1	6	0
Cloathing James Nightingale	1	0	0

The travelling expenses of the surveyor are given in detail. We select a few:—

	£	s.	d.
Going to Bolton	0	1	0
Going to Mr. Andrew's (Rivington)	0	0	6
Going to the Overseers of Westhoughton	1	0	0
Going to Wigan	0	1	0
Going to Chorley	0	1	0
Going to Brindol (Brindle)	0	1	6
Going to Munchester	0	2	6
To Saml. Kershaw for going with mee	0	2	6
To expenses	0	4	6

There is a quaintness in the business transactions which not only tends to show the straightforward character of such, but illustrates the simple methods by which such business was conducted. From many we give the following :—

"May 2nd, 1743. To the churchwarden and overseer of the Township of Horeg. This from Thomas Ormerod to pay to William Parr, of Woorsley, the sum of one pound, in full, which was dew to mee or my orders Aprill ye 1, which said sum pay upon sight, as witness my hand, THOS. ORMEROD."

CHAPTER XXII.

The Indentures, to which we have already referred, were not of that formal character which their very abundance would have a tendency to create. A "poor" child was protected by the power and under the majesty of the law. However obscure or plebian such child's origin, it was nevertheless in a most emphatic manner the child of the town or village, to which by notice of its birthright it claimed citizenship. The "master" in taking over an apprentice increased the liability in a legal form of the place to which such child or apprentice might be removed, and though by the "Law of Removal" such child or apprentice could not be a burden to them, yet betimes through the lapse of years and other causes the liability under such law was disputed, and led to litigation, as in the following case, which will sufficiently illustrate the position :

"As to the settlement of Isabella, the wife of John Lusty, otherwise John Lurky, and Mary, their daughter, aged about three years, and Peter, their son, aged about three-quarters of a year, between the inhabitants of the township of Horwich, in the County of Lancashire.

Removants.
and
The Inhabitants of the township of Clayton-in-le-Woods.
Appellants.

Take notice that you are to produce upon the trial of this appeal at the general quarter session of the peace to be holden by adjournment at the New Bayley Court House, within Salford, in and for the said county of Lancaster, on Wednesday, the Seventh day of May, now next ensuing, the deed, indenture, instrument, or writing whereby the said John Lusty, otherwise John Lurky, was bound apprentice to Thomas Houghton, of

Newton-in-the-Willows, in the said county (since deceased) as therein is mentioned, in order that the same indenture, deed, instrument, or writing may, if the counsel for the said appellants shall think it proper, or advise the same, be read, and given in evidence for the said appellants on the trial of the said appeal, and if you refuse so to do, that parol evidence will be given thereof. Dated the Twenty-fifth day of April, in the year of Our Lord 1794.

JOHN WOODS."

The following refers to illicit sale of exciseable liquors, and to many of our older readers it will be known that Horwich in the past has not enjoyed perfect immunity from these unlicensed dealers.

County of Lancaster } To the Constables of the town-
to wit.   }   ship of Horwich.

Whereas, Peter Bentley, of the Township of Great Bolton, in the said County, innkeeper, hath this day made information and complaint in writing, as well for his Majesty as for himself unto, and before me Robert Dean, clerk, one of his Majesty's Justices of the Peace and Quorum in and for the said County, whereby it doth appear that on the twenty-seventh day of December now last past, at Horwich, in the said County of Lancaster, James Hilton, of Horwich aforesaid, labourer, did sell ale being an exciseable liquor by retail, and that unlawfully without being duly licensed so to do, contrary to the statute in that case made and provided. Whereby he the said James Hilton hath forfeited forty shillings together with the costs and expenses of convicting him of the said offence. And thereupon the said Peter Bentley, who as well for his said Majesty as for himself, exhibited the said information prayeth judgement of we, the said justice in the premises, and that he may have one moiety of the said sum of forty shillings, and also the costs and expenses of such connection as aforesaid according to the fform of the statute in that case made. These are therefore in his Majesty's name to require and command you on receipt hereof, to summon the said James Hilton personally to be, appear before me or such of his Majesty's justices of the Peace for the said County, as shall be assembled at the house of George Monks, the

Boar's Head Inn, in Great Bolton, in the said County, on Monday the sixteenth day of January instant, at ten o'clock in the forenoon of the same day, then and there to answer the matter of the before-mentioned complaint, and be further dealt with according to law; and be you at the time and place last aforesaid with the precept, then and there to certify what you shall have done in the premises by virtue hereof. Given under my hand and seal, at Little Bolton, in the said County, the twelfth day of January, in the thirty-second year of the reign of his Majesty King George the Third, and in the year of our Lord 1792.

ROBERT DEAN (seal)."

Few localities can boast, with greater cause, of such noble thoroughfares, well paved, well sewered, clean and excellent streets than Horwich. However beneficial, or however much the Public Health Act might be needed in other and less favoured districts, this creditable aspect of the public streets dates far anterior to such Act. Its principal streets were formed long before the law regulated their width, and yet in few places can such expansive thoroughfares be seen. Yet some of the more "ancient" of the villagers declare that to-day the public roads—notwithstanding that a more or less costly local council rules the village—are not so well kept as in the days when Peter Heyes, Hibbert, and other old surveyors were the only authority responsible to a not over critical "town's meeting." But even in those "good old days"(?) any dereliction of duty was visited by the terrors of the law, as take the following :—

"At the General Quarter Session of the Peace, held by adjournment at Manchester, in and for the County Palatine of Lancaster, the 23rd day of July, in the twenty-ninth year of King George the Third's Reign.

The King against the inhabitants of Horwich, in the said County. { The said Inhabitants are presented at April Sessions, 1787, for not repairing an

Highway beginning at the northerly end of a dwelling-house called the Crown and ending at Barker's Platting—the boundary between Horwich and Blackrod. And a fine will be imposed and estreated upon them unless good cause shall be shewn to the contrary at the sitting of the Court at the next General Quarter Session of the Peace, here to be holden by adjournment or so soon after as Council can be heard, due proof being made of the service of this notice twenty days before the same session.

TAYLOR."

We have before us two documents respecting the bridge known in the district as "Red Row Bridge," the said bridge marking the division betwixt Horwich and Blackrod in the above referred to Crown-lane. Some little divergence will be noticed, but this, perchance, will disappear if we consider what is common in trade—a sub-contracting for the work required; we leave our readers full freedom to their conclusions.

"At a meeting held the 11th day of May, 1780, by the Landowners and other Ley payers of the Townships of Horwich and Blackrod in order to lett to the best Bider a Bridge according to the following Articles, at a place called Barker's Platt, betwixt the said Townships, and as John Sharples, of Horwich, afforesaid, is Deemed and accepted to be the person appointed to undertake the said bridge as above mentioned, at and for the sum of Ten Pounds and Ten Shillings, and to finish it in a masterly and workmanlike manner on or before the first day of September. (Specifications)—

(1.) That from the Springers to the crowning of the Arch shall be four foot.

(2.) That the said Bridge shall contain sixteen foot from outside to outside of the Battlements, and the Battlements to be two foot high.

(3.) That if it should so be when the Ground work is made to the depths as in the first Article, and not found sufficient to sett the Bridge upon, that in that case the Townships aforesaid shall be at the expense of procuring Piles and Planks, or Flags for the better support of the said Bridge.

(4.) That from the bottom of the groundwork to the said Springers the thickness of the wall shall be one yard at least, pursuant to the plan, and the top of the Battlement to be sixteen inches thick, and covered with further coverers of sixteen inches broad, and four inches thick."

The second document is as follows:—"Know all men by these presents. That I, Thomas Lee, of Rivington, in the County of Lancaster, Mason, am held and firmly bound to John Lee, of Blackrod, and Robert Eatough, of Horwich, both in the county of Lancaster, Supervisors of the Highways in the Townships of Blackrod and Horwich, in the county aforesaid, in forty pounds of good and lawful money of Great Britain, to be paid to the said John Leigh and Robert Eatough, or either of them, or their certain attorney-at-law, executors, administrators, or assigns. For the payment whereof I bind myself, my heirs, executors, administrator, firmly by these presents, sealed with my seal, this seventeenth day of February, in the twenty-second year of the reign of our Sovereign Lord George the Third, by the grace of God of Great Britain, France, and Ireland King, Defender of the Faith, and so forth, and in the year of our Lord one thousand seven hundred and eighty-one. Now the condition of the obligation is such : That provided the above Bounden Thomas Lee, his heirs, executors, or administrators, or any of them, shall, at their own proper cost and charge, keep up, hold, and maintain from time to time, and at all times as often as need shall require, a new stone bridge by him newly erected and built, consisting of one arch, with battlements, &c., as now complete, over a small brook, called or known by the name of Barker's Brook, dividing the townships of Blackrod and Horwich, in the county aforesaid, free from all damages that may happen unto the said bridge or any part thereof by inundations or overflowing of the said waters, that may happen at any time within the space of seven years next ensuing the date hereof. And if the said bridge with every part shall at the end or expiration of seven years appear to be sound in all its parts, according to the judgment of any one or more competent workmen that may be called to view the same, and the same being perfectly sound, then the above obligation to be void and of none effect, or else to remain in full force and virtue.

Witnesses
Wm. ———
Robert Sharples.

{ THOMAS LEE. (seal)

CHAPTER XXIII.

Before advancing into consideration of the more general history of the village, it may prove of service to our readers, and be explanatory reference to many incidents to which we have referred, and to which we may refer, if we place before them a list of the "overseers" so far as we have been able to glean them with any degree of certainty:—

Name.	Date
P. Boardman	1683
James Bolton	1684
Hugh Whittle	1685
George Marsh, Augustus Greenhalgh	—86
Thomas Rothwell, Gyles Gorton	—87
John Knowles, W. Makinson	—88
Dockter Anderton, Peter Longworth, de Walker Fould	—89
Jonathan Markland	—90
Richard Pilkington	—91
Oliver Greenhalgh	—92
Thomas Nightingal	—93
Rob. Greenhalgh	—94
Adam Horrox	—95
Peter Longworth, Wilson Fould	—96
Peter Boardman	—97
Thomas Roscoe	—98
John Greenhalgh	—99
Augustus Greenhalgh	1700
James Greenhalgh, for Wilson Fould	—01
P. Hart	—02
John Greenhalgh	—03
Widow Turner	—04
Thomas Knowles	—05
Robert Pendlebury	—06
Mr. Charles Willoughby	—07
Hugh Whittle	—08
Edward Vause	—09
James Hart	—10
John Williamson	—11
John Hodkinson	—12
Peter Hart	—13

Name.	Date.
J. Halton	1714
Ortine Greenhalgh	—15
Henry Walker	—16
Lady Willoughby, for ye Old Squires (Lord's)	—17
Nicholas Hunt	—18
George Marsh	—19
Jonathan Knowles	—20
Mary Gorton, widow	—21
Edward Boardman	—22
James Marsh	—23
Robert Gillhouse	—24
Peter Longworth	—25
Mr. Markland, for Wilderswood	—26
Richard Pilkington	—27
Oliver Greenhalgh	—28
Thos. Nyhtingale	—29
John Halton	—30
Hugh Whittle, for ye Lower House	—31
R. Greenhalgh	—32
Christopher Horrocks	—33
Jas. Longworth	—34
Widow Boardman	—35
John Pilkington	—36
David Makinson, for John Makinson	—37
Christopher Horrocks, for Urmston's House	—38
Willm. Hart	—39
John Hodkinson, for Turner's	—40
Thomas Knowles	—41
Peter Longworth, for Robert Pendlebury	—42
Peter Longworth, for Robert Greenhalgh at Nery Fold	—43
James Nightingale, for the " Old Lord's "	—44
Hugh Whittle, for ye Lower House	—45
Ralph Vause, for his father's estate in Wilson Fould	—46
Willm. Hart, for James Hart	—47
James Ashcroft, for Mark Low	—48
Roger Haslam, for Scowles Bank	—49
James Pilkington, for Thos. Greenhalgh	—50
Robert Estock, for his own estate	—51
No entry	—52
Henry Hodkinson	—53
Will Hart, for his own estate	—54
Peter Vause, for Halton's estate	—55
John Hokinson, for Bolton's estate	—56
Willm. Longworth's (Walker's Fold)	—57
Roger Greenhalgh, for Mr. Wilson's estate	—58
John Peak, for his own estate	—59

Name.	Date.
Willm. Pendlebury, for Mr. Markland	1760
John Blackledge, for Peter Gorton's New House (Gorton Fold) estate	—61
Samuel Sandford, and James Stones, sen., served jointly for either or both of their estates	—62
Willm. Pendlebury, served for the Town jointly	—63
John Knowles, for his estate	—64
John Knowles, for Peter Gorton's estates called by the name of Gorton's (fold)	—65
Richard Thornley, for John Turner's estate	—66
Richard Thornley, for Robert Boardman's estate, commonly called Makinson's	—67
Henry Pilkington, for his own estate called Sephton's	—68
James Schofield, for his own estate	—69
John Mason, senr., for his own estate	1770
Richard Pilkington, for his own estate	—71
Richard Worthington, for Thos. Nuttal's estate	—72
Richard Worthington, hired for the whole town	—73
Will Pendlebury, for his own estate	—74
James Turner, for James Lomax's estate in the Lee	—75
Hugh Makinson, for that part of the Stocks called Nightingales	—76
Hugh Makinson, served for the town generally	—77
Hugh Whittle, for Whittle's higher house	—78
Robert Greenhalgh, for his own estate	—79
Thomas Kershaw, for the Horroxes	—80
" " for Margaret Wright	—81
" " for the town	—83
" " " "	—86
John Hilton, for his own estate	—87
Thomas Kershaw, for the town from 1688	—94
John Horrocks, for Longworth's Tennement at Wilson Fold	—95
Robert Pendlebury, for Makinson	—96
Thomas Kershaw, for Urmston's house	—97
" " for Turner's part of Stock's Farm	—98
Thomas Kershaw, served for the town	—99
John Pilkington, served for the town	1800
Thomas Schofield " "	1801-5
John Turner " "	1806-8
Robert Whowell " "	9-12
Joseph Crowther " "	13-15
George Vause " "	16-18
William Bennett, W. Smith	1848

Name.	Date.
Peter Hayes, J. Pendlebury, rateable value £10,620	1850
W. Longworth, Christopher Howarth rateable value £11,051	1852
W. Longworth, Christopher Howarth, rateable value £11,317 9s. 11d.	1854-8
W. Smith, W. Greenhalgh, J. Pendlebury, rateable value £11,387 1s. 0d.	1859
W. Smith, W. Greenhalgh, J. Pendlebury, rateable value £11,430 1s. 1d.	1860
Thomas Howarth, Richard Harrison, rateable value £12,729 16s. 6d.	1870
John Evans, J. Ramwell, rateable value £15,186 19s. 0d.	1880
John Evans, Moses Kay, " "	1883

Some of the names given above are almost lost to the recollections of the present generation. Hugh Whittle is spoken of in reference to "Y" Lower House." If we ask to-day where is the "Lower House" we are pointed to the spot where once it stood, but not a vestige remains. Our readers may remember that only within the last few years a lane leading on the south west side of Sharrocks Farm to Sharples Fold, with its high "Cop" looking like an ancient entrenchment, has been levelled, and only a slightly used footpath marks the spot. At the terminus of this ancient lane stood "Lower House." "Sharples Fold" is the modern name which has been acquired through a family of recent date living there, but in the more ancient geography of the village, they will find "Sharples Fold" to be the "Hilton House" above referred to. "Urmston House" is the somewhat antiquated looking farmhouse standing on the upper plateau of "Lord's Height," and now in the occupation of James Owen. The "Greenhalgh" referred to are returned as being "overseer" in respect to "Nevy Fold." This ancient family, who had their residence at "Coleman's," would, doubtless, considering its proximity, have the whole of the adjoining lands, and "Nevy Fold" would be a farmstead. Its position is close to the Primitive Methodist Chapel at "Bottom-of-Moor," and its occupant James Ramwell. "Peter Gorton, New House estate," is in keeping with the date of the erection of the property known as "Gorton Fold," close by the village station. "Bolton's estate" adjoins "New Chapel." The farm and buildings in Wilderswood known as "Beddow's Fold" is the more ancient "Hodkinson Fold," and "Sephton's" is the farm which closely adjoins Leetock, and in the occupation of Titus Barlow. The liability to serve as overseer was not so much a legal requirement in its application as a matter of custom. Fulfilling the conditions which the law then, as now, required was not obviated or delegated to a proxy. In the list we have given above, and considering the population, we may almost infer that every one who was liable served in their "call" the office of overseer in the earlier period, but gradually we see the system developing by which the duties and responsibilities appertaining to the office became narrowed, and instead of individually serving their term others were appointed. The "rentallity" of a place, the ownership or holding of land or property of a given value carried with it a liability. But though such liability was, as a rule, then discharged by the individual, we can scarcely say that such rule had no exceptions, or otherwise "Widow Turner" and "Lady Willoughby" would in turn be overseers for Horwich. Certainly we have no evidence to prove either the one or the other, but yet this fact remains that the duties and requirements were by custom regulated so that each liable to serve was called upon to know something of local necessities and local requirements. This subdivision would betimes be not only irksome to the individual, but prejudicial to the interest of the town, and in 1763 we find "William Pendlebury served for the town generally," and in 1773 "Richard Worthington was hired for the town." This was the beginning of a new system, which was so far adopted that in the first year of the present century the overseers were elected "to serve for the town," a system which is still preserved.

CHAPTER XXIV.

In these pages we have repeatedly referred to churchwardens and constables. These two offices were sometimes held conjointly, and the duties and requirements which past custom demanded can scarcely be inferred from the position and the duties of the office yet continued. Ere referring to the more striking and unique surroundings of the honourable and exalted office of churchwarden, we will place before our readers a somewhat incomplete list, and in so doing we must incidentally refer to the broken chain, which bespeaks the history of the church and its officers, clerical and lay. The continuity which marks the other portion of the history of Horwich is lost in relation to the church and its history. We are met with the startling fact that the history of the most venerable and worthy of the village institutions is broken and battered. From its shreds only can we get the patchwork of its history. Dr. Hallam, in his "History of Nonconformity," has shown that Horwich Church was nothing more than a Dissenting meeting house, that only the fear of costly litigation and the terrors of the law made these plunderers give up the spoil. In this fact we have the why and wherefore of the barren position of its history. It would have been contrary to the polity and traditions of these interlopers to have a record, if such a record had been possible, by those to whom the ministry (?) was entrusted. We could scarcely expect that those who had assumed an illegal position would so far give testimony to their doings as might bring upon them the result of their malappropriation of funds and ecclesiastical revenues. The tendency and teaching of the period was fatal to the preserving of church records and church history, and if in places where the authority of these Puritan zealots was not so supreme we yet find how much of value was destroyed, we could scarcely expect them to be less chary where the power supreme was theirs, as at Horwich. From old village records we extract the following: "These are the houses and persons liable to serve the office of constable and churchwarden, as follows:—

Name.	Date.
Gyles Gorton	1732
John Markland	—33
Hugh Whittle	—34
John Stock	—35
John Hodkinson	—36
James Marsh	—37
Mt. Walton	—38
John Holton	—39
William Hart	—40
Robert „	—41
William „	—42
William Bolton	—43
Hugh Whittle	—44
Edward Boardman	—45
Edward Vause	—46
Mark Low	—47
John Mason	—48
John Makinson	—49
William Greenhalgh	—50
Robert Pendlebury	—51
Thos. Greenhalgh, Old Lord's	—52-3
Richard Pilkington	—54
John Pendlebury	—55
Richard Longworth	—56
James Hulton	—57
Samuel Sandford and James Stones jointly	—58
James Turner, for Hole Hill Constable, and James Stones, for Horwich Moor Gate Churchwardens	—59
Edward Vause, Constable for Horwich Moor Gate, and Samuel Pilkington, Churchwarden for Mr. Bolton's higher house	—60
Ralph Vause, Constable for Horwich Moor Gate, and James Turner, Churchwarden for Hole Hill	—61
John Turner, for his own estate	—62
James Hilton, „ „ „	—63
Urmston House	—64
Richard Turner, for his own estate	—55
John Sephton, for part of his own estate	—66
John Sephton, for one part of his own estate that was his, but now is Henry Pilkington's	—67
John Sephton, for James Lomax's estate in Peak Lee	—68

Name.	Date.
John Sephton, for Peter Gorton's new house at the Three Lane ends	1789
John Sephton, for James Lomax's Higher Estate	—70
John Sephton, for Robt. Greenhalgh's estate where Hamolett Low dwells	—71
John Sephton, for Robt. Greenhalgh's estate where Thomas Grime now dwells	—72
John Sephton, for the town,.............................	—73-9
Hugh Makinson and Robt. Greenhalgh jointly, Hugh for Nightingales, Robert for his own estate	—80
Thomas Kershaw, for town	—81-4
Will Thornley, for John Knowles	—85
Thos. Kershaw, for Robert Greenhalgh, or Boardman's estate	—86
James Schofield, for Byrom's estate	—87
James Schofield, for Mr. Longworth's estate ...	—88
Thos. Kershaw, for Rob. Pilkington's estate ...	—89
Thos. Kershaw, for Schole Bank	—90
Thos. Kershaw, for Gorton's estate	—91
John Mason, for his own estate	—92
Robt. Whittle, for Whittle's higher house	—93
Timothy Eatock, for his farm	—94
John Hodkinson, for his estate	—95
Timothy Eatock, for the Constable, John Hodkinson, Churchwarden. This last year's was done for the estate called Walton's	—96
John Longworth, for John Hilton's share of Sharrock's farm	—97
Thos. Kershaw, for Icabod Kershaw, or part of Horrox's estate and town	—98
Sam'. Kershaw, for town	—99-1800
Thos. Schofield, for town	1801-3
Thos. Schofield, Churchwarden, for town. W. Turner, Constable for town	—04
John Brownlow and Saml. Kershaw, Churchwarden and Constable	—05-7
Hugh Whittle, Churchwarden and Constable ...	—08
Willm. Hutton, Churchwarden and Constable ...	—09
James Bolton	—10
James Bolton, Thomas Kershaw, Churchwarden and Constable	—11
James Bolton, Thos. Fletcher, Churchwarden and Constable	—12-13
George Vuose and John Kershaw, Churchwarden and Constable	—14-18
John Sharples, Churchwarden	—20
Richard France "	—24-25

Name.			Date.
Thomas Plumpton	„	....	1826-32
Richard Franco	„	....	—32-39
Charles Howarth	„	....	—39-46
„	„	W. Longworth, W. Bennett......	—46-53
„	„	„	„ ...... —54
„	„	„	.... —55
„	„	„	W. Greenhalgh —56
„	„	„	„ —57-8
„	„	Joseph Buckley...................	—59
Christopher Howarth, W. Greenhalgh			—60-1
„	„	Thos. Lever Rushton	—63-9
„	„	John Longworth	—70-3
Joseph Howarth, John Longworth			—74-83

In 1875 sidesmen were first appointed, Thos. Howarth and T. B. Greenhalgh being chosen. In 1876 John Evans and T. B. Greenhalgh were appointed, and have been unchanged. The position and duties of churchwardens have been clearly defined by canonical law. Within the last few years the gentlemen holding the office perambulated some portions of the village during divine service, carrying with them their wand of office, a silver-mounted staff. In thus perambulating they were extending the law, which requires "That churchwardens or questmen, and their assistants, shall not suffer any idle persons to abide either in the church yard or church porch during the time of Divine service or preaching, but shall cause them either to come in or to depart." (Constitutions and Canons Ecclesiastical— 19.) Since the introduction of the police system this perambulation might not be so much required, but undoubtedly the mission was not altogether unheeded, for at the time prescribed for these perambulations the idlers at street corners vanished, and it may perhaps be an open question if the village has gained in moral dignity by the discontinuance of this "good old custom." In fact, so far was the "virtue" acknowledged that at a period in the history of Lee Chapel certain officials that more nearly correspond to the canonical churchwardens began the practice at the lower end of the village, which was then only sparsely populated, and seldom visited by the more exalted officials. It is said that on one occasion this assumed officialism received a check from a quarter little expected. On this occasion they met a man named Saul Stones, an eccentric character, and with mock gravity demanded why Saul was not, as in duty and law bound, at Divine service. Saul laid aside his usual pliant disposition, and looking as grave as these "worship hunters" themselves, thus replied to that oft-repeated and threatening interrogation, "I am Saul, the son of Kish, come to seek my father's asses, and lo I have found them," pointing ominously to the discomfited officials. At this period, when the old "justice" held his court at the Black Bull, the offence and punishment was of rapid development, and in one of the churchwarden's books we find the following lines :—

		£	s.	d.
July 20, 1822.	Joseph Hart, Sabbath breaking	0	1	0
Nov. 30 ,,	Andrew Orrell, for killing game...	1	15	0
Jan. 22, 1823.	Doctor ——, being drunk on Sabbath day	0	3	4
Feb. 1, 1823.	J—s. H—r—n, ditto	0	3	4
,,	Peter Deotson, for Sabbath breaking	0	1	0

Sabbath breaking to our immediate forefathers consisted in abstaining from Divine worship without reasonable excuse, and the punishment consequent on this breach of duty was meted without the costly surroundings of our modern courts of justice. Previously the village stocks were used for the condign punishment of the man who had the misfortune to lose "his equilibrium." These stocks consisted of upright stone posts, in which were fitted slotted timber, the unlucky individual being held fast by the hands and feet, the observed of all observers. The village constable, without the machinery of the law, save only that which was invested in him by virtue of his office, marched the Sunday tippler to the stocks, and there for a given period he was held in the embrace of these wooden shackles. We have no direct proof of the exact period when the stocks ceased to be used, but it is said that about the year 1805 the last man named Worthington was incarcerated therein. This man is handed down principally from the cool philosophical resignation he displayed under the trying ordeal. "Ike," said a passer-by, "they corn'd ston to pud thi in thee 'er." But "Ike" felt that his position denied that assertion, and replied, "Hab but they nev dun." We have before referred to the fact that magisterial

authority was largely invested in the churchwarden or
constable for the time being. Authority was not so far
centralised or consolidated as at present. A Sunday
tippler, a Sabbath breaker, or "drunk and disorderly"
case required not a given notice ere he was called upon
to answer the charge against him, but his punishment
was swift and sure, though perhaps not so costly, relatively, judging from the examples above, as the "10s.
and costs" of the present day. Even at a comparatively
recent period many of the gleanings from the churchwardens' account show the marked contrast and diver-
gency which exist betwixt then and now. The manners
and customs of society have undergone a change, and a
rapid development has been displayed such as no equal
period in our country's history has witnessed. Go back
60 years in the history of Horwich, and the legislation
which has given us the Wild Birds Preservation Act
would have been treated with scorn, as contrary to the
teachings or experience, and the requirements of society.
To them birds were destructive agents, the enemies of
the farmer, and the scourge of the horticulturists.
" Dicky Bird Societies" would have been impossible to
youths, and the law of protection to the feathered tribes
been iniquitous to "eager mortals." As the butcher
had a price for his slaughter, so the bird killer had his
price ; and so great an evil were they considered that
" whoever will might kill a bird and receive the stipu-
lated price of one half-penny (0½d.) each bird. For
killing a hedge hog, 4d. ; for killing a filmert, 8d. for
killing a weasel, 3d." In 1820, we find the following
entries :—

	£	s.	d.
Birds Bill (killing birds)	0	11	8
Hedge Hogs	0	2	4
1822—B—n, K—1 for 1 Hedge Hog	0	0	4
„ —R. T—l—r, 31 Birds	0	1	3½
„ — „ „ i 21	0	1	0
„ — „ „ One Filmert	0	0	8
„ — „ „ One Weasel	0	0	3

In one page we have no less than 343 birds paid for at
one half-penny each, yes, whole pages similar to the
examples given above follow each other. In 1824 we
have 5s. 6d. paid for an almanac, probably for the vestry
use ; and in one of the old town records we find that
"Thomas Howell be employed to catch moles in the
township for 7 years for a sum of £3 per year."

CHAPTER XXV.

Few marriages are chronicled in the Parish Register prior to 1738, and even after this date, marriages from the district were solemnized at the "Parish" Church at Dean. Yea, up to 1853, when Horwich became a separate ecclesiastical district, the major part were solemnized at the "Mother" Church, the Curate-in-charge at Horwich being required to preach at Dean "at least once a year" in submission to its authority. The marriages solemnized at Horwich were generally those of the "higher order," the "double dues" demanded rendering the expense too great for the less wealthy; and even to-day amongst the older inhabitants there are only isolated cases that have been married at Horwich. The respect which was paid for these valuable village records in the past—the reason of which we have already referred to—may be gathered from the following:—"Francis Crook, of Cripple-gate, was married on the eleventh day of Nobodies Day, and on ye 11th of fast Assleep;—day of our Defence, In ye 11th year of ye Reign of King George."

"WEDDINGS AT HORWICH OLD CHEAPEL IN YE YEAR 1738."

John Pendlebury and Ails Whewel, both of Horwich, was married May—

Peter Gorton and Margaret Green, both of Horwich, June the 27 Ins. 1738 year of our Ld. Gd.

Roger Green and Mary Gorton, Aug. ye 23d.

Adam Crompton and Margaret Dickson, of ye Parish of Bolton, December ye 11th.

John Boardman and Mary Eckersley of Dean Parish, was married at old Horwich, April ye 23, 1739.

Mr. Henry Norris, of ye Parish of Brindle, and Mrs. Catrine Shaw, of Anderton, of ye Parish of Standish, married Feb. ye 13th.

Richard Green, of ye Parish of Standish, husbandman, and Jane Knowles, of Horwich, of ye parish of Dean, spinster, was married Nov. 11th, 1740.

Mr. Thos. Greenhalgh Gamman, man, and Mrs. Mary Boardman, of Horwich, of Dean Parish, was married att old Horwich, Nov. ye 27, 1740.

Robert Blackburn, usher, of Rivington, and Elisabeth Sympson, both of ye Parish of Boulton, married at old Horwich, Dec. ye 23, 1740.

Rich. Kirkman, of ye par. of Middleton, and Mary Hurst, of Dean par., married a' old Horwich, May ye 4th, 1741.

Thos. Anderton and Elizabeth Kershla, of ye Parish of Boulton, was married att Horwich, Aprel ye 18, 1745.

William Sicksmith and Margaret Lummard, of Rommath, was married May ye 5th, 1745.

Rodger Hart and Ann Penelebury, of Horwich, was married May 7, 1745.

Edward Hart and Margaret Walker, of Boulton, married May 21, 1745.

James Pilkington and Ellanor Hodkinson, of Horidge, married April 91, 1747.

Peter Walker and Ann Raskow was married at Horwich, 25 June, then both of Wesbauton, 1749.

Immediately under the above we find the following notice, which, no doubt, was written by the clerk for the purpose of better giving expression to his instructions:—"I am to give notice by yᵉ direction of yᵉ vicker and other inhabiters of this parish that (there) is to be no parish meetin at yᵉ church on yᵉ 29th instant; for yᵉ afair about yᵉ galery was determined at a parish meeting upon yᵉ 12th of November last past, and those who here legally opposed it will be answered in yᵉ Chancery Court at Chester."

The manorial rights and estate of Horwich were for many generations in the Anderton family. In 1593, at the death of Christopher Anderton, we have Lostoke, Heton-Subtus-Horwiche, and Tyldsley referred to. The fortunes of the Andertons were of a variable character, their devotion to the religion of the pre-Reformation period leading to much of their misfortune. The connection of Sir Francis Anderton with the rebellion of 1715, though only of a brief and unimportant character, led to the sequestration of the estates. In the traditionary records of the district, Sir Francis is spoken of as being far from being in unison with the object of the rebels, and that upon their approach he rode round his extensive park or grounds three times in succession, his countenance betraying his agitated feelings. His loyalty to the Monarchy as such could not be doubted; his loyalty to his religious convictions was of a higher order. In the person of the Sovereign he, in common with many Roman Catholics of the period, recognised a usurper more in a religious than in a civil sense; take away the religious disability, and their loyalty would have been secured. Baines remarks "that Sir Francis Anderton lost a valuable estate through being with the rebels for one day." With the sequestration came litigation. Sir Lawrence, brother to Sir Francis, claimed the estate, and various trials ensued, the fact of Sir Lawrence being a Roman Catholic being relied upon by the Attorney-General, who appeared for the Crown. But the difficulty was removed, and the disability destroyed, by Sir Lawrence conforming to the Church of England, and receiving the communion according to her rites. At his death in 1724, he devised the estates to his nephew, Robert Blundell. Again costly litigation followed, the Crown setting up a prior claim, the counsel for the Crown contending that according to the law of entail Sir Lawrence had died without issue, the only legal claimant being Sir Francis Anderton, and he being attainted of high treason was debarred and legally incapable of holding the estates, or of claiming any right as heir by and through such attaintment. If Sir Francis had a male heir, than he would become the possessor. Sir Francis, however, died without issue, and the manors of Horwich, Lostock, &c., were conveyed indisputably to Robert Blundell, from whom they descended to Henry Blundell, who, by his will dated 24 July, 1809, devised the manors of Horwich, &c., to his daughter, Catherine, wife of Mr. Thos. Stoner, father of Thomas Lord Camoys, and Elizabeth, wife of Mr. Stephen Tempest. This will also was disputed, and a trial took place at Lancaster in 1812, the plaintiff being C. R. Blundell, son of the testator, against whom a verdict was returned, the verdict being confirmed by the Court of Chancery on 8th April, 1815. We have before us a (copy) lease from the Crown relative to the above, and though the length precludes us giving it entire, such portions as bear any interest to the matter before us we now present:—

"8th April, 1755 (copy). Lease from the Crown to John Formby and John Knight, at the nomination of Robt. Blondell, Esqr., of manors and lands at Lostock, Horwich, others and for 31 years, if Francis Anderton Anderton should so long live, or untill he should have a child born."—George the Second, by the grace of God, of Great Britain, France, and Ireland, King, Defender of the Faith, and so forth. To all to whom these our letters patent shall come greeting, know ye that we, as well for and in consideration of the great trouble, charges, and expense our beloved subject, John Formby, of Formby, in the county of Lancaster, gentleman, and John Knight, of Liverpool, in our same county, gentleman, will best, in ; and about the recovering the Premes hereinafter mentioned, to be hereby granted as for and in consideration of the yearly rent hereinafter reserved, and of the conditions, covenants, and agreements herein contained. And also by and with the advice of our dearly beloved cousin and Counsellor, Thomas, Duke of Newcastle, Knight of the most noble Order of the Garter, First Commissioner of our Treasury of Great Britain, and of our trusty and well beloved Henry, Earl of Darlington, Henry Bilson Legge, Esqr. (Chancellor and Under Treasurer of our Exchequer), Thomas Hay, Esqr., commonly called Lord Viscount Dupplin, and Robert Nugent, Esqr., Commissioners of our said Treasury, have devised, granted, and to farm letter, and by these presents for ourselfs, our heirs, and successors, do devise, grant, and to farm let (at the request and nomination of Robert Blondell, of Ince Blondell, in our said county of Lancaster, Esquire) unto the said John Formby and John Knight, all those the manors, or lordships, or reputed manors or lordships, of Lostock, Anderton, Heaton, Horwich, and Rumworth, with their appurtenances, in our said county of Lancaster, and also all that capital, messuage, or mansion house commonly called or known by the name of Lostock Hall, with the park, demesne, lands, thereunto belonging, situate, lying, and being in Lostock, Horwich, and Heaton, in the parishes of Bolton and Dean, in our said county of Lancaster, which said premes, by the particulars thereof, are of the yearly value of two hundred and one pounds, eight

shillings, and sixpence, or thereabouts, and all other
messuages, lands, tenements, rents, tythes, and hereditaments, situate, lying, and being, coming, growing,
renewing, arising, or happening, in Bolton, Dean,
Standish, Horwich Moore, Horrockford, Clithers,
Manchester, and Farther Heaton, and in the parishes
of Bolton, Deane, Standish, Clithers, Eccles, and Manchester, in our said county of Lancaster, all of which
said last-mentioned premses by the particulars thereof
are of the yearly value of three hundred and eighty-four
pounds, nine shillings, and tenpence, or thereabouts.
. . . . And all those messuages, lands, tenements,
rents, boons, and hereditaments, and the reversion and
reversions thereof, situate, lying, and being in Horwich,
in our said county of Lancaster, heretofore lett on
several leases for lives or for long terms of years, determinable on lives at and under several reserved rents,
amounting in the whole, as appears by the particulars
thereof, to the yearly sum of eleven pounds, one
shilling, and tenpence, or thereabouts. . . . . And
all and singular the tythes and rents, of what nature
or kind soever, yearly, coming, growing, renewing,
arising, or happening, in, upon, or out of the lands in
Westhaughton, Heaton, Horwich, Halywell, Farnworth, Rumworth, Kearsley, Middle Hilton, Over
Hilton, Lower Hilton, Worsley, and Blackrod. . . .
And all other messuages, mills, lands, tenements, rents,
tythes, and hereditaments late of Sir Lawrence Anderton, in the said county of Lancaster, to the rents,
issues and profits whereof, we (after payment of the
growing interest of the debts, legacies, and encumbrances affecting the same estate and other annual
outgoing) by reason of the attainder for high treason of
Francis Anderton, brother of the said Sir Lawrence,
are entitled during the life of him, the said Francis
Anderton, or till he shall have a child born. . . . .
Whereto we, by reason of the attainder of the said
Francis Anderton, are entitled as aforesaid. Together
with all and singular edifices, buildings, houses, barns,
stable, dove-houses, curbtages, lands, meadows, pastures, feedings, commons, common of pasture, woods,
underwoods, rents, reversion, reversions, revenues, services, boons, royalties, hunting, hawking, fishing, fowl-

ing, tolls, duty, mulcture, courts, and all profits of courts, waifs, estrays, deodands, goods and chattels of felons and fugitives, felons of themselves, royalties, privileges, pre-eminences, and apparts to the said several manors, messuages, lands, tenements, and premes, or any of them, or any part or parcel of them, or any of them belonging, or in anywise appertaining, or therewith, or with any part or parcel thereof used, occupied, or enjoyed. . . . . . . Nevertheless to be void, frustrate, and determined on the death of the said Francis Anderton or on his having a child born. . . . . . The said John Formby and the said John Knight doth promise, &c. . . . . at his or their, or some, or one of their own proper costs and charges well and sufficiently repair, amend, support, uphold, maintain, scower, clense, and keep, as well as the several messuages, &c., now being in and upon, as also all and singular the hedges, ditches, walls, pales, rails, gates, fences, &c. . . . . . Provided also that if the said yearly rent, or sum of thirty pounds in by these presents reserved as aforesaid, or any part thereof shall at any time hereafter happen to be in arrear and unpaid by and during the space of sixty days next after either of the Feasts or Feast Days of St. Michael the Archangel and the Annunciation of the Blessed Virgin Mary, at or upon which the same ought to be paid as aforesaid, or if these our letters patent shall not be enrolled before our auditor of these premes, and a minute or docquet thereof entered in the office of our surveyor-general of our land revenues for the time being, within the space of six months next after the date of these presents, that then, and from thenceforth in any such case or on any such default, these our present demise, and grant, shall, and maybe, and be accounted, null, void, and of no force or virtue, anything in these presents to the contrary thereof in anywise notwithstanding. In witness whereof we have caused these our letters to be made patent.

Witnesses—

Our above-named right trusty and well-beloved Commissioners of our Treasury aforesaid at Westminster, the eighth day of April, in the Twenty-eighth year of our Reign, 1755.

By Warrant of the Lords Commissioner of the Treasury, ARUNDELL.

Examined by Christopher Denton; Deputy Clerk of the Pipe."

CHAPTER XXVI.

In one of the old town books we find the following entries, which will doubtless throw some light upon the salaries paid to town officials, and also relatively give the taxation for the purposes implied in the official position:—

"Dec. the 31st, 1745. Peter Gorton and Will Turner, surveyors of the highways this year, have agreed them the sum of four pounds, five shillings and sixpence (£4 5s. 6d.), after the rate of two shillings in the pound, by us,

Thomas Knowles, John Peak, Hugh Whittle."

"Jan., 1748. Thomas Knowles and John Crompton, surveyors of highways this present year, have assessed them the sum of £4 7s. 6d. in the pound, by us,

John Knowles, Richard Pilkington."

"Jan. 2, 1749. Thomas Knowles and John Crompton, being surveyors of the highways for the last year, have made up their accounts to the town, and have collected £8 14s., disbursed £9 9s. 7d., and out of purse, 15s. 7d.

John Knowles, Richard Pilkington."

It would be impossible to describe the bleak and cheerless surroundings which made up the hamlet of Horwich about this period. As we gaze upon it to-day we see little signs that would indicate any ancient characteristic; a few scattered and widely-separated buildings tell but too plainly its then insignificance, but yet in these scattered and unarchitectural buildings we see the germ of its history. We have seen that to its forests it doubtless owes its position as one of the earliest, if not the pioneer, of the cotton industry. Its natural position would hold out attractions when water became essentially the motive power. Its overhanging hills, feeding its numerous rivulets and streams, would command the attention of enterprise and lead to its choice; in fact, most of the buildings of the more ancient type possess certain characteristics that plainly bespeak their origin. A spinner or manufacturer in those early days were modest in their requirements and limited in their capacity. A good-sized cottage of the present period would have given "standing" to the owner, and been the means of disbursing a certain amount of labour which modern requirements have concentrated. To speak of some of these ancient buildings as factories are inconceivable in juxtaposition to a modern mill. One of the oldest of these factories existed in what is now a couple of cottages immediately under the present Wilderswood Mill. Another of these ancient factories has been metamorphosed into a more questionable purpose, the original Bay Horse being erected and used for such purpose. The tall three-storeyed buildings at Bottom o' th' Moor tell of the same origin. In fact many of these more ancient factories are to be seen in the valley, their inaptibility for their present use being manifest, and their more than incongruousness with their present surroundings being plainly visible. At the Bottom o' th' Moor, Mr. Robert Greenhalgh carried on the trade of a fustian manufacturer, fustian then being much in vogue. The Hopwood family we find included in a list of Manchester merchants in 1788, whether as bleachers or manufacturers is not stated, but we may presume that the former was their avocation, as we find that Horwich Bleachworks—better known locally as Longworth's Croft, from the fact that it passed by purchase into the hands of an ancient village family of that name—was originated and owned by one of the Hopwoods, but in a future chapter we shall more largely refer to this well known bleachworks. In the same list we have "John Whitehead, of Horwich and of Horwich Moor." It is certain that this Whitehead possessed a bleaching croft at Horwich about this time. Its position, however, is open to question; but the fact is nevertheless allowed that this croft was the largest of any then in the village. This perhaps is only a vague definition, unless we bear in mind the vast difference between a modern bleachworks and its ancient prototype. Then the mode of bleaching was by spreading the cloth on the grass, and by atmospheric influence effecting a change in colour. These bleachworks were in close proximity to a running stream, though doubtless some little of chemical aid was even at that time bestowed, and the area of such bleachworks was sometimes extraordinarily great, as the requirements of the connection might determine, whole fields being thus brought into requisition, and this operation gave the name to the position and also to the persons employed, hence the name "crofters" or "fielders." This system of grass bleaching by its very dilatoriness was sure to evoke a desire for a change, and as the demands for the bleached material increased, the artificial requirements of society gave an impulse to genius, and many and varied plans were tried for a more scientifiq and more speedy operation. This scientific mode was at length brought into prominence by a Frenchman, M. Vallete, who found a ready patron in Mr. Richard Ainsworth, of Halliwell, himself a bleacher. With the introduction of the new system a complete and radical change was effected; the chemical appliance achieved in a few hours what needed more than an equal number of days to effect by atmospheric aid. Crofting or fielding, as such, died, and left no trace behind it but its name, which even yet is continued. With the scientific mode came other changes; the limits of each establishment became narrowed, and machinery was called into action. This further development led on and on, and still greater changes came, but of them anon. The spot now known as "Grundy Hill" was also a croft, and we have in a former chapter referred to others contemporaneous. From a croft Grundy's Hill became a place where manganeze was manufactured, and even the euphonious "Tottering Temple" had its bleaching croft abutting "Scowl Bank" (Scholes Bank). Scholes Bank stands upon an eminence somewhat abrupt, but ere its declivity was broken by the more modern road known as Chorley Road, its position would seem to command an extensive swoop of the expansive valley beneath; its bleak, cheerless, black-scowling appearance giving this uplifted promontory the name of "Scowl Bank." This acceptation of its name is rendered all the more easy by the name given to the land immediately abutting—Dig

Leech—which conveys its own definition. At this period when crofts, from their peculiar position and expansive and unprotected character, were subject to frequent depredations, it was necessary that stringent laws should be promulgated for their protection, hence it became a capital offence to break into a croft. In 1798 Messrs. Tipping had a bleaching croft at the spot now covered partially by what is known as Horwich Vale Works. This was said to be the largest in the district, and in connection with this croft, in August, 1798, a man named John Eccles was charged at Lancaster assizes with breaking into and stealing calico out of the bleaching grounds of Messrs. Tipping, Horwich, and also with committing a like offence in the bleaching ground of Mr. Entwistle, of Rivington, the result being that he was condemned to death, a sentence which was duly carried out in September. The condemned man, it is said, "acknowledged the justice of his sentence." The sparseness of inhabitants which characterised Horwich about this period may be gathered from the following daring robbery:—

" Highway Robbery at Horwich, Nov. 12, 1764.

Whereas Henry Marsden, of Cross Hall, within the township of Chorley, in the county of Lancaster, miller, was on the 5th day of November inst., between the hours of six and seven o'clock in the evening, attacked by two foot-pads, at a place called Old Horwich Chapel, in the road between Chorley aforesaid and Bolton-in-the-Moors in the said county, and robbed of thirty pounds, nine shillings. One of them appears to be about thirty years of age, broad-set, and tall, had a ding on his left eyebrow, without his right hand; had then on a light grey coat, a red and white striped double-breasted waistcoat, red plush breeches, and light blue stockings. The other was tall and lusty, thin-visaged, long hair, tied behind, and had on an old soldier's coat. Whoever apprehends the said robbers, or either of them, so that he or they may be prosecuted to conviction, shall receive a handsome reward from the said Henry Marsden, over and above what is allowed by Act of Parliament for apprehending robbers."

In 1781, the Horwich Vale Bleach Works were advertised to be sold, the following bill of sale having been kindly supplied to us :—" To be sold to the highest bidder. In Hulton, near Chowbent, on Thursday evening in Easter Week, a freehold estate in fee simple, situate, lying, and being in Horwich, six miles from Bolton, Wigan, and Chorley, all market towns, and good roads thereto, be the same more or less of eight yards to the pole or perch, now let to a very substantial tenant for the term of twenty-one years, from May Day next, at the clear yearly rent of fifty pounds, on which estate there now has been laid out several hundred pounds since Michaelmas last, by converting one part of the estate into a printing ground, which is likely to turn out to very great advantage. For further particulars enquire of Mr. Walton, the owner thereof; or of Mr. Charter, the tenant." About this period, "Wilderswood Mill" was worked by Messrs. Crowther and Wingfield. Of course, in speaking of "Wilderswood Mill" we do not refer to the structure which is now thus designated, as the early one was as much unlike the present mill as the present is to the more modern and capacious one.

On February 9th, 1765, the remains of the "Right Honourable Hugh Lord Willoughby, of Parnham F.R.S., and President of the Antiquarians, London," (Parish Register) were interred under the chancel of the chapel. We have already referred to this family, and how it became connected with Horwich through the marriage of Sir Thomas Willoughby with Eleanor, daughter of Hugh Whittle. This Sir Thomas was called to the House of Peers as Baron Willoughby, in 1685—being the 11th Baron. This assumption of the title was ill-requited; its dignity and social position being much of a mistake. Erroneously called to occupy the position, it descended to several other barons who were distinguished only by their strong Presbyterian leanings. Being devoid of estate the title rested heavily upon them, till at length the family was restored to lineal order. It is beside our object to further refer to this ancient family, who can only be said to have a remote connection with Horwich. In 1786 Mr. Richard Pilkington, of the White House, died at the advanced age of 93 years. These were the good old coaching days, and relays of horses kept at the Crown Inn, the Lancaster coach passing through Horwich. In 1793 an accident occurred through the coach being overturned just below Horwich Moorgate, which was then quite a famous and conspicuous hostelry. Horwich then presented tokens of rapid development; a development which owed its origin in a marked degree to the energy of a family who were comparative strangers; a family which, so far as the history of Horwich is concerned, have left their footprints indelibly stamped thereon, a family who from a wilderness evolved a village, and verily turned the desert into a fruitful place. Whatever their mistakes may have been, or however open to criticism, viewed in the light of the present day, many of their actions may be, we cannot look upon the result without acknowledging their claims, for if he who causes two ears of wheat to grow where only one grew before is truly great, because a benefactor to his species, surely the Ridgways have some claim to such distinction.

CHAPTER XXVII.

We can scarcely conceive of the aspect of Horwich immediately prior to and with the advent of the Ridgways. Horwich Moor was something more than the limited area which now receives the designation. Wilderswood, Foxholes, and other surroundings in their wild, rugged, cheerless aspect, their barren, bleak appearance, and chilly cliffs, were not inaptly named. As we gaze upon this spot, notwithstanding the marks which tell of its changes, yet the evidence of its progress, the signs of its cultivation, bear the impress of the more modern type. The exact date of the migration of this family into Horwich cannot be given with certainty, but evidence would seem to favour the statement that a short time previous to 1777 saw the advent of this remarkable family. Of their antecedents we know but little with that certainty which would warrant the retailing of such information as we possess to our readers. We had hoped to have placed before them such a genealogical record of the family as their merits demand, but having failed in our efforts to examine the Bolton parish register for that purpose, we could not venture upon a record which might mislead. The Ridgways were, however, a family of some local distinction in Bolton previous to their removal to Horwich; in fact the evidence would seem to warrant the assertion that the Ridgway family had representatives in Bolton and Horwich at one and the same period. At this time they possessed a bleaching ground, or croft, at Dog Brow, better known as Ridgway Gates, from the fact that the entrance to these grounds was protected by gates. The position then was a deep gully, and the river Croal, which ran between the uplifted ground, found the water required in the operation. It is said that owing to a fire destroying some portion of their stock-in-trade, the

Ridgways were induced to look out for a better position, and one that would command greater advantages, but of this we have only traditionary testimony. The present Market Hall in Bolton covers the exact spot where the bleachworks of the Ridgways stood, the "Dog Brow" property being sold to the Corporation of Bolton for £300. We have already seen that a John Ridgway had a bleaching ground in Horwich at a spot other than that so closely associated with the family, and where their vigour, their business tact, and genius have been so successfully and permanently developed. In order to understand the surroundings of the family at this period, we shall have to examine the records. The first lease was betwixt Henry Blundell on the one part, and John and Thomas Ridgway on the other part, for a period of 99 years. This lease was duly signed in 1777; but in 1801 this lease was abrogated, and a fresh one made out to Thomas Ridgway alone, the length of the lease being likewise much extended. From this we gather that the brothers John and Thomas Ridgway had a conjoint lease of Wallsuches—Makinson Moor estate—in 1777, but we find also that the former was at the same period carrying on the business at Bolton in his own name, that of "John Ridgway" alone. The reason for this change and renewal of lease was the death of the first-named John Ridgway, who died at his residence, Chamber Hall, Bolton, on November 2nd, 1800, and was buried in the parish churchyard, Bolton. This John Ridgway was a man of some local standing. He was a trustee of the Bolton Grammar School, and took an important part in the election of one of its most distinguished masters, the learned Lempriere, author of the classical dictionary bearing his name. In an advertisement for a head master of Bolton Grammar School in 1790, testimonials were to be directed to John Ridgway. This John Ridgway had several children, and if the traditionary ownership of the bleaching grounds already referred to were owned by a Mr. John Ridgway, we may presume that a son of the above was the owner and occupier. That a second Bolton John Ridgway was in existence at this period we have every proof, for on the occasion of a loyal address to His Majesty from the Inhabitants of Bolton in 1803, in respect to the late conspiracy against his person and government, we have Mr. John Ridgway as chairman. In an old lease, bearing date of 1801, in reference to Chamber Hall, leased for a term of 5,000 years, we have "John Ridgway, son of John Ridgway," and from a copy of exchange of lands and purchase for the purpose of road improvements to Dean, in this vicinity, we have proof of the local standing of the family. But we are not concerned to prove—what at best is a questionable distinction, if alone and unadorned--their ancient lineage, though perchance it might be found, as we have every reason to assume, that their claim in this respect might overshadow many whose only pride is to point to a barren, unfruitful, and cumbering ancestral tree. We venerate and respect our ancient aristocracy, but that veneration can only increase, and their influence be but duly felt when—though guarding zealously and justly their traditionary honours—they take up manfully their position in the social struggle, and either at the bar, in the senate, in the church, yea in the counting-house, show that they are of the people and with the people. Mr. Thomas Ridgway was distinguished for his unostentatious demeanour; his character was exemplified in that energy which not only manifested itself in the success which attended his mercantile efforts, but also in that still greater development, a prosperous village. That energy which was so essentially manifested in his career, he, by the very force of his example, communicated to others, his sons, Thomas and Joseph, in a most marked degree exhibiting this trait. Following the Wallsuches estate, the "Stocks" lease was taken 1787. To those who look upon the extensive property to-day can scarcely conceive of its appearance then. The roads were wretched and uncared for; property was a commodity of little value. Only the few houses which even to-day bear their ancient names relieved the bleak and cheerless surroundings; no distinguishing mark to break the monotony; the moorland, with its heather covered back-ground, and rocky cliffs gave a barren aspect to the landscape. To-day many of the more ancient names of localities are misnomers. To speak of "Grundy Hill" is a contradition to its present position; but in the early days of the present century, instead of being somewhat in a declivity, to gain it then was torture to man and beast. Lee Lane was a narrow, undignified thoroughfare, with some three or four houses at considerable distance from each other. The "Black Bull" stood upon a "tower" eminence, and though Horwich had ceased to be a forest, it was indeed much of a wilderness. A small, simple, hut-like structure is pointed out to the visitor as the beginning of those large and concentrated buildings which form the "Wallsuches" of to-day; but this concentration is the further result of a rapid development of trade. Signs of progress speedily manifested, and employment was freely offered. A great change came over the village, the wave of prosperity (as then understood) swept over it, and a new and a strange life was dawning. It is necessary when a sudden transition —a change which revolutionises the social structure— occurs, whether in States or the more minor concomitants thereof, that a strong hand should direct the result. Prosperity might intoxicate and destroy that equilibrium which alone preserves society under changed conditions from sinking into a chaos. The very kindness of success might engender a transmittible, a chronic evil. At such times a kind of social providence provides the strong will and the resolute arm. True, their actions are liable to be misconstrued and their motives freely challenged, their necessary firmness becomes despotism, and their restraints tyranny. But history unfurls a truer story, and in weighing the result gives forth a verdict. The "Ridgways" for a time were undoubtedly the "Uncrowned Kings of Horwich." They possessed a power which none could gainsay. Betimes this power may have been arbitrarily employed, and viewed in connection with the more advanced present, many of their proceedings may appear harsh and high-handed; but circumstances had combined to give them power, and perhaps in juxtaposition with prevailing customs, the spirit of the age, and the tendency of the period, we may find much more of that moral dignity of character than may be superficially observed. We have already glanced at Hrowich as it existed ere the Ridgways first came; its sparseness of Inhabitants, its wild and rugged aspect. The aspect of its natural surroundings was but too truly reflected in his moral and intellectual status. Education was not a necessity, nor yet was it a right; it was more of a privilege, but this privilege existed as a kind of divine right for a favoured few. Some village dame, "who had seen better days," had the semblance of a school, but faint and slight her own attainments, she failed to inspire her charges with anything more than alphabetical aspirations. Family feuds existed, and were handed as legacies from sire to son; these feuds were sometimes fought out, if not with clannish ferocity, yet with all the malice that a brutal and unrestrained disposition, fed and nurtured by hereditary animosity, could command. The energy of the Ridgways caused a migration from Blackrod, Rivington, and the surrounding districts, and even to-day many of the more aged can trace the families by name who thus migrated. With this sudden development came increased responsibilities. Mine hosts of the Bull and Crown were receiving golden tokens of this advent of prosperity, and though in comparison with the surroundings of to-day the villager's position was meagre, his fare simple, and many articles now in daily consumption were luxuries, and bread a reserve for the Sunday meal, yet we are not to suppose that our forefathers were so far the creatures of circumstances as to some extent not be responsible for their position. To be "mine host" at either of the two hostelries we have referred to was virtually to be in possession of the alchemist's stone, and many of position, though perhaps a little needy, through family influence found thereby a sure means of possessing a banker's account. Handloom weaving was then, and for a long time afterwards, the common employment, and few cottages existed that had not one or more pairs of looms, which were either auxiliaries or the sole "bread-winning" provision of the family. A manufacturer then had a number of these home employés, who brought in their "cuts" at stated periods. With their first success, the Ridgways began to consider their responsibility, and, seeing the lamentable ignorance which prevailed, as early as 1792 they began to encourage the means of education. As men of tact and wise discretion, they knew that any effort of theirs, unless supported by the sympathy of those for whom such effort was made, would only prove futile, and they first gained such sympathy by creating an individual interest and rousing the active co-operation of their workpeople, with the result that in 1793 the present "Old School" was opened for educational purposes. Having thus provided the means of instruction, they began to inculcate lessons of thrift, and in 1802 they formed a kind of "building club," offering portions of the "Stock's Estate" on long leases, on easy terms. To further develop this provident scheme a committee was appointed and payments made much after the manner of modern building societies, the committee being as follows:— Joseph Howarth, John Horrocks, John Whitehead, James Grundy, John Lowe, Rev. Leonard Redmayne, Joseph Ridgway, Thomas Ridgway (treasurer). From this society sprung that cluster of houses now known by the name of "Club houses." Leases were granted as under, their length being from 286 to 290 years, the ground rent being merely nominal:—John Eatock, 1803; Thomas Plumpton, 1804; Thomas Schofield, 1805; Christopher Petty, 1808; Edward Wilsden, 1809; Leonard Redmayne, 1809; William Pass, 1809; Thomas Macon, 1809; James Grundy, 1809; John Hampson, 1809; Alice Entwistle, 1809; Thomas Schofield, 1813; Edward Ashton, 1839; William Eaton, 1839; Samuel Pennington, 1839, &c.

CHAPTER XXVIII.

With the migration into Horwich which followed the advent of the Ridgways came two families which were looked upon much in the light of a social phenomena— two Catholic families—the names of which for obvious reasons we suppress. At this time those holding Papistic views were the living embodiment of treason— treason not only to the king, but to the freedom and well-being of the nation. Hatred of the Papists was not a mere feeling, but a social creed, and in subscribing to its tenets society sought a protection against the fierce bigotry which had lit the fires of Smithfield, and by the rough hand of torture had sought to eradicate the "rights of conscience." Religious teachers of the Puritanical mould had not only cultivated this feeling, but fed it by false deductionable facts. Then cruelty and persecution were exhibited as the twin sisters of the Catholic hierarchy, forgetful of the fact that their own history was equally crimson-stained, and their own deeds of a darker hue. Even to-day the feeling which was more pointedly displayed at the beginning of the present century is not altogether lost, for even with the enlightened teaching of the present day, which recognises patriotism as apart from creeds, and social worth as distinct from religious theories, amongst those who know little of the higher atmosphere, the refined and soul-strengthening teachings of this truly ancient Church, the votaries thereof live under a kind of social ostracism. In this the religious instruction (?) imparted has much to answer for, for that which robs the State of the full moral, social, intellectual power which any integral part thereof might more readily and successfully have given, is an assassin to its interests and an enemy to its progress. We are not pleading for any particular church or system, but for that perfect freedom which enables a system to gain power and influence only by its innate worth and adaptability.

Nearly a century had elapsed since Horwich had within it an open upholder of this ancient faith; for with the attaintment of Sir Francis Anderton and the action of the Commissioners, who sought out those of this persuasion, and subjected them to a certain impost because of their alleged connivance and aid to the Rebellion, it became a matter of policy and an only escape from ruin to cloak or hide their views or reasons. That our readers may better understand the position at the time to which we refer, we place before them the following documents:—

Coun. Lane's. } To ye King's Rememberancer of y^e
Salford Hundred } Court of Exchequer at Westminster.

We, whose hands and seals are hereunto set, Commissioners amongst others appointed by Act of Parliament, made in the ninth year of ye Reign of his Present Mag^{tie} by laying a tax upon Papists, and for making such other persons as upon due sumons shall refuse or neglect to take ye oath therein mentioned to contribute towards ye s^d tax for reimbursing to ye Publicke Purs of ye great expeness occasioned by y^s late conspiracies, and for discharging ye estates of Papists from ye two-third parts of the Rents and Profits thereof one year, and all arrears of same, and from such fortitures as are therein more particularly described. I do hereby certify (that) att a meeting for puting ye s^d Act in execution had at Manchestr within ye said Hundrd of Salford ye 23 day of Sepr In ye tenth year of His Mag^{tie} Reigne, an dupon examination of tou credible wittness upon oath, pursuant to ye Directions of ye Said Act, It Appears unto us (that) ye Said Lands and tenements, situate, lying, and being in Heaton, Horridge, and Halliwell, in ye s^d Hundrèd of Salford, of ye yearly value of about iii. 8s. 4d., late belonging to ye Lord Viscount Falconberg, which was registered pursuant to an Act made in the first year of his said Mag^{tie} Reign, entituled an Act to oblige the Papists to Register their names and real estates is now really and bona fide vested in and belongs to Mr. Joseph Byrom, of Manchester, a Protestant by alcenacon, really and bona fide mad before ye twenty-filth day of December, 1722, which said lands and tenements is charged with ye sum

of 45—0—5—½, as its part or proportion of ye sum of
85—5—0, charged upon ye said town of Heaton,
Horridge, and Halliwell afforesaid toward ye sd ald,
which said sum of 45—0—5—½ we do hereby declare to
be a deficucy within ye intent of ye sd Act first
mentioned, and do certify and return ye same according.

Given under our hands and seals ye day and year
above written.

(Signatures erased.)

With this digression we proceed with our sketch of
the Ridgways. To trace in detail the development of
" Wallsuches," which name probably refers to a locality
rather than a definition, is not our purpose ; but their
rapid and successful career, whatever other claims they
may possess, show them at least to be of Nature's
aristocracy, which ever blesses while it receives. Down
the deep valley (now almost obliterated) a copious
stream of Nature's fluid ran its merry course, and to
make this stream subservient to their purpose both the
genius and the energy of the Ridgways were fully
employed. The "dash wheel" system of washing—an
adjunct to bleaching—was brought into requisition,
various erections followed the course of the stream,
which buildings were known as No. 1, 2, 3, 4, 5 and 6.
The water when discharged from the first was made
subservient to the needs of others in rotation, for which
purpose "bucket" wheels were adapted, and literally
not a drop of water was allowed to depart ere it had
fully met the design of the Ridgways. A then large
building of some five stories in height was erected,
which was designated the "Gingham House," from the
fact that ginghams were principally finished here, and
the first glazing callender erected. The bleaching
works situate at Shaw Brook, midway on the boundary
water line of Horwich and Rivington, had already one
of these finishing machines, which were then looked
upon as a remarkable invention, being so adapted that
heated irons were inserted into their hollow cylinder,
like metal bowls, and a greater polish or finish given to
the cloth. At this place, in additon to a large water
wheel, the steam engine was introduced, the peculiarity
being that a good portion thereof was made from timber,

a huge baulk supplying the beam. Bleaching and finishing became virtually a trade; lads were bound by indenture, and new hands signed articles of agreement. When such articles were duly signed and attested a kind of enlistment shilling was given, and when this shilling had been taken the new hand knew that he was irrevocably pledged, the wages being on a kind of a sliding scale. Then no Act of Parliament existed to regulate the hours of labour, no holiday, nay Sunday was not a day of rest only during the hours of Divine Service, any curtailment of the hours of labour being met with the objection that only a given time was allowed from the date of receiving to the date of despatching, and other interests would suffer, notably the shipping interest, by any such curtailment. We need not blame the Ridgways in this, for they were bound to follow where competition led, and surely if the recently developed ten hours' bill for bleachworks could be so strenuously opposed as, say yesterday, on the same grounds we have little room to throw dirt at the byegones. We know, however, that the boon was only granted when a stronger power exercised its authority; and even young men and those of riper years can remember that to see the daylight free from the trammels of work was impossible, and a Friday morning's beginning only ended late on a Saturday night; even young boys of some eight or ten years of age being called upon to stand upright and follow their occupation without any relaxation for meals or otherwise; fearful of short Sunday being over, knowing that Monday would introduce a mystery of labour unfathomed and unfathomable, as the writer of these pages has experienced. Wages were then paid monthly, and £11 and £12 were often gained; and the writer remembers a story told by his grandfather, who worked for the Ridgways during a lifetime of long duration, that he recollected the "stovers" refusing to fetch £13 as their month's wages. We have introduced this collateral matter to refute the aspersion that we have read that "only starvation wages were paid." "Pilkington's estate" was leased in 1801. Upon this estate, upon the higher ridge of ground, the "White House" stood, the public road passing close by its front door. Upon this

spot stands "Ridgmont," the public road being
diverted, and an extensive park surrounding the
mansion. Thomas Ridgway, the founder of that
portion of the Ridgway family to which our reference is
made, died on the 30th August, 1816, aged 77 years.
His will bears date of 16th April, 1814, and was duly
proved in 1817, and by this will his two sons, Thomas
and Joseph, were left share and share alike, without
distinction, no specification or definite share being
named. This led to a dispute, and Mr. John Ashworth,
of Turton, was called in as arbitrator, and fixed the
boundary by the Chorley road site, that on the north
side to Thomas, and that on the south side to Joseph;
the latter, however, to have all the timber. Few of
our readers but will remember the Ridgway crest and
motto, the latter, it is said, being compiled by a
Horwich schoolmaster, to whom Mr. Thomas Ridgway
gave twenty guineas. By a peculiar transposition of
letters, the motto spells "Thomas Ridgway." This
will be more easily seen when we bear in mind
the more modern introduction of the "u" as used
in *Deus*, the motto being as follows: *Mihi* (to
me) *gravato* (when weighed down) *Deus* (there is
God), or, " God is with me when I am weighed down." *
In 1818, a large portion of Horwich Moor was purchased
from the " Commissioners appointed by Act of Parliament," by Mr. Joseph Ridgway. The following
document relative thereto will perhaps possess some
interest :—

"We, whose names are hereunto subscribed, Commissioners appointed for carrying into execution an Act
of Parliament passed in the 55th year of the reign of
his present Majesty King George the 3rd, intituled
"An Act for enclosing Horwich Moor, in the Parish of
Dean, in the County Palatine of Lancaster, do hereby
give notice that we have set out, and appointed such
private roads and footways over, upon and through, or
by the side of the allotments to be made and set out in
pursuance of such Act, as we have thought required,
and have ascertained the said private roads by marks

---

* Translated for the author by the Rev. H. S. Pigott, M.A.,
vicar.

and boards, and have prepared a map in which such
private roads and footpaths are laid down and described, and have caused the said map to be deposited
with our clerk at his office in Wood-street, Bolton, for
the inspection of all parties concerned, and which
private roads and footways and the general lines thereof
are hereinafter specified and set forth, that is to say, Roads
—a private carriage road leading out of the Bolton and
Chorley turnpike road to another enclosure in Horwich,
8 yards wide and which road is called upon the map
Coal-pit Road. Another private carriage road leading
out of the said turnpike road to other ancient enclosure
in Horwich, 10 yards wide, called Greenhalgh Road.
Another private carriage road leading out of the said
turnpike road along the site of ancient enclosure and
being in Horwich, and ending at an allotment intended
to be set out and allotted to the heir-at-law of the late
Thomas Ridgway, Esq., deceased, and to Joseph Ridgway, 10 yards wide, called Moor Side Road. Another
private carriage road out of the said turnpike road to a
road leading to Wallsuches Bleach Works, 10 yards
wide, called Wallsuches Road. Another private carriage road leading northward from the Wallsuches Road
last described to two Stone Quarries, and to an allotment intended to be set out and allotted unto the heir-at-law or devisees of the said Thomas Ridgway and to
the said Joseph Ridgway, 8 yards wide, called Delf
Road. Another private carriage road leading southwards from the said Wallsuches private carriage road
to a cottage, 4 yards wide. Another private carriage
road leading from publick carriage road called North-easterly Road along the western boundary of the Moor,
beginning at White Gate and ending at Stone Pit Road,
8 yards wide, called Makinson Road. Another private
carriage road leading also from the north-easterly road
past the public Stone Quarry to the western boundary
of the Moor and from thence along the said boundary
to where it adjoins Heaton's ancient enclosure, 10 yards
wide, called Stone Pit Road. Another private carriage
road leading northwards out of the north-easterly road
along ancient enclosure from Cow-Hey-Nook, the
northerly side of John Longworth's farmhouse, 4 yards
wide, called Longworth Road. Another private car-

riage road leading southwards out of the north-easterly road along ancient enclosure belonging to John Longworth from Cow-Hey-Nook to ancient enclosure belonging to Henry Blundell, Esq., deceased, 8 yards wide, called Cow-Hey-Road. And another private carriage road leading out of the north-easterly road to the Bolton and Chorley turnpike road, 6 yards wide, called Moor Gate Road. Footpaths—A public footway beginning at ancient enclosed land belonging to the devisees of Henry Blundell, Esq., deceased, at the end of the Cow-Hey private road (carriage), along the said Cow-Hey-Road to Cow-Hey-Nook, and continuing from Cow-Hey-Nook along the Longworth private carriage road and along the side of the ancient enclosure to the end of the Stone Pit Road. And another public footway beginning at Heaton's ancient enclosure at the end of the footway last described, along part of the private carriage road called Stone Pit Road to where it adjoins the private carriage road called Makinson Road and ending at a place called White Gate. And we do hereby further give Notice that we have appointed a meeting of the said Commissioners to be held at the house of Thomas Nelson, the sign of the Queen Anne, Gt. Bolton, 15 Mar. next, for the purpose of receiving, hearing, and determining the objection or objections of any person or persons who may think himself or themselves injured or aggrieved by the setting out of the said private roads or footways or any of them.

          R. A. FLETCHER.
          JOHN ASHWORTH."

Feby. 20, 1818.

CHAPTER XXIX.

The brothers Thomas and Joseph, on the death of their father, succeeded to the estates, and also jointly to Wallsuches, and to their energy is due that undying association which the Ridgway family have with Horwich. Joseph, the more distinguished of the brothers, married for his first wife Miss Ellen Hudson, daughter of a merchant residing at Caton. On her decease he married Annie Maria, daughter of Mr. Peter Wittenhall, of Rushton, county Chester. The first Sir Henry Mainwaring was a Wittenhall, but took the name of Mainwaring in consequence of succeeding to the title and estates. Mr. Peter Wittenhall married Frances, daughter of Mr. Thomas Ravencroft, of Leftwich Hall, Cheshire, and Pick Hill, Flintshire, having with other issue a son and five daughters; Annie Maria, above referred to, and eldest sister of the late Mrs. Pigott. Thomas married Miss Gill, of Bolton, and through this line the Ridgways were continued. Of the brothers, Joseph was perhaps the more noted, his connection with the magistracy, his bequests to the Church, and other outside agencies to which we have referred, his position as deputy-lieutenant of the county, and his passionate devotion to hunting, have all conspired to give him a county name. As early as 1823 we find that his hunting proclivities had so far ingratiated him into the high esteem of the gentlemen who composed the "Ridgway Hunt," that they invited him to dinner at the Commercial Hotel, Bolton, and a writer in the "Annals of Sport" for 1824 thus refers to the Ridgway pack: "Having a little business which took me to Bolton-le-Moors, Lancashire, on my way I fell in with a pack of harriers belonging to Joseph Ridgway, Esq., who resides at Ridgmont. Ridgmont is situated at Rivington (Horwich), three or four miles from Bolton. They consisted of about fifteen couple of the finest harriers I have seen for some time;

they are very handsome dogs, and if they have a fault it is that they are too much of a match for a hare; they are large, bony, powerful animals, and I should suppose that with a good scent few hares would stand up more than fifteen or twenty minutes before them. Upon enquiry I find the kennel consists of 25 couples, which three times a week hunt the circumjacent neighbourhood. It may, perhaps, be justly remarked that if the hounds are strong the country they hunt is not only very heavy, but very hilly also, and therefore the former are united to the latter." Thomas, through the result of an accident which caused him to be somewhat lame, and denied him the pleasures of the hunt, displayed the same characteristic in his patronage of coursing, and the Ridgway meet owes its birth thereto; and the second son, Joseph, son of Thomas, held his father's predilections, and the kennels at Wallsuches became famous through the entire county. In the early part of the century (April, 1803) Mr. Thomas Ridgway, of Wallsuches, lost his wife (Mary), and though the epitaphist may not be a critic of life with all its faults and failings, true worth is ever embalmed in that casket of affection which survives any tangible record. An old print of the period thus refers to her death:—"On Saturday se'n night died Mrs. Ridgway, wife of Mr. Ridgway, of Wallsuches, near Bolton. She was eminently distinguished for her piety, benevolence, and charity. Her heart melted at the tale of woe, and her hand sought every opportunity to relieve the needy. She was a faithful wife, an affectionate mother, and kind and indulgent to her servants." The Ridgways, by the exercise of that consummate energy which had given and rewarded them with success, became veritably a "Saul" amongst their fellows, and in all trade matters to them were relegated duties and responsibilities that were general to the trade. At this stage in the history of bleaching were exhibited those outward signs which told of a more powerful invisible agitation, an agitation which later on became thoroughly developed. In connection with Wallsuches a Sick Society had been formed, and under its shadow a trade organisation grew and prospered. Wallsuches, however, has been singularly free from those melancholy trade disputes that have riven asunder those mutual ties that bind together capital and labour. The Chartist agitation had blown the loud blast of alarm to a class who elected to govern by a "divine right" principle, and jealous of its authority, and caring not to divide its privileges, any action of the working classes was watched with suspicion. To the programme of the agitators the labour class gave a ready sympathy, and though few were brave enough to court results in their adhesion, yet the spirited utterances which were wafted from this then broad platform led many to think who had not dared to think before. One grievance discovered leads to many others, and in every period of the national history, in every effort that may in itself command sympathy and deserve support, we find agitators, like cancers, throwing out their feeders, and insidiously sapping the purity and worth of their votaries. At this period there were none of those mutual guarantees that determined the respective position of employer and employed as at present. Labour had no rights, and consequently no privileges. The workman was much of a legalised machine, to be used at his master's pleasure. Capital alone was the recognised factor to be employed in the service of the State, or in the good of the Commonwealth. Its authority was paramount in the Church; its power was irresistible in the Legislature; it stained the ermine and tore away the badge of justice. Yea, submissive obedience was more than a creed to the working classes themselves; combination for mutual protection was then a crime; to protect the interests of the working class was the voice of a phantom. Interests! They had none, and how could protection be afforded to that which did not exist? To whisper their grievances to each other was to court danger, and yet these combinations grew apace. Notwithstanding a vigilance which would seem to defy detection, their illicit meetings were discovered, and the discovery laid open the fact that the agitation at Wallsuches was but a branch from a hidden trunk. Ere we blame the Ridgways in their efforts to stamp out this agitation, let us just appositely view the present, and our judgment will be much mollified. With the discovery came the result; three of the more active were taken

before Messrs. R. Fletcher and J. Watkins, two of the
petty sessional J.P.'s, and by them duly convicted on
the 19th of March, 1821; the three men being named
respectively Tom Peak, W. Rutter, and Edward Roper.
An appeal against the decision on a technical ground
was made to the King's Bench at the ensuing Hilary
Term, Thomas Ridgway being the respondent, and the
"journeymen bleachers" appellants, the charge being
"that they had attended a meeting on the 9th of
March last past, for the purpose of obtaining an increase
of wages." The appellants had appealed against the decision of the magistrates to the Salford May Sessions, when
an informality was urged "that the count was for
attending a meeting convened for the purpose of obtaining an increase of wages," and the words of the Act
under which they had been convicted were "A meeting
convened to obtain an increase of wages." The Session
quashed the conviction subject to the opinion of the
"Court of King's Bench." Mr. Williams and Mr. Denman appeared in support of the order of the Sessional
Court, and Mr. Scarlett, Mr. Coltman, and Mr.
Starkie appeared for Mr. Ridgway, the decision of the
Court being "that the conviction was good." The following from the *Bolton Express* of March 6th, 1825, will
perhaps illustrate the position of the workman at that
period.

Submission: Whereas, I Thomas Drinkwater, of
Rivington, when in the employ of Messrs. Thomas
Ridgway and Nephew, of Horwich, did absent myself
from their service without any just cause, or without
permission to me given by my said masters, for which
offence they have very justly commenced a prosecution
against me, but on thus publicly expressing my contrition for the past, paying all expenses incurred in the
prosecution, and the expenses of publishing this my
submission in the *Bolton Express*, they have consented
to forego the said prosecution and all proceedings
therefrom. As witness my hand this first day of
March, 1824.

THOMAS DRINKWATER.

Witness—George Vause, Constable, Horwich.

We have already referred to Mr. Joseph Ridgway's
Court as held at the Black Bull, and sometimes at the

"Moor Gate," but in his character as a Petty Sessional Magistrate the "Old Justice" was best known. He was for a lengthened period chairman of the bench, and in his decisions he generally maintained a high character for wise discrimination, a judicious and calm judgment, and ever ready to "temper justice with mercy." Many stories are told of his connection with the bench, the following being amongst the number. At the Petty Sessions in July, 1839, John Andesty, an Irishman, was brought before Mr. Ridgway and Mr. W. Hulton, charged with being drunk and disorderly, when the following dialogue took place betwixt the prisoner and the bench:—Mr. Ridgway: What trade are you? Helpin' to dhrive the pigs yer honer, my Lord Mayor. (Laughter.)—What do you say about being troublesome? Prisoner: Why yer honer, my Lord Mayor, ye see I only jist came into the town on Sunday last, and on Monday I jist get a dhrop to dhrink in helpin' some pigs, yer honer.—Mr. Ridgway: Where do you come from? From Liverpool, yer honer.—What were you doing there? Dhriving pigs, yer honer.—Mr. Ridgway: I think you ought to abstain from drink then? Well, yer honer, my Lord Mayor, ye see I've got a bad coff.—If you promise to leave the town and go home we will discharge you? Mr. Hulton: He will come again next year.—Prisoner: Maybe I won't be alive, yer honer.—Mr. Ridgway: Well, you will have to leave the town, and we will discharge you.—Prisoner: Arrah, gud luck to your gud lookin' countenance, and I'll do that same.—Mr. Ridgway: You will have to pay the expenses? Prisoner: Did you say that same? I haven't got a fardin' in the world.—Mr. Ridgway: Never mind the expenses then, we will forgive you.—Prisoner: Gud luck to ye, may the—and ere the sentence was finished the prisoner was shown out of court.—Mr. Ridgway in politics was what to-day would be called a Tory of the old school, whatever that may mean, but even this term, surrounded with its modern definition and clothed in the language of the hour, is both misleading and delusive. To speak of Toryism in the past, with its modern acceptance, is to conjure up a picture of a drone reclining in ease and surrounded with plenty, his only thought how to gather around him a host of parasites able and willing to protect him from the angry wolves which gnash their teeth in hungry revolt. Such a picture reflects not the character we have before us. That he governed with a limited despotism, and ruled with the power of his will cannot be questioned; but yet Mr. Ridgway was a pattern of progress, the village that he and his family veritably and truly made is proof positive. That he lived before his day, and died in the very youth of his success, would be the record of fact. That the spirit of progress should be cultivated the united efforts of the family in the cause of education is sufficient evidence. Within the village and without this fostering band was ever visible. When we view, as view we must, the mistakes of the immediate past, we must be ready to deal justly, if not charitably, with those noble characters whose higher self was lost in the whirl of partizanship, and the lustre of whose lives was dimmed by a creed, political and religious, which but too truly recognised only "one faith, one hope, one baptism." To make political capital out of the past is impossible, unless we imitate that which we condemn, for at this period the working classes were simply the tools of both the ruling faction, and also the more dangerous, because more designing, agitator; both alike courted their smiles and enticed their sympathy for selfish ends. On the occasion of contested elections, when the scenes around the hustings were of a character at once revolting and deplorable, both contending parties marshalled their forces, and the old story of being prepared for war, &c., was a political text, paraphrased by bludgeons and handy weapons. On these occasions the sturdy crofters at Wallsuches were sent to Bolton with the name of the candidate in whose service they were drafted conspicuously displayed on their hats, and "true blue" colours flashing in martial style. Their zeal was only equalled by their ignorance, for few of those hardy crofters could have deciphered unaided the name they so conspicuously displayed. To them it was a mere pleasure, a pastime, a delight; patriotism was submerged within the limits of a pint pot or pewter, and their rights and privileges were no greater than the limits of a good feed, for which due preparation had been made in the ordeal of a free break-head fight, and the beginning and end of their duty to the State was the parrot cry of "Bolling for ever." In 1835 the ordinary quietude of the village was disturbed; and early on that January morning the bells of the church rang out a merry peal, while the steeple itself was gay with blue and white flags. The village itself was gaily decorated, the occasion being that Mr. Ridgway had invited those electors who had accompanied him to the poll and voted for Lord F. Egerton and the Hon. H. B. Wilbraham, successful candidates for South Lancashire, to dine with him at the Black Bull, then under the charge of Mr. Bilsborrow. His brother Thomas was equally active. In 1834 he was president of the Bolton Cattle Fair Society, whilst for many succeeding years he represented Horwich on the Board of Guardians, and in the debates which ensued in consequence of important alterations in the administration of the poor laws he took a leading part, his arguments being generally of that cogent style which command attention, and from an old town's record we find that in 1837 he was elected "Constable;" in fact Mr. Thomas Ridgway was the last gentleman who held that position. At that time the position of constable was of an honorary character, much as that of the higher office of sheriff at the present day, the more onerous duties being performed by deputy. In 1838 he appointed Richard Gregory as his deputy, and with him ceased this antiquated office in Horwich.

CHAPTER XXX.

Of the two sons of Thomas Ridgway, of Wallsuches, in whom survived the hopes of the Ridgway family, Thomas, the elder, was killed in early manhood whilst hunting at Euxton, near Chorley. Joseph, the remaining son, known more popularly in the village as "Young Joe," in many respects imitated his progenitors, being ever ready to assist in any movement the object of which was to improve and cultivate the masses around him. With this object in view, twelve scholars from the poorer class were taught in the village school at his expense. Nor was this an irrevocable number; the master had power in deserving cases to forego the school fees and apply to the cashier at Wallsuches for the amount. In those days, schooling was scarcely so costly an item in the domestic expenditure as at present. Books, slates, pens, and all requirements, and the modest sum of 2d. per week, covered an education which, judging by results, was equal, if not superior to the present. Much of the needful came from the charity sermon fund, which, we may say by the way, was not so large as at present, for as the result of the sermon by the then incumbent (Rev. D. Hewitt), on July 21st, 1839, the collections realised £32, in 1840 £37, 1845 £55, 1846 £60, whilst in 1883, when the vicar (Rev. H. S. Pigott) preached, the collections amounted to £116.

This second Joseph was married twice, and had issue by his first wife, a son and a daughter, Thomas Hastings Ridgway, and Cecily, married to the Hon. J. Stuart Hardy. On the occasion of his first marriage, to Selina Harriet, youngest daughter of Sir Francis Hastings Doyle, Bart., which was solemnized at St. James's, Piccadilly, the Rev. Edward Girdlestone, Vicar of Dean, brother-in-law to the bridegroom, officiating, the village put on a very gay appearance, the bells, the gift of J. Ridgway, sen., rang out merry peals throughout the day, and flags and banners in rich profusion decorated the streets and public thoroughfares. The cannon at Wallsuches, made from a "press ram," belched forth its echoing sound; the employés at Wallsuches were regaled at the Bull, Brown Cow, and Crown Inns, and the culinary arrangements taxed to the utmost to provide for the unlimited repast to which the employés were invited. At the former place Mr. Charles Howarth presided (Messrs. Charles and Christopher having been taken into the firm as partners), and the first toast was "Mr. and Mrs. Ridgway, may they live long in the perfect enjoyment of every domestic happiness, a blessing to the neighbourhood and themselves," the toast being honoured with "three times three." The employés at Wallsuches after enjoying the repast were marshalled in processional order, and wended their way through the village to the front of the hall, where cheers were given for Mr. and Mrs. Ridgway, and also "three times three" for the mother of Mr. Ridgway; after this they returned to their respective rendezvous. Amongst other toasts was the following, "Messrs. Charles and Christopher Howarth, our highly respected masters." This young Joseph Ridgway married for his second wife the sister of Lord Colville. In 1860, acting under the advice of his physician, Mr. Ridgway went to pass the winter on the continent, together with his wife and son. He subsequently visited Egypt, and whilst at Thebes Mr. Ridgway had another attack of sickness. There is something touching in the almost tragic ending of that journey to Egypt. To watch over her husband and son, the devoted wife forgot herself in those noble traits which ennoble the feminine character in whatever station they are exhibited. Alone in the squalid tent of a wandering Arab, unable to communicate her needs, or by intelligible language evoke sympathy for her position; there denied of those aids so important to the success of her heroic mission, the noble lady cheered husband and child, till at last an English clergyman at Cairo heard of their position and went to their aid, but, alas, too late, her unaided exertions had made her susceptible to her husband's disease, and with her husband's daily improvement she sickened and died, a martyr to her devotion. The son also died at

the early age of 17. Their remains were subsequently
brought to Horwich and laid in the family vault. With
his marriage Mr. Ridgway left Wallsuches and went to
reside at Fairlawn, Kent, but shortly after his return
from Egypt he went to reside at Goudhurst, having
purchased the estate, and by means of a faculty had
the remains of his wife and son removed to the mauso-
leum he had erected. He died on the 20th of January,
1879, at Eaton-place, London, in the 59th year of his
age. The first Joseph died at Leamington, June 26th,
1842, aged 77 years, and was buried July 6th. Mrs.
Joseph Ridgway (the elder) died at Hatton Hall,
Northamptonshire, 14th November, 1860.

Horwich Bleachworks, from its name would be
implied the oldest in the village, and consequently one
of the pioneers of the bleaching business. It would be
difficult to say with chronological exactitude when the
operation of bleaching first commenced in what is now
embraced within the limits of Horwich Bleachworks,
but local titles are oft suggestive of date, and give a
definition both to period and position before their
changeable deeds and shifting transfers. While not
prepared to say that here bleaching was first introduced
into Horwich, we should not question the assertion
that here a longer continuity may be found than elsewhere. We have already referred to a " Hopwood "
whose name appears in the list of merchants frequenting Manchester market at the close of the last century,
and ere we refer to the names introduced, we may
just glance at its changing history. From Mr. Hopwood the bleach works passed into the hands of a Dr.
Pilkington, who resided and then held the Stock's
estate, this lease passing into the hands of the
Ridgways in 1803. The other estate adjoining on which
stood the " White House " was named the Pilkington's,
and passed into the hands of the Ridgways in 1801.
On May 31st, 1820, the bleach works and circumjacent
land passed into the hands of Messrs. France and Pass,
Mr. Longworth purchasing the estate in October, 1840.
Mr. Longworth was the descendant of an ancient
family, who though not really residing in the village,
had yet sufficient interest therein, as to be considered
one of its inhabitants. But it is scarcely necessary to

refer to him in these pages; his memory will ever be
green in the annals of local history. In every position
in which he could serve the village, there was he to be
found. In the board room as guardian for Horwich, as
chairman of its local meetings, as churchwarden, as
master or employer he was distinguished alike for his
urbanity and kindly disposition; to the poor he was a
councillor and friend, and yet his stern unflinching
character could ever be evoked where the interests of
the villagers were concerned. Though his connection
with the village became more directly allied with the
purchase of the bleachworks and estate, yet we find that
he had important connections therewith before. In the
Bolton Chronicle of May 26, 1838, we find the following
reference to the "rent audit." "On Monday
last, W. Longworth, Esq., of Land, Heaton
and his sister held their rent - day at the
house of Mr. Yates Bilsborrow, Black Bull, on
which occasion upwards of 70 of their tenants sat down
to a plentiful and substantial supper. Mr. Longworth,
in his usual affable manner, remained during the
evening, and defrayed all expenses, which has always
been his practice every rent day.". Not only as a
bleacher and landed gentleman was Mr. Longworth
known, but also as a colliery proprietor. At Doffcocker
and Westhoughton, pits were opened out under his
guidance, and the more widely known Brinsop Hall
Collieries owe their existence to his energy. To the
friendly societies he was a ready patron and an
honorary member, acting as treasurer, and rendering
every assistance for the consummation of their success,
and notwithstanding his social position, he deemed it
no slight on that position to take part in their
gatherings and be a leader in their processions. To
view the surroundings of the Bleachworks of to-day is
only to have a faint conception of what they were in
the past, when the mill known as Foxhole Mill was
part thereof. Now they have a compressed and modern
aspect, which little illustrates its scattered portions in
its more early history. The works are now the property
of his only surviving son, who resides at the ancient
seat of "The Knowles."

The following may perhaps interest our readers, and convey some information:—

Tax Office. Know all men that we, Thomas (Royal Arms.) Baldwin, the younger, clerk, and Thomas Barton, Esquire, two of the Commissioners appointed for the purposes of an Act, intituled "An Act for making perpetual, subject to redemption and purchase in the manner therein stated, the several sums of money now charged in Great Britain as a Land Tax for one year, from the 25th day of March, 1798, for the County of Lancaster, do hereby certify that in the execution of the said Act, and of two other Acts for extending the powers of the said Act, and for explaining and amending the same, we have contracted with Richard Pilkington, of Horwich, in the said county, for the redemption of six shillings and elevenpence farthing (6s. 11¼d.) land tax, being the land tax charged upon a messuage, barn, and sundry other buildings, with eleven acres of land situate in Horwich aforesaid, occupied by John Hopwood, also a messuage and carding house occupied by John Eatock, with six cottages and a smithy in Horwich aforesaid, occupied by Samuel Irlam and others. The consideration for the redemption is declared to be so much of lawful money of Great Britain to be paid to the Receiver-General, or his deputy, for the said county of Lancaster, as according to the current price of stock transmitted to such Receiver-General—£12 14s. 4¾d. will be sufficient to purchase twelve pounds fourteen shillings and fourpence three farthings capital stock in the three pounds per centum consolidated bank annuities, on the 11th day of May, 1799, such price to be estimated according to the current price of stock transferred in the week preceding the 20th day of May, 1799.

Witness our hands and seals ———

(Attached Certificate.)—We, two of the commissioners of the land tax for the division of Bolton, in the county of Lancaster, do hereby certify that a messuage, a barn, a shippon, and stable, two buildings for finishing muslins, and other buildings, and eleven acres and a half, or thereabouts, of arable, meadow, pasture, and croft land, after eight yards to the perch, situate in Horwich, in the division aforesaid, the inheritance of Richard Pilkington, and in the occupation of John Hopwood, and one carding house and messuage in the occupation of John Eatock, six cottages and a smithy in possession of Samuel Irlam, Ellen Renshaw, William Greenhalgh, Samuel Hodkinson, and Mary Hampson, are charged with the land tax to the amount of 6s. 11½d.

JNO. WOODS.
23rd April, 1799.   THOS. FOGG.

To this said Richard Pilkington the town's memorandum is indebted for this singular entry : —" I Richard Pilkington Remembers that I have been told that I suppose fifty years ago, when Mr. Richardson was Stuard, they stopt paying the lay for Lostock, and that Christopher Horrox, William Hart, and myself went to Lostock to meet Mr. Richardson and took and shewed him the Rentally which is in the old Town Book which was thought to be Mr. Brigg's writing, and that no more was said, but Paid their Lay as usual, as witness my hand,   RICHARD PILKINGTON."

This Richard Pilkington was also a benefactor, as we have seen, to New Chapel, and the following extracts from his Will may be interesting :—" I, Richard Pilkington, of Horwich, in the county of Lancaster, gentleman, do make and publish my last will, and my general and testamentary expenses to be paid out of my personal estate. I give and bequeath unto John Mason, of Sharples, in the said county, yeoman, and Richard Mason, of Horwich aforesaid, yeoman (which said John Mason is one of the trustees of the chapel called the Horwich New Chapel for Protestant Dissenters or Presbyterians), their executors, administrators, and assigns, the sum of one hundred pounds, to be paid within six months after my decease out of such part of my personal estate as shall be legally applicable for that purpose in preference to any other legacy given by this my will. Upon trust that the said John Mason and Richard Mason and survivor of them and the executors and administrators of such survivor and the trustees and trustee for the time being acting in the execution of the trusts of an Inder. bearing date on or about the 25th day of December, 1719, for the management of the said Chapel, do and shall pay out and invest the same at interest in their or his names or name, and do and shall pay the interest of the paid sum of £100 to, or permit the same to be received by the person who for the time being shall be minister of the said chapel, so long as the Assembly Catechism shall be taught to the children, and the doctrines expressed in the said Indenture of the 25th December, 1719, be taught, held, and preached to the congregation frequenting the said chapel. I give and bequeath to my housekeeper, Amelia Roscoe, her ex-administrators and assigns, the sum of £80, to be paid to her out of my personal estate at the end of twelve months after my death. I also give to the Amelia Roscoe a suit of mourning; and after devising specified sums to his nephews, Richard Pilkington, of St. Helens; William Pilkington, of St. Helens; and Joseph Rylands, linen manufacturer, of Wigan, and legacies to his great nephews, John and Joseph Cross, with further instructions for the division in the case of the death of any of the interested parties, with powers to provide for the education out of the estate for those younger who might have a claim under the said will, it concludes as follows:—"And I hereby revoke all former wills by me at any time heretofore made, and declare this only to be my last will and testament." The will bears date of 4th June, 1832, witness A. L. Howarth, attorney, Bolton, James Pickup and James Gorton, clerks. A codicil was added on the 18th July, 1838, witnesses J. H. Johnson, clerk, Thomas Jolley, weaver. The will was sworn under £4,000.

"By the tenor hereof, we, Henry Raikes, clerk, Master of Arts, vicar general and official principal of the Right Rev. Father-in-God, John Bird, Lord Bishop of Chester, lawfully authorised, make known unto all men, that upon the 12th day of May, in the year of our Lord 1840, the last will and testament with a codicil of Richard Pilkington, late of Horwich, gentleman, deceased, was intebuated, proved, approved, and declared valid, and administration of all and singular the goods, chattels, and credits of the said deceased was granted unto Richard Pilkington, William Pilkington, and William Wilding, three of the executors named in the said will and testament, being first sworn upon the Holy Gospels, well and truly to administer the said goods, &c."

CHAPTER XXXI.

At the latter part of the last century the village, along with the country in general, was roused into that state of martial ardour which speaks a dangerous crisis. Patriotism is the full energy, the combined flow of the multitudinous streamlets, which give united vitality to the national life. At its shrine crimes have been condoned; and blood guiltiness metamorphosed into heroic actions. The ambitious designs of the "First Napoleon" had inspired the nation with courage, and the "nation of shopkeepers" had suddenly developed all the pomp and state of mighty war. Then telegraphic communication was unknown; the dangerous forces of the air had not become subservient to the use of man, but the "sea-girt isle" was alive both to its necessities and its dangers. The old system of signalling was revived, and Rivington Pike once more prepared to send forth its forked tongue of flame. Contributions for war purposes were made, the moiety from Horwich being as follows:— Rev. Samuel Johnson, M.A., curate in charge, £5 5s.; Adam Howarth £1 1s. 0d., John Hopwood £1 1s. 0d. and 55 lesser sums amounting to £10 11s. 5d., the appeal being "for subscriptions to support war with France," date 1798. The volunteer movement was brought to the fore, and Horwich and district had its volunteer contingent, to which we have already referred. Press-gangs became the terror of the district, and many were suddenly drafted from home and sent to bear a part in the great struggle. Lots were cast for recruits, and "subs" only could meet the exigencies of the country's needs. The more wealthy—at least those wanting in military ardour—paid heavily betimes for the privilege of remaining purely civilian. Considering its then population, Horwich received back a fair share of war's heroes. Its Wards, Houghtons, Rawlinsons Wilkinsons, &c., came fresh with the "scars of glory," and over many a pot of beer in the village inn they mounted afresh the ramparts of Badajos, renewed anew the deadly struggle at Salamanca, rang out victory's cheer as at Vittoria, and fought, yea won afresh, the glories of Waterloo. The temporary peace which followed the brief exile of Napoleon to Elba, caused unusual rejoicings. The privations of the working classes had been severe. Bread was a luxury reserved for a Sunday meal—if at all. The capture of "Europe's dictator" sent a cry of joy throughout civilisation, and England felt revivified in the prospect of a much-needed peace, and need we wonder that a day of "General Thanksgiving" was set apart by Royal command for Thursday, July 7th, 1814, when the following sermon was preached by the Rev. Samuel Johnson, M.A., perpetual curate of Horwich. The rev. preacher selected for his text, Deuteronomy 33 c., 29 v.: "Happy art thou, Israel: who is like unto thee, O people saved by the Lord, the shield of thy help, and who is the sword of thine excellency; and thine enemies shall be found liars unto thee, and thou shalt tread upon their high places." It is well known that the Jewish state was a Theocracy. God, who had a long time presided over it in a peculiar manner, commanded Moses to "Get him up into the mountain Abarim, unto Mount Nebo, and behold the land of Canaan, the good country, which he gave unto the children of Israel for a possession," and then "die in the mount, whither he went up." (Deut. xxxii., 49-50.) The illustrious prophet and servant of the Almighty, anxious for the welfare of the people, and now sensible of near approach of his dissolution, after the example of Jacob takes a solemn leave of them, in a prophetic blessing pronounced upon each of the tribes, into which they were divided. Being, however, unable to express their happiness, he thus breaks out into admiration of it:—"Happy art thou, O Israel: who is like unto thee, O people saved by the Lord, the shield of thy help, and who is the sword of thine excellency, and thine enemies shall be found liars unto thee, and thou shalt tread upon their high places." In applying which words to ourselves on the present truly important occasion, I shall consider our own happiness and the source from which it springs, and conclude with an application. Our situation in itself is truly desirable fenced by the waters of the surrounding ocean, we live securely in a country where commerce is extensive and advantageous, whose land is fruitful, whose climate is temperate and friendly to the health and long life of its inhabitants, now more especially renowned as well for their bravery as their sagacity. Thus situated we are blessed with such a Constitution of Government as every considerate person would wish to be born under. An admirable Constitution, the work of much wisdom and virtue, in which power and liberty are so happily balanced that, as Sovereignty cannot rise into tyranny, so neither can obedience sink down into slavery. Many years' experience have now proved it highly conducive to our happiness. It is a compound of blessings, the value of which it is not easy to express. It imparts a relish to all the other comforts which we enjoy, and is as requisite to our well being as our daily sustenance. It is our preservation in the day, our protection in the night, the security of life and property, of religion, of all that is dear and sacred. To this let it be added, that we are members of a primitive and apostolic Church, which teaches all that is necessary to salvation, and yet nothing that is unsound and unscriptural. Her doctrines are built upon the true rule of faith and practice, the Word of God, and explained agreeably to the sense of the first and purest ages of Christianity. Her worship is unencumbered by superstition and divested of enthusiasm, is solemn and devout, plain, and yet truly sublime. Her ministers are lawfully ordained, and her sacraments rightly administered. In a word, her instructions, which breathe holiness and charity, cannot fail to make those who seriously attend to them ' "Wise unto salvation," and lead them in the way of everlasting bliss. But in taking a view of our own happiness, it is necessary to add to the blessings by which we have been continually surrounded, the mercies by which we have been occasionally distinguished. Far removed from the seat of war, we have only felt its expense, a very trifling affair, when compared with the miseries with which it has been attended, and which we have never been laid under the dreadful necessity of beholding. But whilst we have rested under our own roof in security and peace, how often have our ears been filled with the joyful tidings of victory over the proud insulting foe! Many deliverers, no less sagacious than valiant, have been raised up for us, whose exertions have been crowned with success. But in how short a space of time has he who had subdued empires been himself subdued by the wisdom and valour of injured nations. In the moment of prosperity, they who had long groaned under the iron rod of oppression, rose up against their vile oppressor, and threw down the aspiring military adventurer from his seat. Thus has our inveterate enemy been "found a liar unto us, and we have trodden upon his high place." His best formed designs have been baffled, his vain boastings have been exposed, and we have lived to see the long wished for return of peace and plenty. Such is our happiness, considered with relation both to the ordinary and extraordinary mercies showered down upon us. It is indeed so great that, adopting the very words of the text, we may with great propriety thus address our nation "Who is like unto thee?" Where is the people upon the face of the earth which can be compared to us in the undisturbed possession and secure enjoyment of the gifts and blessings which every returning day has brought with it, even in times of general terror and distress? In what region has there been so unexceptional an exposition of the religion of Christ or so excellent form of government as in this happy island? We know by peculiar experience the wide difference between Kings and Tyrants, Subjects and Slaves. Ruled by wise and equitable laws, here we may do what we will, if we do what is right; and, defended from the encroachment of violence, can look around on our possessions with the pleasing reflection that whatever we possess we can truly and properly call it our own. May the nations of the earth rescued from oppression and misery ever be sharers in our happiness. "Filled with the knowledge of the glory of the Lord as the waters cover the sea." (Hab, ii., 14). May they continue to enjoy, in prosperity and peace, the blessings of a well regulated liberty, and worshipping God according to the dictates of a rightly informed conscience, "worship him in spirit and in truth." It is time now to consider the source from which our happiness has flowed, and this, surely, is no other than the care and goodness of the over-ruling Deity. To show in how particular a manner the Providence of God watches over every one of us our Saviour tells us that "the hairs of our head are numbered." And if men, in their private capacities, are thus regarded by the Almighty we may well conclude that public societies, states, and kingdoms are so in a more eminent manner, inasmuch as the fortunes of all the individuals that made up such aggregate bodies are included in them, and improved or impaired in proportion to the prosperity or adversity that befalls them. Accordingly the Spirit of Truth assures us that "if any evil happen in a city it is the Lord that doeth it—he maketh peace and createth evil;" is the defender of all the public blessings that befall a nation. (Amos iii., 6. Isa. xliii., 7.) That "the Most High ruleth in the kingdom of men, and giveth it to whomsoever he will." (Dan. 4, 7.) And that "the kingdom is the Lord's, and He is the Governor among the people" (Psalm 22, 28). Can it be doubted, then, who is the Author of our present happiness? We ought certainly to ascribe it to the superintending goodness of the All-wise and All-powerful God, and gratefully acknowledge ourselves to be a "people saved of the Lord;" by His creative power, which has surrounded us with the turbulent ocean, we are defended from the sudden incursion of destructive arms. By the kindly and salutary influences of His "heavens, even the works of His fingers" (Psalm 8, 3 v.), our climate is healthy and our land fruitful. Through the favour of His Providence our lot has been cast into a country where we are governed and supported by wise and equitable laws, and enlightened and animated in an Apostolical Church by the genuine religion of our blessed Redeemer. To His blessing upon our uninterrupted exertions to preserve the Constitution uninjured, it is owing that it remains unimpaired, and that we are still an independent people. Extraordinary praises ought, doubtless, to be given to the policy, constancy, and perseverance of our excellent statesmen; and especially to the wise forecast and firm conduct of one super-eminent patriot, whose splendid talents, so anxiously employed for his country's good, can never be forgotten. Not a little commendation is to be ascribed to the bravery of our forces, both by sea and land, and many honours are due and have indeed been justly paid to the sagacity, magnanimity, and fortitude of our commanders and allies, displayed in the hour of danger. But whilst we are mindful of rendering the just tribute of gratitude to those illustrious instruments in the hands of the Lord, let us never forget to acknowledge ourselves a people "saved" by Him, "the shield of our help and who is the sword of our excellency." It is He who hath given us wisdom in council, courage, and conduct, and victory in the day of battle; and by the marvellous operations of His providence, made all things work together for our good. "Not unto us, therefore, O Lord, not unto us, but unto Thy Name give the praise, for thy loving mercy and for thy truth's sake." It now remains only to conclude with an application. It is a notorious truth that the last and present century have been distinguished by a series of events unexampled in the annals of history. In consequence of a three-fold conspiracy, which had long meditated with delight upon the overthrow of the altar, the ruin of the throne, and dissolution of all civil society, the French Revolution at last broke out with sudden and irresistible fury. It is impossible to particularise in a small compass the atrocities of that dreadful scheme of Liberty and Equality, which could be fully accomplished only by desolation. Let it suffice to observe, it is well known, that a tragical scene of misery has been realised, in which, whilst revolution followed close upon revolution, even the tyrants themselves devoured one another. Desolation and distress, aggravated by an almost hopeless prospect of termination, were, however, to be yet widely diffused over the world. The miseries and perplexities of foreign countries continued under the dismal reign of one upstart ruler, who was as successful in the management as he had been ingenious in the contrivance of a most dreadful warfare. A short time has passed since his rapid victories, which at the expense of slaughtered thousands upon thousands, had revolutionised a considerable part of Europe, and still threatened the remainder. But behold "the goodness of God which endureth yet daily." The righteous Governor of the world hath not suffered this blood-stained invader of human happiness to triumph finally. Having made this wicked and aspiring mortal the instrument of his vengeance upon impiety and iniquity, he then permitted him to be infatuated, defeated, confounded, totally overthrown. Thus has the impending storm of evils been dispersed by a gracious over-ruling Providence, and we have lived to see the downfall of tyranny, the deliverance of nations, the revival of commerce, the return of an honourable, and, it is hoped, an enduring peace. Who, except even the bitterest enemy to his own country, can forbear to exult in the view of its rise in the scale of happiness and importance? What heart can be so cold as not to glow with satisfaction at the consideration of the situation of the nations abroad so happily improved by the delightful accession of freedom and independence, tranquility, and prosperity; and so likely to be blessed by a far more extensive influence of the mild and benevolent, and purifying principles of Christianity. For his various accumulated mercies, suddenly rushing in upon the world, from under the gloom by which it had been long overspread, what thanks are due to the great Giver of Good? What return shall we make unto the Lord for all His benefits? Let us give Him all that we have to give, a heart and life truly devoted to His service. Obedient to His will in all things, as far as human frailty will permit, let us be "followers of that which is good," (1 Peter 3, 13 v.) Guarding with the utmost vigilance against those vices, and those neglects of duty, whatever they may be, to which we see others, and may feel ourselves inclined. Whilst we "Fear God" let us also "Honour the King" (1 Peter 2, 17 v.) persuaded by the remarkable events of the times in which we have lived, never to "Meddle with them that are given to change" (Prov. 20, 21 v), but always to submit, as our holy religion directs us, with cheerfulness to the rulers of this world, for the good of society, and for conscience sake. Grateful for the signal successes with which the

Almighty hath crowned our king and country, let us serve Him faithfully all our days, worshipping Him in spirit and in truth, in our Apostolical Church, which His own right hand has planted, and for so many ages preserved and shielded against the secret designs and open attempts of her inveterate enemies. And whilst we praise and serve the great Author of our happiness, let us love and serve one another, and "live in peace" that so "the God of love and peace may be with us." So may we hope for a continuance of our present happy situation. So may we trust that the Divine judgments will be removed far from us, at least that "the Lord, the shield of our help, and who is the sword of our excellency" will be evermore our Mighty Protector and Deliverer, and that boastful enemies will at all times "be found liars unto us." So may we sit as on safety's rock, pouring forth those triumphant strains of the Psalmist: "God is our hope and strength, a very present help in trouble, therefore will we not fear though the earth be moved, and the hills be carried into the midst of the sea, though the waters thereof rage and swell, and though the mountains shake at the tempest of the same. It is God who maketh liars to cease in all the world, he breaketh the bow, and snappeth the spear in sunder, and burneth the chariots in the fire. The Lord of Hosts is with us, the God of Jacob is our refuge."

CHAPTER XXXII.

The following case will to some extent illustrate the custom of the period, and show the manner of dealing with cases that now perhaps too frequently are treated as purely accidental. At this period (1823) juries dealt with cases without any of those surrounding guides which more refined feeling, and the concomitant tendency of a charitable civilisation (!) have invested them. The verdict which denied the higher principle of Christianity, and refused "Christian burial" could then be given without any outrage on the national conscience. Justice was more than proverbially blind; fact, not sympathy, moved the balance. On September 11, 1823, an inquest was held at the Black Bull, touching the death of a child named Noah Turner, aged three years, which had met with its death by being run over with a cart, the horse and cart being in charge of a man named Thomas Rimmer. The evidence went to show that the carter exercised reasonable care, but the child was killed, and the verdict was one of "Manslaughter." Rimmer was sent to Lancaster Castle, and was finally tried before Mr. Justice Bailey (Joseph Ridgway, of Ridgmont, being one of the jury,) and received a sentence of three months imprisonment.

Horwich, as we have seen, was largely interested in hand loom weaving, and a fair share of prosperity had followed, but the important change which had followed the introduction of the "steam loom" began to have its effect. Meetings were held throughout the country, and petitions to Parliament were adopted asking the aid of the Legislature for an equalisation of price, such equalisation to be the result of a tax put upon all cloth woven by steam power. Of course the numerous petitions failed. The Legislature itself was powerless to impose a tax which would have warred against the best interest of society for the benefit of a class, and that not the most numerous, and better arguments were required to upset the commercial traditions of the country than those set forth by the Hand-loom Weavers. In 1829 great distress prevailed in the manufacturing districts, riots being frequent, wages were at the lowest, and poverty and discontent followed. From a manifesto issued by the weavers we find it stated that calico, 30 yards in length, were woven for a shilling, out of which shilling 2d. was paid for winding; the position of the weavers being well summarised in the sentence "that a man must work early and late to get four (4) cuts per week, or virtually 3s. 4d." However strong to-day such a statement may appear, collateral facts proclaim its genuineness, for such was the state of privation, that the poor rates were requisitioned and the earnings made up to 1s. 6d.—one and sixpence per head. The cause of all this misery, in the then perverted state of the public mind, was attributed to the introduction of machinery, and where such existed, in whatever shape, there danger existed. Factories were pillaged and machinery destroyed, and it became a standing requirement that a provision for defence should exist. Cannon sometimes, of a rude shape, were mounted on a kind of a rampart overlooking the entrance to the works, and strangers were warned that such "due provision for protection had been made." But at this period the distress was not confined to a class, or to a section of the community; trade and manufactures as well as agricultural stagnated: "whole parishes were reduced to a state of beggary," pauperism in its worst form existed, whole parishes being subject to its desolating blight. People were compelled to seek the aid of neighbours little, if any, better off than themselves and already overburdened by the rates, out of which their own poor had to be maintained. Tenants could not pay their rents, farmers were too poor to effect improvements in their holdings, the farm labourer was a casual pauper, his miserable earnings supplemented by the parish dole. The operatives of Lancashire and Yorkshire were starving on wages which only amounted to a few pence per day (often no more than threepence or fourpence), though they worked for 12 hours. O'Connell declared in the House of Commons that in Ireland 7,000 persons were subsisting on three-halfpence a-day each. At the opening of Parliament in 1830 the Government in the "Royal Address" approached the subject of the "wide-spread distress" in such apathetic terms which led the discontented multitude to the belief that they were careless alike of their miseries, and callous to their sufferings. The national temper was strained, and the hidden volcano already gave signs of a danger which threatened such an upheaval as would have sunk the social fabric into irremedial confusion—confusion in which they who taught, and they who preached the doctrine, "that the aristocracy were made to govern and the people to obey," would themselves have been the greatest sufferers. The creed which involved the theory that it was the duty of the aristocracy to care for the people, had been weighed in the balance and found wanting. To their guidance and control, to their great and all powerful share in the government of the country, the present calamities were assigned, and a spirit powerful and bold was then abroad, which taught that the people had something more to do with the laws than simply to obey them. To this period is assigned two of the most powerful and, we may almost say, peaceful agitations—for where such failed the fault was beyond and apart from the agitation—that has marked an important crisis in the history of any country—the Chartist agitation and the Anti-Corn Law League. From 1823 down to the final repeal of the Corn Laws by Sir Robert Peel, the agitation was ever popular amongst the working classes. On the other hand, the ruin of the nation was prophesied by many of those who were considered both sagacious and patriotic. There was not a form of ruin to farmers, to merchants, to manufacturers, to shopkeepers, to peasants, to working men, to throne, and army, to Church and State that was not prophesied, decade after decade. Not one, however, of these direful forebodings has been realized. In 1828 Parliament so far acquiesced in the popular demand that a medium or post duty of between 64s. and 65s. was introduced, but this was insufficient for the popular demand. In 1838 the list of the Manchester Anti-Corn Law Association was published, and the working classes in the manufacturing districts, of which Manchester was the centre, joined the Association, and perhaps in few places was the movement more popular than in Horwich. The symbol of the Association was unknown, and a great many joined the movement, which doubtless has proved of incalculable blessing to the community. The productions of Ebenezer Elliott, the "Corn-law Rhymer," showed up the impulse, and paved the way for the Anti Corn Law orators. Such productions, with all their faults and failings, as the following, in the then excited state of the public mind, could not fail to impress :—

>Child, is thy father dead?
>   Father is gone,
>Why did they tax his bread?
>   God's will be done.
>
>Mother has sold her bed,
>   Better to die than wed.
>Where shall she lay her head,
>   Home we have none.
>
>Father clamm'd thrice a week;
>   God's will be done;
>Long for work did he seek,
>   Work he found none.
>
>Tears on his hollow cheek,
>   Told what no tongue could speak.
>Why did his Master break;
>   God's will be done.

A commercial panic followed the temporary prosperity of 1835, and many of the so-called "monied classes" were landed in ruin through the collapse of many bubble companies; this, added to the failure of the harvest, led to an unnatural pressure on the money market, and in its train followed bank failures, and commercial panic with its consequent distress. 1836 was a year of loss and ruin, 1837 was even worse, and Mr. Cobden estimated the losses at a very high figure. This year the harvest was a poor yield, and that of 1838 was one-fourth less than that of 1834, "the most deficient crop of any since 1816." No wonder, then, that the note of dissatisfaction was ominous and deep, factories running short time, some four days a week, and thousands of operatives unemployed, and those working receiving a very low rate of wages. No wonder that in this great distress the death knell of the "bread tax" was sounded, and the people ready to take up with any cause that even gave a promise to better their position. The position at Horwich may be gathered from the fact that, as a subordinate aid to other "helps," a charity ball was held in 1839. In 1837 the prospectus for the Bolton and Preston Railway was issued, and in this many recognised the sign of the good time coming, Thomas Ridgway, of Wallsuches, being one of the provisional committee. In 1841 the railway from Bolton to Horwich and Blackrod was opened, the service being as follows from Bolton :—8 15 and 11 a.m., 2 15 and 6 p.m. ; Sundays 8 30 a.m. and 6 30 p.m. On Sunday second class passengers were taken at third class fares, the rates being as follows :—First class 1s. 6d., second class 10d., third class 8d. On Saturday, April 30th, 1836, a storm of a violent character, attended with fatal consequence, passed over Horwich. A house occupied by a man named Joseph Hough, situate a little above Wallsuches, was almost entirely wrecked; two sons were standing together when the electric fluid struck the house, the elder, aged 14, being killed on the spot, fragments of slate, glass, and furniture being carried a distance of a hundred yards, and forced into the ground. The boy's body was burned to a cinder, every part of his clothing was consumed with the exception of part of one stocking; two others in the family were injured, but ultimately recovered. A subscription to cover the loss of furniture, &c., was set on foot, and the following appeal appeared in the *Bolton Chronicle*, of May 7th, 1836 :—"To the Humane. Melancholy visit by Lightning. The attention of the humane public of Bolton and its vicinity, proverbially alive to objects of real commiseration and compassion, is especially invited to a consideration of the awful dispensation of Providence manifested to the family and property of Joseph Hough, of Horwich, a poor, industrious, labouring man, whose residence on Saturday last, April 30th, was struck by lightning, his son instantly killed on the spot, two other of his children injured, all the furniture in his humble dwelling destroyed, and his looms and the work in them greatly damaged. Subscriptions may be paid to Messrs. Hardcastle, Cross, and Bankers, or to Mr. Woodhouse,

solicitor." The subscription in Manchester amounted
to £17 6s. 6d. At this period the Chartist agitation
was at its height, and we who look back upon the
immediate past, wonder why such agitation should
destroy the equanimity of our fathers, remembering
how much then denied, we enjoy. Chartism appealed
rather to the passions than to the intellect, and the
advocacy of the "People's Charter," and that which
in itself appealed to the nobler instincts of the nation,
was environed by a virulence and crippled by the very
infatuation it created. When at the Monmouth
assizes, in January, 1840, Frost, Williams, and
Jones were sentenced to death, the national
feeling gained in sympathy, but the Government
was spared the mistake of making the trio "Martyrs
for the people," and Chartism, as a public working
force, began gradually to decline, and it was only a kind
of flickering of the expiring flame, that agitated Horwich and the surrounding district, when the Chartists
held a camp meeting at Westhoughton, on Sunday,
August 13, 1843. In 1822 the Horwich Building Club
ceased to exist, and the property it then held was
brought to the hammer at the Black Bull, accompanying
the placard announcing the sale was a map, showing
the surroundings of the property, and in an artistic
manner conveyed each particular to the would be pur-
chaser. With the advent of the Rev. David Hewitt,
in 1826, came an agitation encouraged and promoted, as
we have already seen, by the Ridgways. Of the old
chapel various relics are now to be found in the park
attached to Ridgmont, some of which we have
examined, and here we may refer to what has been
termed the "Legend of the Old Chapel," a legend
which perhaps may contain more truth than is generally
associated therewith. It is said that the "first chapel"
was built by a tailor, his remuneration being twopence
per day, the condition being that the builder should be
allowed to display the emblem of his handicraft in a
conspicuous place. We shall, however, give a description of the stones as we have seen them, leaving the investigation in the hands of our readers. The first
stone, which appears to have been a kind of "key stone,"
has sculptured a large pair of "Scissors," another,

somewhat worn, has upon it what may be typified the "goose," the understone being inscribed Anno Dom. 1588. Some portions would seem to indicate a connection of the Derby family with Horwich, for here we have the Eagle and Child and Manx Crest with the mottos "Fear God, Honour the King." On the stone lintels, the figure of Christ holding the world in His hand, with the monogram I.H.S. On the opposite, "The Crucifixion." At the foot of the cross, the lion and the lamb are peacefully reclining. On another of equal dimensions, we have a penitent kneeling, the priest with outspread hands giving the blessing. Another bears at one end the word "WARRAW," at the opposite end "ALEMENDROS," at one end "MDOO," at the other 1662. The following word square being in uplifted characters in the centre:—

     S A T O R
     A R E P O
     T E N E T
     O P E R A
     R O T A S

which has been translated "The Sewer (tailor) accomplished his work."

CHAPTER XXXIII.

In October, 1834, great excitement was caused in the village by a new "claimant" to the Anderton estates, giving notice against the payment of rents, &c., to any other "than the agent appointed by the said claimant." Minus the excitement, nothing occurred to disturb the ownership. The excitement was all the more intensified by a rumour "that not only was the claimant the undoubted heir" to the vast Anderton estates, but that a man named Harrison had found in a certain house in Lee-lane deeds and documents that would give full power and authority to this claimant. So strong did the feeling prove that a certain amount of pressure was needed to entice from the more cautious their rents, &c.

On Friday, November 9th, 1838, occurred one of those mysterious murders which ever impress a lasting sensation in the immediate neighbourhood. The morning was clothed in gloom, and a dense fog hung over the hills, and wrapped the valley in obscurity. Perhaps many others of equal density had environed Horwich and its surroundings, but never before had they been registered in such tragic characters as on this Friday morning, 1838. Even to-day a gloomy, foggy November atmosphere brings out the remark, "It's just sich another day as wen Scotchman wur shot." Few even of the younger portion of the villagers but are acquainted with its ghastly details, and its mysterious character gives its prominence which must be our excuse for referring at length thereto.

The *Bolton Chronicle* of November 10th, 1838, thus refers to the murder:—"Yesterday, about one o'clock, one of the most dreadful and atrocious murders was committed in our neighbourhood which has ever fallen to our lot to report. It is with no common feelings of regret that we now sit down to make public this gross act of turpitude. Up to this time the deed is wrapped in mystery. By the kindness of two medical gentlemen we have heard the particulars of the event, and we are grieved to be compelled to make them public. All who know this country know that there are parts which are secluded and wild. Imagination pictures many deeds of violence as we pass over such tracts. In one of these bare and barren spots was this murder perpetrated. A poor itinerant Scotchman is the victim. With another of his countrymen he was in the habit of travelling the country. The deceased was going by appointment to meet a friend at the Five Houses, near the "Two Lads," crossing from Horwich to Belmont. The non-appearance of the deceased induced the other Scotchman to go in search of him. The unhappy man was discovered lying by the roadside in a dying state, a shot having passed under the right ear, and, making its way through the head, found its vent through the left eye. The face was terribly blackened. When found he only uttered 'I am robbed, I am killed.' His friend states that having to meet him he went to the Black Dog in Belmont, where they ought to have dined—the dinner being ordered, but finding he did not come he went in search of him. He states that while on his road he met a tall man in shooting coat with a gun, and after walking for some distance, he turned round and saw the point of the stranger's gun directed at him. The stranger immediately lowered his gun, and he saw no more of him. He sought for his friend, but never heard of him till he heard of his death. No suspicion of the man being bad who gave this evidence, he was allowed to go on his way, and went, as he said, to Blackburn." The name of the unfortunate man was George Henderson, and he was 20 years of age. The *Chronicle* in its notice of the inquest says: "About ten o'clock in the morning Mr. Benjamin Birell—the friend referred to—arrived at the "Five Houses," and went into the beer shop kept by Mr. James Garbret, where he waited half an hour. We have to add that Roger Horrocks, who was found in a "turfcess" with a gun at his side, was at one time supposed to be the guilty person, but closer evidence fixing upon a man named James Whittle, the former was liberated and the latter arrested. On Tuesday, November 13, an inquest was held on the body before Mr. W. S. Rutter, coroner, and seventeen jurymen drawn from Horwich, Halliwell, Heaton, and Sharples, at Mr. Lambert's, Horwich Moor Gate, the following being the names of the jury: Richard France (foreman), Thomas Barlow, John Pendlebury, Will Longworth, John Hopwood, Roger Walsh, Robert Barlow, John Knowles, Richard Booth, Thomas Markland, William Pendlebury, Hugh Gruôdy, Richard Crankshaw, Robert Orrell, Joseph Winder, James Spencer, and William Longworth. The following magistrates were also present: Joseph Ridgway, Esq., P. Ainsworth, Esq., M.P., Robert Andrews, Esq., and Robert Derbyshire. So widespread was the melancholy interest taken in the proceedings that reporters were present representing the Bolton, Manchester, Liverpool, and Blackburn press. In consequence of the reports current on Friday and Saturday, Thomas Wright, Esq., and Peter Ainsworth, Esq., M.P., had thought it right to direct the arrest of a collier named James Whittle, in the employ of the latter. Thomas Whowell, a lad, fourteen years of age, was the first witness examined, and deposed to seeing the deceased previous to the murder. When witness returned from taking his brother's dinner to a coal pit close by, he saw the same Scotchman, and heard him moaning, and saw blood upon the ground. He heard someone in the gutter on the other side of the road, and, without stopping to look, he ran off for assistance. James Fletcher was the next witness, and spoke to Whowell fetching him from the pit, where he was banksman. Mary Entwistle deposed to seeing Whittle, the prisoner, with a gun, at half-past eight on the morning of the murder. W. Garbut, beerseller and master collier, said he lived at Five Houses, Horwich. There were no houses on the road but those between Horwich and Belmont. A girl informed him that somebody had killed the Scotchman. James Whittle, the prisoner, was within three yards of his door when the girl came in. He had seen him in the forenoon of that day. He recollected seeing him fire a gun at the bottom of his garden on Friday morning. He saw Whittle pass by his house while the Scotchman was in. There was no other company. Many people came to see the body, but he did not see Whittle amongst them. Benjamin Birrell, the surviving Scotchman, said as he was going to Belmont he saw a man very near the place where Henderson was found. He was above the hill, and had a gun. He was dressed in blue clothes. Witness, after leaving the man, who made inquiry from him; turned round and saw the prisoner with the gun pointed towards him. The prisoner on being observed lowered his gun. He then came up to him and asked him if he had seen two birds fly past, to which he replied "No." Whittle being ordered to stand up, witness said he was like the man he had seen on the moor, but he could not swear positively. He was about the same height, wore a similar hat, and wore the same sort of clothes. Dr. Wolstenholme, of Bolton, described the fatal injuries. William Simm, of Aspull Moor, said that as he was going to his sister's at Belmont he saw James Whittle with a gun in his hand. He was then about 350 yards from the place where Henderson was found. A Scotchman came into Garbutt's as witness went out. (Witness identified Whittle.) William Slater, a lad about thirteen, said he saw Whittle along with a tramp in the coal pit cabin. At the adjourned inquest, Matthew Lambert, landlord of the "Moor Gate," said he had lent the prisoner a gun on several occasions. On the day in question witness and prisoner should have met on Brownlow's Close, but about one o'clock he came to his house, and told the witness that he had brought home his gun. He stopped till four o'clock, when they went out together. As they went prisoner said he would never have a gun in their house again, and he would never shoot from one again. Lambert was subjected to a long examination, and gave his evidence under much pressure. A verdict of "Wilful murder" was returned against Whittle. The trial took place at the Crown Court, Lancaster, on Tuesday, April 9th, 1839, the court being crowded, the counsel for the prosecution being Mr. Dundas, Mr. Peel, and Mr. Cross; Mr. Wilkins (afterwards Serjeant Wilkins) being for the defence. Whittle being found "Not guilty," the presiding judge remarked that they had taken the safest side. The following verses were written on the occasion, the original being in possession of Mr. J. C. Scholes, by whom we have been privileged to copy :—

THE TRAGEDY ON HORWICH MOOR.

Horwichian hills, Belmontian dreary plains,
  To your dread names two tragic names belong;
O, could my muse pourtray in living strains
  Your fate should flourish and look green in song.

Your snowy cliffs and monumental piles
  The dreadful story of the "Two Lads" tell;
And on your swampy heaths and lone defiles
  By murderous hands a Caledonian fell.

But unborn ages shall the story hear
  In legends handed from sires of old,
While listening youth will drop the flowing tear,
  Nor leave to future sons the tale untold.

Thus execration will attend your way
  Till cycling years and hoary time shall end,
Till the last trump shall sound the judgment day,
  And nature's groans to heaven's high throne ascend.

Here aërial sprites that shun the face of day
  And skip the plains in Luna's silver beam;
Here fancied ghosts that on the mountains stray
  Will fright the natives—down Time's moving stream.

Strangers, beware, let bygone deeds suffice,
  No more let parents weep, nor kindred pain;
In some dark cavern, hid from mortal eyes,
  The Fates, relentless, hold their deadly reign.

When dark November wrapp'd the world in gloom,
  And murky clouds obscured fair Nature's face,
A vile assassin seal'd thy earthly doom,
  Ill-fated youth, of Scotia's noble race.

Scarce twice ten seasons had their courses run
  Since that first joyous morn, which gave thee birth,
Till the last rising of the noonday sun
  Which saw thee lifeless, on thy parent earth.

'Twas thine to journey from thy native clime,
  And seek thy fortune in a Southern land;
In Blackburn town to pass thy vacant time,
  'Midst generous friends—thy country's social band.

'Twas thine to range the jocund country round,
  The flow'ry meads, the plains, and fertile vales,
To taste the stores—where rosy health is found,
  The balmy breezes, and the ambrosial gales.

'Twas thine to climb the rugged mountain's side,
  To hear the rock-man in his dreary glen;
To view the landscape, far and wide,
  Free from the noise and busy haunts of men.

'Twas thine to cross the misty moorlands high,
  Thro' devious paths and winding ways to tread,
To hear the wakeful night-bird's warning cry,
  Steal on thy ear from yonder roofless shed.

Here—solitude in death-like stillness reigns,
  No shielding arm, no guardian angel nigh,
A savage murderer stalk'd the lonely plains,
  And here, ye powers, it was thy fate to die!

Weep Scotland's sons, and loving kindred weep
  On this sad spot a brother's blood doth cry;
His corse was doom'd to eternal sleep,
  His soul was raised to realms on high.

Perhaps, some father or some mother dear,
  Still live to mourn their son's untimely death;
Perhaps, some brother or some sister's tear
  Will flow in memory till their latest breath.

The Great Jehovah, w' o doth all things scan,
  Hath loud proclaim'd—and is His justice dead?
That he who sheds the vital blood of man,
  By man's strong arm his blood shall yet be shed.

CHAPTER XXXIV.

Few events connected with the history of Horwich were so well calculated to be remembered as the "Horwich races." Their short existence—a period of 10 years—may suggest a want of the sympathy and aid so necessary for such institutions, but in glancing over the records such aids will be found to be many and powerful, and their decline must be ascribed to a cause inspired more by the moralist than the sportsman. The first Horwich races took place on the 22nd August, 1837, the ground being that immediately under the "Manor House," upon the spot now covered by Blackrod waterworks. We have before us as we write the "Admittance card, grand stand, price 2s. 6d." This and the following have been kindly supplied us by Mr. Brownlow, Rock Haven, a gentleman who took the liveliest interest in the races from their conception to their close. The second Horwich races took place August 2nd, 1838, in a field adjoining Anderton Hall, Messrs. J. Radcliffe and P. J. Monday, stewards.

A Hurdle Sweepstakes of 4 sovs. each, with 50 added from the fund. Ten stone each. Thoroughbred horses 7lb. extra, and a winner of any previous steeple or hurdle race 7lb. extra. Mares and geldings allowed 3lb. Heats, twice round and a distance. Hurdles not to exceed 4ft., two in the round. Gentleman riders.

    Mr. J. Munday's Jereboam, scarlet.
    Mr. Brownlow's Lucks-all blue and white cap.
    Mr. Bindle's Blucher, black and blue.
    Mr. Mascall's Miss Julia Wriggles, blue and white.
    Mr. Chew's Tom Thumb, tartan and black.

The Horwich Stakes, of 5 sovs. each, h f. with 50 added from the fund. For horses of all denominations. Four years 9st. 5lb., five years 10st, six years 10st. 6lb., and aged 11st. Gentleman riders.

    Mr. Brownlow's Lucks-all, blue and white cap.
    Mr. Hindle's Blucher, black and blue.
    Mr. J. Monday's Jereboam, scarlet.
    Mr. Mascall's Unknown, blue and white.
    Mr. Chew's Doctor; tartan and black cap.
    Mr. Moreton's Signorina, black and white cap.

A Pony Race, of 3 sovs. each, h f, with a Purse added from the fund. For ponies not exceeding 14½ hands. 13½ hands to carry 9st. and 7lb. extra for each inch.

    Mr. Munday's Fairy Queen, scarlet.
    Mr. Brownlow's Paddy, blue and white cap.
    Mr. Radcliffe's Blank, green and scarlet.
    Mr. Howard's Creeping Jinny, purple and white.
    Mr. Moreten's Put, black and white cap.

A Consolation Race of 2 sovs. and Purse.

J. HEATON, clerk of the course.

The races, which yearly grew in popularity, were removed to what is to-day known as the "Racecourse," being then an expansive field, but now more or less divided. The local press began to have full reports of its proceedings, and Horwich races occupied a fore place in the betting list. In 1840 we have the following reference in the *Bolton Chronicle*:—This spirited "little affair" came off on Thursday, July 30. The beautiful sunshine of the day before raised up the spirits of the sporting gentlemen, and grateful expressions were unduly indulged in, that a fine day would charm the "Horwich Races" with the warmth of summer rays just cooled with gentle breezes. The sad and doleful aspect of Thursday morning, however, damped their zeal a little, but towards 10 o'clock the clouds were observed drifting before an easterly wind, and here and there a sudden burst of light proclaimed the approach of "Old Dan Phœbus and his fiery car." As 12 o'clock approached the roads—old and new to Chorley—became animated by pedestrians and vehicles, and many a sage and sober person expressed their delight at the aspect of the upper region, and the gratifying appearance of a "bit of blue." The turnpikes threw open their arms with wonder and the milestones grinned again at the sight of so many carts, shandries, carriages; the occupants of the shandries attested by their agitated and convulsive motion their strong repugnance to the supposition that their drags could be considered no great stakes. Merry throngs were soon seen approaching the field of action from all parts, over hedge and ditch they came as well as by road and highway. The sound of the clamorous drum was now heard, contesting with the loud-lunged trumpet the dominance of noise. At a distance was seen the

Union Jack floating on the grand stand, which by halfpast one was well filling with visitors. The course was not all that could be desired; to improve it funds will not be wanting to support a national pastime, the gentlemen of Horwich and district who have so spiritedly supported in the past will not be wanting in the future. The site of the course was excellently chosen, being situate and surrounded with the sweet scenes at the foot of Rivington Pike. Under the grand stand a refreshment booth was under the charge of Mr. Mascall, Lever Arms Hotel, Bolton. The inns at Horwich were not dissatisfied with the order of the day, if we may judge by the number of their guests. Like loyal subjects many supp'd at the "Crown." Though "bull-baiting" is out of the fashion, many "baited" at the "Bull." It behoved the "Bee-hive" to be on its best behaviour, and "Horwich Moor-gate" was "agate" of emptying its larders and its cellars with expedition. At two the grand stand was well filled, and the course crowded with throngs of various descriptions. Mr. Ralph Clare was judge. In the stewards' stand we observed the following:—J. T. Hindley, F. Gerard, J. Ratcliffe, Esqrs., Captain Hay, &c. W. H. Hornby, Esq., and a party of guests from Blackburn occupied carriages on the course, and many distinguished sporting gentlemen from Bury, &c., were present.

Hurdle Sweepstakes—Mr. Parker's Duenna 1st
Horwich Stakes—Mr. W. H. Hornby's Champagne......1st
Hunter's Stake—Mr. Hollingshead's Little Peter 1st

In 1841 the stewards were Messrs. F. Gerard, W. H. Hornby, J. F. Hodson, H. B. Hollinshead. Aug. 4th. The above meeting, which has ceased to be called a "Little go," had on this occasion the aid of the railway to bring sportsmen, &c., thereto, 12 carriages being required, and the course presented a more lively appearance than ever before. "Huts" were in abundance, and "stalls" of every description were visible, every thing being offered for sale, from the inviting roast beef of old England, and the temptingly displayed ham, down to "toffy Harry," who had the startling announcement in front of his booth, "Storming of Canton every Wednesday and Friday evening at the Millstone." The magnificent view on and adjoining the course cannot be excelled, if equalled, on any other turf in the kingdom, the "Pike," "Winterhill," and the beautiful outline of hills give a most romantic effect which cannot be easily described. In addition to the committee and stewards were the officers of the 60th Rifles, R. Towneley Parker, Thos. Carr Standish, Duxbury Hall, and family, J. Ratcliffe, Esq., &c. The band of the 60th Rifles stood on the grand stand and played during the day, the races lasting two days."

The Tradesman's Gold Cup of 60 sovs. added to sweepstake of 15 sovs. each.
Mr. Peace's Lord Mayor .... 1st.
Hunters' Stake.
Mr. Parker's Sam Weller .... 1st.
Hurdle Sweepstake.—(Thursday).
Mr. Parker's Sam Weller .... 1st.
Horwich Stakes.
Mr. Lee's Little Mary .... 1st.
Ladies' Purse of 15 sovs. added to sweepstake of 3 sovs.
Mr. Mascall's Maid of Kent .... 1st.

In 1842, Aug. 3, the stewards were Messrs. W. Standish Standish, F. Gerard, W. H. Hornby, C. Edmondstone, and H. B. Hollinshead. In 1843 the above-named with Mr. J. H. Hindle added. In addition to the usual events were "The Willoughby Stakes of 5 sovs. each with 20 sovs. added from the fund," and a "Gold Cup, value 50 guineas, given by W. S. Standish, Esq., added to a sweepstake of 10 sovs." In 1844 evidence was given of the growing popularity of the races, the attendances being extraordinarily large. Mr. W. S. Standish, one of the stewards, and family appeared on the course in a carriage drawn by four horses, and attended by a large party. On Wednesday, the Willoughby stakes, the tradesman's gold cup, the hunters' stakes and sweepstakes were run off. On Thursday, the ladies' purse and hurdle sweepstakes. On Aug. 6, 1845, the surroundings of the races were of the most brilliant description, and the interest was keenly intensified as was shown in the fact that a week before the event 50 stalls had been taken for racers, whilst space for the undescribable *cœteras* which alone give a perfect reflex of such gatherings had grown anon. The stewards were Lord Newport, M.P., and Messrs. W. S. Standish, J. Nowel Farrington, F. Gerard, T. Towneley-Parker, and A. Graham, 1846. The races commenced on Thursday, August 6th, and continued on Friday and Saturday. Stewards: Messrs. W. S. Standish, J. Ridgway, and J. Meiklam. The weather being fine, the trains from Bolton and Manchester were crowded, and every horse that could be spared was yoked to some sort of conveyance, to convey the teeming multitude to the races, every vehicle from a carriage to a sand cart being brought into requisition. The respectable families in the district were well represented, a portion of the family of the Earl of Balcarres being present. The "Blackrod Band" in full uniform played a number of delightful airs.

The Champagne Stakes of 15 sovs. ft. with 30 sovs. for 3 year old colts, sst. 7lb., fillies 8st. 5lb. The Crown Course, a new ¼ mile. The second to save his stakes, and the winner to give one dozen of champagne to the club.

 Mr. Cranston's Comme-il-faut (Noble)............ 1st
 Mr. White's Infringe (Owner) 2nd

The Tradesmen's Gold Cup of 100 sovs. in specie, added to a handicap stake of 15 sovs. each, 10 sovs. ft., and 5 sovs. ft. if declared by 18th of July. From Blue Post, and twice round, 1½ miles. Second to save his stakes, winner to pay 10 sovs. towards expenses.

 Mr. Whitworth's Lady Sarah (Abdale) 1
 Mr. O'Brien's Jonathan Wild (Ryder) 2
 Mr. Standish's Little Hampton (Francis) 3
 Mr. Worthington's Sharston (Edwards).............. 4

The Scurry Stakes of 5 sovereigns each, with 20 sovereigns added. To be ridden by gentlemen qualified as for the Garswood Cup at Newton, officers of the Army or Navy on full pay, or members of the Harwich Racing Club.

 Mr. T. Towneley Parker's The Snob 1
 Mr. Rothwell's Drayton...........................2

The Hunter's Stake of 10 sovereigns each, with 20 sovereigns added by club. Same conditions as above, and to produce certificate of having hunted six times during the hunting season ending 1846.

 Sir John Gerrard's Perpetual Motion (Owner) ... 1 1
 Hon. J. Erskine' — (Erskine) 3 2
 Mr. T. T. Parker's (half-bred) 2 3

Willoughby Stakes of 5 sovereigns, with 20 sovereigns added from Fund.

 Mr. Osborne's Miss Cantling (Abdale)............ 2 1 1
 Mr. Walker's The Nobbler (Winteringham)... 1 2 2
 M. W. Thompson's Bran (Turner) 3 3 3
 Mr. Thompson's Stansty (Williams) .... 4 a a

On Friday, the morning opened gloomily, the cloud-capped towers wore their prophetic hoods, a great thunderstorm broke over the district, and the rain fell in torrents. About half-past one the weather improved, and the following events followed :—

The Bolton Purse of 10 sovereigns, with 20 sovereigns added, for two and three years old; the winner of Champagne Stakes to carry 4lbs. extra.

    Mr. White's Infringe (Williams) 1
    Mr. Cranston's Comme-il-faut (Abdale) 2
    Mr. Thompson's Stansty (Templeman).................. 3

A Cup, value 50 guineas, gift of W. S. Standish, Esq., added to a sweepstakes of 10 sovs., 5 sovs. ft., the winner of any stake of the value of £100 to carry 5 lb. extra.

    Mr. A. Johnstone's Fair Helen (Ryder)............... 1
    Mr. Clarke's Maid of Lyme (Templeman) 2
    Mr. Walmesley's Miss Castling (Abdale) 3
    Mr. Standish's Little Hampton (Francis) 4

Manchester Handicap of 100 sovs., added to a sweepstakes of 20 sovs. each, 15 sovs. ft.

    Mr. Parr's Dulcet (Butler) 1
    Merklam's Godfrey (Templeman) 2
    Sir John Gerrard's Quebec (Abdale)................... 3

The Ladies Purse of 5 sovs. each, with 20 sovs. added, to be ridden by gentlemen qualified as for the "Sourry and Hunter's Stakes," the winner to be sold for £40 if demanded in the usual way.

    Mr. Taylor's Charley (Erskine) 1
    Mr. Barton's Ibrahim Pacha (Young) 2

The Selling Stakes of 5 sovs. with 20 sovs. added, the winner to be sold for £120 if demanded in the usual way, the allowance in weight being in proportion to the value set on them.

    Mr. Walker's The Nobbler (Winteringham)... 1 0 1
    Mr. Brown's Ferona (Abdale) 3 1 2
    Mr. Thompson's Lavender (Francis) 0 0 2
    Sir J. Gerrard's Fair Rossmond (Templeman) .... 0 2 d
    Mr. Thompson's Hudibras (Williams) ...... 2 d 0

Saturday, August 8th, match for 25 sovs., 10 sovs. ft., riders to be gentleman as under the Sourry Stakes.

    Mr. Young's Victoria (Young) 1
    Mr. Dorning's The Potter (Hon. S. Erskine) 2

Whip Stakes of 3 sovs., with splendid gold mounted riding whip.

    Mr. Rothwell's Drayton (Erskine) 0 1 1
    Mr. Smith's Olly Gammon (Smith).............. 1 2 2

The Innkeepers' Purse of 20 sovs., with handicap stakes of 3 sovs., for the beaten horses of the week.

    Mr. Walker's Ibrahim Pacha (Smith) 1 1
    Mr. Young's Victoria (Hon. E. Erskine) 2 2

The last Horwich races were run on Thursday, August 5th, 1847, but owing, it was said, to the "elections" having only just been finished the attendance was not so large as usual. The usual Horwich race weather—rain with thunder—prevailed, and the damping influence of the atmosphere gave a damping effect to the result.

The Champagne Stakes took the lead as usual with the following result:—

Mr. Meiklam's Melenden (Templeman) 1
Sir J. Gerard's Hockley (Slippeon) 2

The Tradesmen's Cup.

Mr. Stephenson's Shereaton 1
Mr. Wood's Columbus 2
Mr. Standish's Little Hampton 3
Mr. Driver's Bran 4
Mr. Par's Fruin 5

Scurry Stakes.

Mr. Parker's Vesture 1
Mr. Young's Tribute 2
Mr. Clifford's Vanilla 3

Hunters' Stakes.

Sir J. Gerard's Perpetual Motion, walk over.

Willoughby Stakes.

Mr. Greenwood's Chesterfield 1
Mr. Thompson's Prince Carodoc 2

Bolton Purse.

Mr. Ridgway's Otterburn 1
Mr. Scott's Mrs. Caudle 2

CHAPTER XXXV.

In 1834, the local press began to call attention to the beautiful and extensive landscape view as seen from Rivington Pike, and soon the "Pike" became a place of resort for pleasure seekers, and others whose object was more questionable. The *Bolton Chronicle* in this year reported that "an expanse of 60 miles could be seen from its summit," and on June 5th, 1844, it again refers to its claims as under :—" Parish churches that may be seen with the naked eye from Rivington Pike : Standish, Wigan, Holland (up), Ormskirk, Highton, Weeton, Childaw, Chester Cathedral, Prescot, Winnock, Warrington, Leigh, Broden, Newton, Deane, Stockport, Manchester, Prestwich, Blackrod, Rivington, Chorley, Leyland, Croston, Eccleston, Mall, &c. The following gentlemen's seats or halls may be seen : Haigh, Parbet, Wrightington, Wharton, North Hall, Adlington, Coppull, Rickshall, Hill-hall, Duxbury, Adderton, Old and New Heaton, Lostock, Ince, Gidlan-hall, Highfield (moated), Moss-hall, Park-hall, Chorley, Astley, Hexton, Cross-ball, Shawhill-hall, Latham-hall, Knowsley, Charnock, Bedford, Lightholks, Garswood, Penington, Anderton, Dunham—remarkable for its fine old timber, Garret, Cleworth, Cuerden, Chisnal (moated), Bradley, Tunley, Burch, Byron, Rivington (old and new), Rufforth, Scarisbrick, Lever, Farnworth, Chamber-hall, Ainsworth, Houghton, Weeton, Childaw, Winstanley, Monsborough, Hackley, Bradshaw, Crow-trees, Smithells, Sharples, Breightmet, Langtry. In addition, the following different counties : Lancashire, Cheshire, Derbyshire, Yorkshire, Shropshire, with a great part of North Wales, Westmoreland, and Cumberland. In all, 26 parish churches, 68 halls, 7 counties, and part of North Wales." It will not be necessary to remind our readers that the aspect of surrounding scenery has undergone a great change since the above was written. The progress of civilisation has made great changes, but even yet upon and around the Pike is open to view such an expansive landscape, with its varied characteristics, that few places can equal. "Italy," said a writer in the *Bolton Guardian*, whose extensive knowledge of foreign climes gives him authority, " may possess the more expansive, but none more beautiful." Then the "South Lancashire Lakes," the largest artificial lakes in this country, and, perhaps, in the world, nestled not at its base. Rivington Pike became a place of public resort, and "Pike Fair" was at once the hope and dread of the neighbourhood. This orgie, for thus alone can it be termed, was held on Whit-Saturday and the following Sunday, and the following case from the Bolton Sessional Court may lead our readers to a conception of the "fair" as then held, and the peculiar views of social duty as held only as it were yesterday. In 1835, at the Bolton Petty Sessions, two men, named John Entwistle and William Brindle, of Bolton, were charged "with neglect of Divine service." It was given in evidence that Rivington Pike fair on the Sunday was a scene of rioting and drunkenness, that parties going in carts and other outlandish vehicles became not only a danger to themselves but to the more sober pedestrian, that evils arising from the "orgies" at Pike fair had become a public nuisance, and Hopwood—the constable at Horwich—had brought the case before the magistrates as a "test case." The constable had ordered the two defendants to turn back, but they had refused, and the case was duly tried. Mr. Ridgway, who presided on the bench, declared "that he would put a stop to the scenes of rioting and drunkenness which prevailed on the Sabbath at Rivington Pike." The hills were covered with people that came only for disturbance, carts were upset, and life and limb endangered. The defendants were fined 1s., and 5s. 6d. costs, and summonses issued against them for "exercising their worldly calling on a Sunday." Notwithstanding this act on the part of the magistrates, the Pike Fair carnival grew apace, and only within the last few years, when railway companies have proved successful competitors has it declined. To picture the scenes that crowded the base of the hill, to describe the heterogeneous mass of humanity that gathered underneath its shadow on such occasions, would be impossible. There, in reflex, was humanity in its worst form, there, revolving from a dangerous point, was the concentrated terror of a mighty district, a veritable Babel, harmonising only in their dangerous proclivities, and their scare-crow, crime stained facial index. Here and there the loud voice of the travelling preacher could be heard commingling with the shrill tones of the ballad singer, the professional mendicant, or the unfortunate cripple hurling anathemas at the loud-lunged hucksters, who drowned their whining appeals. The publican and sinner were indeed there. The plateau at the base of the "Pike," with the long curving road, was covered with tents, booths, and structures of an indescribable form. From a score or more of these, intoxicants were virtually hurled at the visitor. Then, a "licence to sell" could be borrowed, and "Pike Fair" brought out many nondescript followers of Boniface. The "Pike," as seen from Horwich, was like an ant-hill, covered with its moving mass, and the village was flooded by visitors whose "room was indeed better than their company." The fame of this beacon-covered hill, however, is still to the fore, but now its visitors are more of the class who come to drink in the health giving breeze which gently fans its summit, and from its ancient watch tower scan the "Ribble" in its wandering course, to view dark, frowning Snowdon on the outstretched horizon, or at day's departing hour to see its mighty monarch retire to rest in the golden glory of the Irish Sea. In the district the "Pike" is looked upon much as a weather indicator

If Riving(ton) Pike do wear a hood,
Be sure the day will ne'er be good.

In the morning, when a fine day is desirable, the older villagers always turn for their prognostication to the over-hanging hills. If they have their "neet-cap (covered with fog) on," there is a questionable aspect; but when this is uplifted, and the hills are plainly visible, then the weather prophet is "more than a prophet," and speaks in a matter of fact-style, for

When Rivington puts on her hood,
She fears a rainy day;
But when she doffs it you will find
The rain is o'er and still the wind,
And Phœbus shines away.

Pace-egging—or Peace-egging—was a pastime much in vogue, and few places took a more lively interest in this ancient custom than Horwich. At this period the higher classes so far encouraged the practice that on the Monday morning preceding Good Friday the lodge gates were thrown open, and the children of the district marched boldly up to the "Hall," where the "Lady" or some important proxy was stationed with the lesser coins, and as the children came and demanded their "pace-egg" and sang,

We'll come no more here
Till this time next year,
Fol-the-da,

each was presented with a copper coin. The shop-keepers also made provision, and he who violated the custom was ostracised. Even females took a lively interest in these proceedings, and custom allowed what modesty might condemn. But to the young men were relegated the more important functions. For weeks, yea months, "Tipton Slasher," or some other semi-dramatic piece was studied and rehearsed, and as much care bestowed upon the "get-up" as more important events could scarcely command. Outside districts were visited in gangs, and sometimes the rivalry betwixt the home "pace-eggers" and the "invaders" from the neighbouring villages could only be appeased in a fight, which generally lasted for successive seasons, or till superiority was acknowledged. "Ball" was an attendant amongst the rougher gangs. This name was given to the "figure of a horse's head" made from wood, having powerful jaws, which was manipulated under cover of a sack or sheet. This important adjunct was termed the "Player," and his identity was protected with scrupulous care. He held a kind of licence for marauding, which might have proved dangerous to his peace had his identity been established.

The friendly societies at this period had remarkable displays. The Female Society, now defunct, had imposing processions, the bells ringing, a sermon preached at the Parish Church, the officiating minister being rewarded with an invitation to dine and a fee of £1. The local gentlemen headed the procession, and village danies carried their staffs as emblems of official dignity with a hauteur unsurpassed by the sterner sex. The other societies followed suit on the second Saturday in August, and in rich paraphernalia and costly costumes paraded the streets. The "Gardeners"—now withered and dead—were noted for their displays. A cart or lurry was enshrouded in evergreens, in the centre of which stood "Eden's forbidden tree," laden with luscious fruit, Adam and Eve being typified by two golden-haired children, the temptress holding the pernicious fruit in tempting proximity to her "sinless" lord. After parading the public streets, the church was visited, and to the beautiful strains of the fine "Old Portuguese" from two trumpeters, "Adam and Eve" were duly escorted into the sacred edifice.

In 1840 the police system was introduced into the village, P.S. Charles Wilson, P.C. Dawson, and P.C. Craig being the first representatives. The abolition of the antiquated office of constable was looked upon with disfavour, not only in Horwich, but more or less throughout the country. The local press abounded with complaints on the doings of the police; everywhere they were looked upon as invaders, as cripplers of liberty, and as deniers of those rights which all Englishmen have ever held dear and inviolable. Terms of scorn were used towards them, and though the system has survived and its adaptability proved, yet the epithets that heralded its advent have continued, and "Bobbies" and "Peelers" are yet terms which show that the distinguished repealer of the Corn Laws was at one time in no great esteem with the populace. Their advent into Horwich was rendered all the more conspicuous in consequence of a "remarkable case"—such the local press termed it—occurring in which they figured in a manner which perhaps did not tend to create a sympathy for this radical change. A man named Shaw was charged at the petty sessional court, Bolton, with assaulting P.C. Craig while in the execution of his duty. Shaw denied the assault, and charged the police

with being drunk and in company of two women at the
Moorgate Inn, where the charge and counter-charge
originated, Joseph Heath, of Horwich, being also impli-
cated in the charge. Thomas Walmsley, son of the
landlord, said the latter (P.C. Craig) had had some
drink but he knew what he was doing. Shaw was
ordered to keep the peace and pay costs. In the same
year (1840), Sunday, August 9th, an event occurred
which threw the higher end of the village into a state
of gloom. On the day named six females, three young
men, and three children left Horwich in a cart with the
intention of proceeding to Lever Bridge, where Ridgway Bridson, a nephew of the Horwich Ridgways, had
a bleachworks, and where many old Horwichers were
employed. They had proceeded on their journey as far
as Darcy Lever, and had stopped at the Farmer's Arms
for baiting. Adjoining this hostelry is a steep incline,
now more protected, and, awaiting the feeding of the
horse, five of the females got out. Incautiously one of
the young men had taken the bridle from off the horse.
The females had returned to their position in the cart
with the exception of the sixth, and in her efforts to get
in she caused the others to set up a loud peal of
laughter, the horse took a momentary gaze and dashed
off. No check to his movements could be given, and
down the incline it dashed, the cart being upset and
two of the occupants killed on the spot, Jane, wife of
Moses Makinson, organist at Horwich Church, and
Mary Ann, wife of John Sharples, crofter; Ellen
Roper, Mrs. Turner, and Mrs. Caldwell being seriously
injured.

The government of the village even up to this period
was conducted on cheap lines, the efficiency of which is
a matter of history. In 1837 "it was moved by Charles
Howarth, and seconded by William Bennett (at an
ordinary town's meeting), that Henry Hibbert be appointed Collector of the Church rate, highway rate,
poor rate, be Guardian for the Poor, look after settlements, and be surveyor of highways at a salary of £35
per annum, he to be paid extra for journeys other than
to Bolton." Our readers have their own materials for
contrast.

On Wednesday, Oct. 9th, 1850, the "Horwich Agricultural Society held its first show and fair, the pre-

sident being Mr. William Longworth, The Knowles, Horwich. Never before had Horwich witnessed such brilliant surroundings. The committee, accompanied by the village band, paraded the streets, the church bells merrily ringing. The entries were 125, as follows :— For drovers premiums 5, bulls 9, calving cows 5, heifers 12, barren cows 7, fat cow 1, entire horses 5, brood mares 15, colts 23, draught horses 8, roadsters 4, boars 4, breeding sows 6, fat pigs 5, store pigs 7, litter of pigs 1, cottagers' fat pigs 4, cottagers' store pigs 4. The sterling worth of the animals evoked the highest admiration, the highway from the "Bull" to the "Bridge Inn" being lined with stalls, &c., and a select company numbering over 100 gentlemen of the surrounding districts met the President at dinner, which was served at the National School, Mr. John Scott, of the "Bull," being the caterer. For a number of years the "show" grew in popularity, and a Floral and Horticultural Society was established ; but Horwich seems fated to throw out brilliant prospects only to see them fade and die ere they reach maturity, and soon this flourishing institution lost its vigour, and the "Cattle Fair" of October is but a puny imitation of its more brilliant ancestor.

1850 is also to be remembered by one of those terrific storms which ever leave a lasting impression on a district. About four o'clock in the afternoon of July 16 the storm burst forth, and for five hours the thunder and lightning played in terrific consonance. Attracted by the overhanging hills, the clouds, draped in blackness, hung like a mighty pall over the village, the "very windows of heaven were opened," and down the rugged slopes, through ravines and dell the clamour of waters could be heard, small streams became like rivers, and down the hills the waters swept like billows of the angry ocean. The usual water-courses were unable to bear the strain, and every obstacle bowed before the fluid monarch ; the valley became as a lake, and waters pressed on with devastating force, trees were uprooted, boulders carried along as though they were pebbles, and great damage was the result. At the "Tigers" in Shaw Brook, the furniture was washed out of the house, and such an uplifting of the bed of the stream that quartz was washed up, and these "gold besprinkled stones" gave rise to singular theories. Wilderswood Mill and Foxhole Mills, then worked by Messrs. Wm. Bennett, jun., and Wm. Bennett, sen., were flooded and great damage was sustained. At the latter mill the lodge embankment gave way ; at Horwich Bleachworks the water flooded the lower buildings, and the garden at "The Knowles" was much damaged. The highway in many places was washed up, and near to Pearl Brook (burned down in 1882) the water was three feet deep in the public thoroughfare. During the storm a house was struck by lightning at the "Higher Barn," but at "Sharrock's Farm" a more terrible visit was paid, by which two children lost their lives. Alice Makinson, daughter of Evan Makinson, of Preston, who resided with her aunt in the capacity of servant; the other being Ellen Longworth, aged eight years, daughter of Mrs. Shaw, wife of John Shaw, who farmed the place.

On April 30th, 1851, the sad railway accident in Sutton Tunnel occurred, in which five lost their lives. Amongst them was Mrs. Wettenhall, widow of Major Wettenhall, and sister to Mrs. Ridgway, of Ridgmont, Mrs. Ridgway herself being amongst the injured. Mrs. Wettenhall resided with her sister at Ridgmont. In the compartment of the first class carriage with the two sisters was Mr. Clarke, a brother-in-law. The train, being overladen, was brought to a stand in the tunnel. After standing in this dangerous position for some time, another train came up and dashed into the standing one. Ward, the coachman, and John Entwistle, footman, were in the private carriage of Mrs. Ridgway (a britizka), which was placed on a truck. The last carriage of the train ran into was that occupied by Mrs. Ridgway and party, they being the only occupants ; the britizka was thrown on the opposite metals, Ward, the coachman, receiving severe injuries, and Entwistle escaping injury. Mrs. Ridgway died November 14th, 1860, at Hatton Hall, Northamptonshire.

The introduction of the "Bessemer" system into the iron industry caused such a revolution, not only in the quality but in the mode and manner of making steel, that other industries were thereby created, and about twenty years ago Horwich became the spot where tuyeres and other requisites were manufactured. There are two places devoted to this purpose, viz., Mr. A. Peak's, and Mr. A. Mason's Pearl Brook Works, a considerable number of hands being employed. We are indebted to Mr. Herbert Mason, of the Pearl Brook Tuyere Works, for much of the information in the following notes. "Tuyere," from the French, means "blast-pipe." Tuyeres are used in the manufacture of Bessemer steel. They are made from a peculiar composition of fire clay, and vary in length from 12 to 24 inches, varying in diameter from 3 to 7 inches, and are round. The clay is prepared in what is termed the pug mill, and from thence it is conveyed to the tuyere maker, and having been knocked into shape, is placed in a mould, and by hydraulic or mechanical pressure perforated with a number of small holes running the whole length of the tuyere. After being dried in what is termed the stove, they are conveyed to a huge kiln, and there undergo the important process of burning. Their mode of use in the conversion of steel is briefly as follows: A number of tuyeres (from 12 to 16) are placed in a converter, a large egg-shaped vessel, generally holding a charge of about eight tons of metal; the space between these tuyeres is rammed solid with gameter, and this forms the bottom of the converter. A blast-pipe is attached to the lower end of the tuyeres, and supplied with air from large engines, the blast of air which passes through the holes of the tuyeres being about 20lbs. pressure. When the tuyeres are duly fixed in their places, the molten iron is poured into the converter and consequently on to the tuyeres (they having to stand both the heat and pressure); the blast is then turned on and continued for about twenty minutes, when the converter is tilted and the "spiegel" is added to the molten mass, which after a further short blowing is pronounced "Bessemer steel." As we have said, tuyeres have been in use over twenty years, and in this period many rivals in the trade have arisen, yet Horwich stands A 1, not only in the quantity but the quality, and, judging from the efforts put forth, the trade will yet continue to be intimately connected with Horwich.

CHAPTER XXXVI.

In 1830 an additional portion was added to the churchyard, which then had become imperatively needed, the township paying £13 10s. as its share of the purchase money. In 1876 further additions were made, and a pleasing transformation effected, a number of trees being planted and the appearance of the churchyard otherwise improved. At the vestry meeting held in March, 1877, Mr. T. D. Eaton, vestry clerk, read the churchyard improvement accounts, which showed that the receipts had been £378 14s. 8d., the expenditure £507 13s. 1d. (of which sum £236 7s. 4d. had been expended in the purchase of the land), leaving an overdrawn balance at the bank of £128 18s. 5d. In this year (May 17th, 1877) a fatal and strange accident occurred in this portion of the churchyard. Two men were engaged in making a vault for the reception of the remains of a young man named Thomas Pearson, their names being Thomas Bath, stonemason, of Horwich, and William Tribble, labourer, of Halliwell. The ground being of a sandy description, the grave had been dug, and Bath was engaged bricking, when the sides of the grave collapsed, and the two men were held fast, and over two hours elapsed ere they were rescued. Hundreds of spectators crowded the churchyard, and every effort was put forth for their rescue, but before this was attained it was evident that Bath had succumbed, he being almost entirely covered, while his companion had his head and shoulders clear. Such a singular fatality evoked a feeling of sympathy with the widow and four young children, and a sum of £80 was subscribed for their needs.

About 1850 and the succeeding year, "hush shops" and illicit distilleries had so far come under public notice that in 1857 a writer in the *Bolton Chronicle* referred to them as "great nuisances." We have seen that Horwich had in the past an unenviable notoriety in this respect, and few places possess more adaptability to the illicit trade. Many of our readers will remember with what tenacity they held their unlawful sway, and how skilfully every effort put forth by the police was defeated; but the raid was at last successful, and Horwich enjoyed an immunity therefrom.

As we have before intimated, the present vicar (the Rev. Henry Septimus Pigot, M.A.) succeeded to the vicarage in 1853. Mr. Pigot is the seventh son of the late Rev. Thomas Pigot, M.A. of Blymhill, Staffordshire, who was born at Peplow Hall, Shropshire, in the parish of Hodnett, that estate having been in the Pigot family for many generations, but has since passed into other hands, though the Pigot armorial bearings still remain on the lodge entrance to the domain. The rev. gentleman had been located at Winwick, and on Tuesday, the 15th of March, 1853, Mr. Pigot visited the scene of his former labours, and whilst in the house of a friend a committee of the parishioners waited upon him, and asked his acceptance of a beautifully decorated Communion Service as a small token of their esteem. Accompanying the more substantial present was a richly designed address, in which was the following prophetically suggestive sentence:—"Most cordially do we wish that in the sphere of labour on which you have just entered at Horwich, you may enjoy the satisfaction of living in the hearts of your parishioners, as you have lived, and ever will live, in the hearts of all at Winwick." On the 21st May, 1858, being Pike Fair Saturday, the first procession of Sunday scholars took place, there being over 600. The procession was headed by the Rev. H. S. Pigot, with his brothers Charles and George, many of the influential inhabitants joining in it. At Ridgmont (Mrs. Ridgway), Moor Platt (Mr. Charles Howarth), Colemans (Mr. Christopher Howarth), The Knowles (Mr. William Longworth), every preparation was made for their reception, the Horwich Brass Band being in attendance. Yearly now the procession on Whit-Saturday is looked forward to with lively interest, and each school has its gathering on the same day. In the year succeeding Mr. Pigot's advent, the noise and pomp of war was heard throughout the length and breadth of the land, and Wednesday, April 26, 1854, was set apart by Royal Decree for a national fast, and on this occasion an impressive sermon was preached by Mr. Pigot from Rev. chap. 12, ver. 11. In the same year Horwich had the honour on Sunday, July 16, of having the learned Very Rev. James Cotton, LL.D., Dean of Bangor, as the preacher of the school anniversary sermon, £73 18s. 0d. being collected. In January, 1878, the Rev. H. S. Pigot, M.A., completed his quarter of a century as vicar of the parish, and such an occasion was not allowed to pass without some tribute from his parishioners to himself and lady. The idea was first mooted by the two superintendents of the Sunday school—Mr. Moses Kay and Mr. Joseph Stubbs. The suggestion was received with an enthusiasm which betokened success, and the parishioners were apprised of the intention, and from the rich and poor came tokens of the high regard in which the vicar was held. The wardens of the church, Mr. Jno. Longworth and Mr. Joseph Howarth, warmly supported this effort originated in the Sunday school, and over £100 was soon at the disposal of the committee, over £25 of which the Sunday school had subscribed, the Rev. W. S. F. Maynard, B.A., curate, and Mr. Samuel Bentley, parish clerk, taking an active part. A service of solid silver was purchased, on which was engraved the following inscription:—" Presented to the Rev. H. S. Pigot, M.A., vicar of Horwich, and Mrs. Pigott, together with a silver tea and coffee service, by the Sunday schools and parishioners as a token of regard, and as a slight acknowledgement of his faithful ministry among them for upwards of a quarter of a century. Horwich, Feb. 16, 1878." In presence of a crowded school the presentation was duly made, the Rev. W. S. F. Maynard, curate, being entrusted with the duty. Both Mr. and Mrs. Pigot were entirely in the dark in regard to the object of the meeting, and the rev. gentleman spoke under strong emotion in acknowledging their kindness to him and "his dear wife." We have seen that under Mr. Ridgway's will the living of Horwich was benefited to the extent of £100 per annum, and a sum of £300 for the purpose of a vicarage provided £400 was raised within a limited period. Of this sum Mr.

and Mrs. Pigot conjointly subscribed £125, Mrs. Pigot collecting over an additional £100, the rest of the £400 being subscribed by the parishioners. Even with the fund at their disposal, the vicarage would not have had the charming and complete arrangement as seen to-day had not Mrs. Pigott out of her own private purse borne the expense of building the surrounding walls, stables, and coach-house, with other improvements. On May 21st, 1880, Mrs. Pigot somewhat suddenly died, and in a former chapter we have given the inscription on the neat little tablet erected by the teachers of the Sunday school.

In 1854 the "Patriotic Fund" was established for the relief of soldiers and sailors' wives and children, £152 being subscribed in Horwich, at Wallsuches Bleachworks £54 5s. 0d., and at the Horwich Bleachworks £16 0s. 6d.

On Monday, March 12, 1855, occurred one of those destructive fires which are ever the bane and terror of a neighbourhood, but in this instance fortunately unattended with that bitterness which springs from a loss of work. At about 15 minutes to six, as the workpeople were wending to Wallsuches, signs of fire broke out in what is technically termed the "Stove," a place where cloth undergoes the process of drying. At the time it was said that about 1,000 pieces were suspended in a dry condition. Under such circumstances the flames spread rapidly, notwithstanding the efforts put forth for their subjugation. In the lower room were five callenders, which were also much damaged. The estimated loss was £3,000, which was fully covered in the Norwich Fire Office.

On Tuesday, September 11th, 1855, intelligence arrived that the Russian stronghold, Sebastopol, had yielded to the Allied Troops, and nothing could exceed the enthusiasm manifested in what at best was only a partial success. From Wallsuches and Horwich Bleachworks flags and banners floated in profusion, and a handsome flag was hoisted from the church steeple, other establishments and private houses being gaily decorated. A number of the inhabitants had in anticipation subscribed for and purchased a monster flag for the tower of the church, but the glorious intelligence coming so suddenly a staff of sufficient length could not be procured. Many of the cottagers illuminated their houses, and bands of music paraded the streets, the church bells ringing and "shooting" till 10 p.m. The "big cannon" at Wallsuches boomed out at intervals, and from innumerable lesser "firearms" the sound of triumph was heard. At Wilderswood a monstre bonfire cast its lurid shade around, loyalty and patriotism ruling predominant. In this year, at the dinner of the Horwich Agricultural Society, Mr. Robert Andrews, J.P., of Rivington Hall, offered to give £10 towards a "baby show," to be held in 1856, but owing to certain representations made to him he consented to give the sum to other purposes in connection with the society. As a manufacturing community any interference with the staple industry of the county, from whatever cause arising, has its effect in Horwich. The "cotton panic," consequent on the American war of 1860, was keenly felt in the village, and the privations endured were those common to Lancashire at that period. The more extensive works in the village were almost entirely idle, and private aid soon became ineffective to meet the great demands made upon it. Relief works were started, and various public improvements were carried out through the aid of Government loans. The more able of the village stepped forward, and in the most generous and munificent manner aided their needy brethren. Many who never before had taken "charity's dole" now partook thereof with gratitude, and the improvements in the highway were crowded by men to whom a barrow and a spade were much of a novelty. The steep declivity leading from Moor Gate to Wallsuches was much lessened, and what had been considered well-to-do members of the village community were engaged in breaking stones at a shilling per load. With the close of the war Horwich resumed its wonted position, but those trying times are gloomy reminiscences never to be obliterated.

In 1872 Horwich adopted the Local Board of Health Act, and by arrangement of public meeting the board was to consist of twelve members, the names of the first representation of the new system being as follows: —W. Greenhalgh (elected chairman), Cooke, Peak,

Hope, Hutchinson, W. Kay, Mason, Calderbank,
Smith, Stead, Howarth, and Nathaniel Longworth.
In 1873 Mr. J. Longworth took the place of his brother,
and was elected chairman of the board in 1882, a position which he still holds. Mr. Stead vacated in 1876,
and Mr. J. Fell, who took up the position, declined
to stand in 1878. The same year Mr. Sydney Kay
entered the board vice Hope, defeated, the board at
present being constituted as under :—J. Longworth
(chairman), Lieutenant-Colonel Ainsworth, James
Beddows, L. Cooke, John Calderbank, John Crankshaw, W. Greenhalgh, Moses Kay, T. Mason, A. Peak,
W. Smith, and James Stones. How far Horwich has
been benefited by the change may, perhaps, be an open
question. But with the promulgation of the Act,
which called it into being, either self-government by
Local Authority or by an Urban Sanitary Committee
was imperative, and Horwich wisely chose the former.
On the score of economy the board certainly stands
blameless. With its advent the two more pressing
sanitary considerations—sewerage and water—came to
the fore, and up to the present the latter boon has not
been fully obtained, though, perchance, ere our readers
glance over these pages the full terms and conditions
for the acquirement of this needful requisite will have
been duly signed, the following being the text of the
agreement :—"That Horwich Local Board shall pay to
the Blackrod Local Board under this agreement for the
supply of water the sum of 7½d. per 1,000 gallons up
to 17,000 gallons a day, 27,000 gallons 6½d., 50,000
gallons 6d., the agreement being for sixty years." To
speak of Horwich buying back its own water may
appear short-sighted policy ; and that which by the
affinity of contiguity could be said to be a natural
legacy, be the property of another, may assume a certain negligence, but its freedom from debt, the comparative lowness of its local rates, are immunities not
enjoyed by its neighbours, and these may be considerations which posterity will more calmly and more
judicially consider.

CHAPTER XXXVII.

We have in these pages repeatedly referred to the friendly societies in connection with the village, and incidentally to the growth and decay of some, which at one period occupied a fore position in these beneficial institutions. But notwithstanding that of the more ancient "some are not," others differing only in their mode of government, and perhaps in what may be termed the externals, have taken their place, and at two of the Sunday schools "sick societies" are connected therewith. That in connection with the "Church" was started in 1855, and in order to gain stability it was agreed that nothing in the way of sick allowance should be paid for a period of two years. In 1881 it consisted of 427 members, with an accumulated capital of £2,730. The "New Chapel" has also an organisation of a similar kind, and at the same period numbered 167 members, and its capital returned at £1,206. The Independent Order of Oddfellows (Ridgmont Lodge), have their head-quarters at the Crown Inn, and at the same period had 333 members, with a capital of £2,071. The United Order of Oddfellows assemble at the Black Bull, and numbered 260 members, with a capital of £1,007. In addition another branch of the Oddfellows meet at the Bay Horse, and the Foresters have their club at the Bridge Inn. The Orangemen have their rendezvous at the Brown Cow, and here also the Free Gardeners held their meetings prior to their dissolution in 1874, when, owing to the paucity of their numbers, they elected to have a division of the spoil, which amounted to £3 per member. It will thus be seen that Horwich is well represented by its friendly societies, and some of them have all the essentials of stability.

In 1860 the first distribution of the "Ridgway Charity" was made. Under the provision of the will of Mr. Ridgway, a sum of £100 was left to be distributed annually in clothing to the "poor of the parish," the distribution to be under the control of the minister and wardens of Horwich Church for the time being. We give a list of articles bestowed at one of these distributions. 30 pairs of blankets, 9 green quilts, 15 alhambra quilts, 14 pairs of cotton sheets, 754 yards of drabbet, 598 yards of white flannel, 16 yards of blue flannel, 4 yards of winsey, 2 dozen of men's stockings, 2 dozen women's and 2 dozen boys'. The recipients vary in number, in 1872 there being 159. Some time before distribution notice is given in the Parish Church of such intended dispensation, and applicants on a fixed day attend at the National School and state their needs, and if, after due consideration, their position is such as to render them fit objects of such charity, then a ticket is forwarded to them, and such an allowance of goods and kind as their circumstances require is meted out to them.

As before intimated, on Thursday evening, June 13th, 1872, a public meeting was called to consider the adoption of the Local Government Act, Mr. W. Greenhalgh presiding, Mr. Greenhalgh, of Bolton also attending to give any legal aid required. Mr. A. Peak, in the blandest manner, told the meeting that he thought Horwich could govern itself, an opinion which the meeting re-echoed in adopting the Act. At a meeting of the local board, held Oct. 29th, Mr. John Evans was elected clerk, at a salary of £25. At a further meeting, December 11th, 1872, Mr. Nevett, of Preston, was elected surveyor, at a salary of £50 per annum, and four per cent. commission. The common seal of the board was adopted, having for a device two men bearing staffs, with a stag in the centre, above being the Royal Crown, the motto being "Labour is wealth." In January, 1873, Dr. Robertson was appointed medical officer of health, at a salary of £20. On his leaving the district in April, 1875, Mr. George H. Whittaker, L.R.C.P., L.R.C.S., Ed., was appointed, and still continues to hold the office. In March, 1873, Mr. Thomas Curwen was appointed nuisance inspector and rate collector, at a salary of £40. In May, 1873, great preparations were made in the district for the approaching visit of the Prince of Wales to open the

Bolton Town Hall, and the surveyor was instructed to see that the portion of the Horwich roads, over which the Prince would have to pass, was put in a thorough state of repair. In December, 1873, Mr. John Longworth and Mr. W. Greenhalgh were appointed under statute which gives Horwich the right of appointing two governors of the Amalgamated Blackrod and Rivington Grammar School. The name of Mr. Adam Mason, a former governor, was also put to the vote, when Mr. Greenhalgh elected himself by the exercise of his privilege of giving the casting vote.

In 1877, Wednesday, February 14th, a meeting of the owners of land, tenements, and hereditaments was held in the Old School, in respect to the Lee Mill ground rent. Mr. John Longworth was elected to preside, on the motion of Mr. W. Greenhalgh.—The Chairman, in opening the proceedings, read extracts from the deed relative to the property, in respect to which such rent is paid, and explained that the same was left solely to the owners of land, tenements, and hereditaments in Horwich, with power to fill up any vacancies in the township. The deed bearing date 1st May, 1851, is entitled a conveyance of a plot of land containing 1,472 square yards, situate in Horwich, in the county of Lancaster, upon the trusts of an Indenture, dated the 13th May, 1802, for the benefit of the owners and proprietors of lands or hereditaments within the township of Horwich, Mr. and Mrs. Bullough (trustees as within appearing) to Mr. Joseph Ridway and others. Mr. A. Mason (joint trustee with Mr. Longworth) said the trustees had no wish but to arrange matters so as to be agreeable to all parties, and in such manner as would produce the greatest amount of good to the township. Mr. Mason produced the bank book, which showed a balance in favour of the trustees of £112 17s. 8d. The trustees had had several meetings to consider how best to apply the money, and he thought the best suggestion was that contained in the resolution he would move. Educationally, Horwich was pretty well provided for, and also with respect to charities. With respect to the repair of the roads, he thought that if applied to that purpose it would almost appear lost. He then submitted the following resolution:—"That this meeting of owners of lands, tenements, and hereditaments in Horwich, having been called by public notice, recommends the trustees of Lee Mill ground rent, after paying for all necessary expenses in collecting the same, to apply the balance, together with any present or future accumulation, towards the founding and supporting of a public subscription library and reading-room, and to combine also on the same premises another larger room in which may be provided lectures," concerts, and other methods of rational instruction and amusement." Mr. William Howarth, of Wallsuches, seconded the resolution. Mr. A. Peek moved "That the money be devoted to the repairing of the highways." He said it would be like throwing the money away to use it for such a purpose. He did not approve of billiards and such like games practised at these Mechanics' Institutions; he thought they did more harm than good. They had had four libraries in Horwich, and they had never lasted six months. Mr. W. Greenhalgh said if there was one thing more than another that Horwich was in want of it was some counter attraction to the public-house. He would gladly give £20 for such a purpose. He thought that if the Public Libraries Act could be adopted in the village, which would cost only a halfpenny rate, and a subscription library connected with it to keep up the books, it would prove of advantage to the township. The chairman submitted the following motion: "That if suitable existing premises unconnected with any religious denomination cannot be found that a site be obtained and a suitable building erected thereon to be called 'Horwich Public Hall,' the necessary remaining funds to be obtained either by voluntary subscriptions or by shares, as may hereafter be determined, and that if it is found that these objects or any of them can be secured, the management be placed in a committee consisting of the trustees for the time being and four or six other persons, being owners of property in Horwich, to be named at a subsequent meeting, and that the trustees be requested to make inquiries as to the practicability of securing these objects or any of them and report to an adjourned meeting." At the adjourned meeting March 14th,

1877, Mr. Mason in the chair, he explained that Mr. Martin, of Rivington, was wishful to do something to meet the public wants of Horwich, and was prepared to erect at his own cost a building on the land in Lee-lane —formerly intended for a temperance hall— in which provision would be made for lectures, &c., and every arrangement for innocent recreation, beverages other than intoxicants might be procured, or he would be willing to relinquish his own scheme and to subscribe to such building £200 on the following conditions :—(1) That it be opened free from debt, the general public being asked to subscribe ; (2) That it should not be used for denominational purposes, but be governed by a representative committee, to be revised every five or seven years. The question, after some discussion, was left over. In 1878 the present beautiful building which adorns Lee-lane was erected by Mr. Martin at his own cost, and the following necessarily brief description may not be out of place. The Hall covers an area of 32 superficial yards, and the offices, stables, and outbuildings cover a further space of 136 yards. The bowling green is 52 yards by 36. The view from the outside is delightful, the hills forming a kind of background to a lovely landscape. The general style of the building is of the Gothic design, Elizabethan type. The front is extremely attractive, being of pressed brick, relieved by terra cotta tracery ; the apex being of Yorkshire stone. The interior of the building is in keeping with its outward aspect, the handsome staircase of polished pitch-pine, together with the other appointments, being most harmonious. On the ground floor is the billiard room, reading rooms, chess and draughts room, and coffee room, over which is a large assembly room of 1,505 square feet, the most striking feature of the building, perhaps, being the turret, surmounted by a weather vane, from which project the points of the compass. On Wednesday evening, April 2nd, 1879, the Hall was duly opened by its generous donor, Mr. P. Martin, J.P., of Heath Charnock, Mr. J. Barlow, J.P., of Bolton, presiding over the meeting, supported by the Rev. H. S. Pigot, M.A., Vicar of Horwich, and a select company. Mr. Martin, in the course of his remarks, said that after many years' experience as a magistrate he had come to the conclusion that 90 per cent. of the cases brought before the bench arose from intemperance. He had erected that Public Hall, in which he hoped the people of Horwich would find ample means for spending a pleasant evening. He had striven to make everything conducive to their comfort and every provision for their enjoyment. There were a reading room well supplied with papers and serials, a room for chess, billiards, draughts, &c. Mr. Martin only survived the opening ceremony a few months, and in 1833 the Hall passed formally into the hands of the local board, Mr. Henry Taylor being appointed hall-keeper, together with the office of nuisance inspector and local rate collector. The new year of 1877 opened with the cheering manifestation that Lee Weaving Mills, which had long been stopped, would soon resume their wonted activity, they having passed into the hands of Messrs. Southworth, of Clitheroe. On January 2nd the winders commenced operations, and the first load of looms was decked by the villagers with flags and other emblems of joy. At a soiree held in the Co-operative Hall in honour of the occasion, it was well said "That they in Horwich had every facility for progress. They had the railway at hand, land cheap, water in abundance, rates low." The hills are rich in materials for building, and an excellent class of clay is located in the valley. Coal is cheaply procurable, and with such adjuncts we look forward hopefully to the future of Horwich, and lay aside our task of writing the history of a village in the hope that we may have proved of some assistance to our successor of days to come, who may perchance learn herefrom how a smiling village became a happy and prosperous town.

WALL, PRINTER, WIGAN.

INDEX

ABBOTT, William (advertisements) p.3
ADLINGTON p.114
ADVERTISEMENTS Follow p.256
AINSWORTH, Lieutenant-Colonel p.250
ALLATT, Mark p.97
AMALGAMATED BLACKROD & RIVINGTON GRAMMAR SCHOOLS p.253
ANDERTON, p.11, 13, 39, 43, 172
ANDERTON FAMILY pp 170-174
ANDERTON, THOMAS p.93
ANDREWS, Robert, J.P. p.249
ASHWORTH, John p.93

BACK-HOUSE FIELD p.140
BARKER'S BROOK p.157
BARKER'S FLATTING p.155, 156
BARLEY CROFT p.140
BARLOW, J p.255
BATESON, Rev. A p.95
BATH, Thomas p.245
BAY HORSE p.176, 251
BEDDOWS, James p.250
BEDDOW'S FOLD p.162
BEE-HIVE INN p.231
BENNETT, William p.241, 243
BENNETT, William, junior, p.243
BENTLEY, Samuel p.247
BESSEMER SYSTEM p.243, 244
BILSBORROW, Mr. p.200, 204
BIRELL, Benjamin p.224, 226
BISHOP PILKINGTON p.36
BISPHAM, Rev. Thomas p.86, 87
BLACK BULL INN p.71, 126, 127, 167, 184, 185, 197,
                 200, 204, 216, 221, 242, 251
BLACKROD p.25, 115, 117, 127, 128, 155, 156, 185
BLACKROD BAND p.233
BLACKROD LOCAL BOARD p.250
BLACKROD WATERWORKS p.229
BLEACHING p.31, 176, 177, 179
BLEACHWORKS (includes Horwich Bleachworks, Longworth's Croft and
     Wallsuches Bleachworks, Horwich Vale Bleachworks, Lever Bank)
     p.176, 178, 179, 192, 201, 203, 204, 243, 248, 249
BLESSED TRINITY CHURCH - see Horwich Chapel
BLUNDELL, Henry p.64-66, 126, 193
BLUNDELL, Robert p.126, 171, 172
BOBBIN SHOP p.98
BOLTON p.32, 33
BOLTON, James p.101
BOLTON'S ESTATE p.161, 162

BOTTOM-OF-MOOR   p.161
BOTTOM O'TH'MOOR   p.176
BRIDGE INN p.242, 251, advertisements p.4
BRIDSON, Ridgway   p.71, 73
BRIDSON, Thomas Ridgway   p.82
BROWN COW INN   p.73, 126, 202, 251
BULL INN   p.202, 231
BULLOUGH, Mr and Mrs   p.253
BYROM, Joseph   p.188

CALDERBANK, Mr   p.250, advertisements p.4
CALDWELL, John - advertisements p.7
CATTLE FAIR   p.242
CHARITIES   p.252
CHARTISM   p.196, 197
CHORLEY NEW ROAD   p.69
CLARKE, Mr   p.243
CHURCHWARDENS 1732-1883   pp164-166
COAL   p.28, 29, 31, 35, 256
COAL FIRES LANE   p.31
COAL PIT ROAD   p.192
COCKER, Moses   p.93
COLEMAN'S   p.161, 246
COLLIER, Rev. F.G.   p.88, 90, 91
CONSTABLES   1732-1883   pp164-166
COOKE, L.   P.250
COOKE, Mr   p.249
CO-OPERATIVE HALL   p.256
COTTON   p.30, 31, 33, 175
COTTON FAMINE   p.249
COUNTING HILL   p.35
COW-HEY-NOOK   p.192, 193
COW-HEY-ROAD   p.193
CRAIG, P.C.   p.240, 241
CRANKSHAW, John   p.250
CROSSLEY, Rev. John   p.87
CROWN   p.155
CROWN INN   p.73, 180, 185, 202, 251, advertisements p.3
CROWTHER, Joseph   p.98, 99 179
CURWEN, Thomas, nuisance inspector   p.252

DANE'S DIKE   p.35
DANE'S DITCH   p.37
DAWSON, P.C.   p.240
DEANE   p.32
DEANE CHURCH   p.43
DELF ROAD   p.192
DERBY FAMILY   p.222
DICKINSON, Mr.   advertisements p.5
DIG LEECH   p.177, 178

DRUIDS p.73
DUTTON, Thomas, A, advertisements p.8

EATOCK, John p.205, 206
EATON, T.D. p.245
ECKERSLEY, Nathaniel p.99, 100
EDGAR HILL p.37
EDGARD DEN p.37
EGBERT DEN p.35
EGERTON, Lord F p.200
ENCLOSURE p.191
ENTWISTLE, John p.243
EVANS, Rev. p.87
EVANS, John p.252

FALCONBERG, Lord Viscount p.188
FELL, J p.250
FEMALE SOCIETY p.239
FISHER, Mr - advertisements p.5
FIVE HOUSES p.29, 224, 225   1850 FLOODS   242
FLETCHER, James p.225
FLORAL AND HORTICULTURAL SOCIETY p.242
FORESTERS p.251
FOREST OF HORWICH pp7-17, 18-23, 24-28, 30-33, 39, 175
FOXHOLE MILL p.204, 243
FOXHOLES p.181
FRANCE, Mr p.203
FREE GARDENERS p.251
FREEMASONS p.73
FRIENDLY SOCIETIES p.239, 240, 251
FUSTIAN p.176

GARBRET, James p.224
GARBUT, W p.225
GARDENERS p.240
GIANT'S STONE p.34, 35
GILL, Miss p.194
GEOLOGY OF HORWICH p.28, 29
GORTON FOLD p.98, 100, 161
GORTON FOLD MILL p.100
GREENHALGH, Robert p.176
GREENHALGH, W p.250, 251, 253
GREENHALGH, William p.206, 249
GREENHALGH ROAD p.192
GREENHALGH SURNAME p.28
GRUNDY HILL p.177, 183

HALLIWELL p.11, 12, 32, 33, 35, 108, 109
HAMPSON, Mary p.206
HAMPSON FAMILY pp.144-146
HANDLOOM WEAVING p.185

HANGING STONE - see GIANT'S STONE
HARDAKER, Rev Mark   p.95
HARDY, Rev John   p.86
HARRIS, Rev Robert   p.95
HARRISON, Mr   p.223
HART, Robert   p.135
HATTON, William   p.100
HEATON   p.7, 11, 12, 32, 33, 43, 172
HEATON OLD HALL   p.69
HENDERSON, George   p.224-226
HEWITT, Rev D   p.70, 72, 73, 76-78, 80, 81, 201, 221
HIBBERT, Rev   p.100
HIBBERT, Henry   p.241
HIGHER BARN   p.243
HILTON HOUSE   p.161
HODKINSON, Samuel   p.206
HODKINSON FOLD see BEDDOW'S FOLD
HODSON, Ellen   p.194
HOLE HILL   p.164
HOOD, John   p.96
HOPE, Mr   p.250
HOPWOOD, Mr   p.203
HOPWOOD, John   p.205, 208
HORDERN, Sharples   p.35
HORROCKS, Roger   p.224
HORWICH (origin of name)   pp.5-7
HORWICH AGRICULTURAL SOCIETY   p.241, 242
HORWICH BRASS BAND   p.246
HORWICH BUILDING CLUB   p.221
HORWICH CHAPEL   p.36, 38, 41-66, 70-83, 169, 170, 245, 247
HORWICH LOCAL BOARD OF HEALTH   p.249, 250
HORWICH MOOR   p.69, 181, 191
HORWICH MOOR ENCLOSURE   p.191
HORWICH MOOR GATE   p.164
HORWICH RACES   pp.229-235
HORWICH VALE BLEACH WORKS   see BLEACHWORKS
HORWICH VALE PRINT WORKS   p.95
HOUGH, Joseph   p.220
HOUGHTON FAMILY   p.208
HOULGATE, Rev W.J.   p.96
HOWARTH, Mr   p.250
HOWARTH, Adam   p.208
HOWARTH, Charles   p.241, 246
HOWARTH, Christopher   p.246
HOWARTH, Joseph   p.247
HOWARTH, William   p.253
HUGHES, Rev John   p.87
HUSH SHOPS   p.245
HUTCHINSON, Mr   p.250

INDEPENDENT METHODIST CHAPEL p.102, 103
INDEPENDENT ORDER OF ODDFELLOWS, RIDGMONT LODGE p.251
IRLAM, Samuel p.205, 206

JOHNSON, Rev Samuel pp.67-70, 75, 208-215
JOHNSON, William p.120
JONES, Rev John p.95

KAY, Moses p.247, 250
KAY, Sydney p.250
KAY, W p.250
KENWORTHY, Rev James p.87
KNOWLES, The p.204, 242, 243, 246
KNOWLES, Thomas p.135

LEE LANE p.99, 184, 223, 154
LEE LANE CONGREGATIONAL CHAPEL pp.91-97, 99, 102
LEE LANE CONGREGATIONAL CHAPEL DAY SCHOOL p.96
LEE LANE CONGREGATIONAL CHAPEL SUNDAY SCHOOL p.94, 100-102
LEE LANE INDEPENDENT METHODIST CHAPEL p.102, 103
LEE MILL p.253, 254
LEE WEAVING MILLS p.256
LIBRARY p.254
LIDDELL, J.P. - advertisements, p.3
LOMAX'S WIFE p.35
LONG MARLED EARTH p.140
LONGWORTH p.11, 35
LONGWORTH, Ellen p.243
LONGWORTH, J p.250
LONGWORTH, James p.133, 134
LONGWORTH, Jno p.247
LONGWORTH, John p.192, 193, 253
LONGWORTH, Nathaniel p.250
LONGWORTH, Peter p.135
LONGWORTH, William, Squire p.82, 203, 204, 242, 246
LONGWORTH ROAD p.192
LONGWORTH'S CROFT see BLEACHWORKS
LORD'S HEIGHT p.8, 161
LOSTOCK p.11, 12, 43, 172
LOSTOCK HALL p.69, 172
LOWER HOUSE p.161

MAKINSON, Alice p.243
MAKINSON, Hugh p.93
MAKINSON, Jane p.241
MAKINSON, Moses p.241
MAKINSON ROAD p.192, 193
MANCHESTER p.7, 8, 13, 27, 32, 38, 39, 67
MANOR HOUSE p.229
MARTIN, P, J.P. p.255, 256
MASON, Mr p.250, 255

MASON, A   p.244
MASON, Adam   p.253
MASON, Herbert   p.244
MASON, John   p.206
MASON, Richard   p.206
MASON, T   p.250
MASON'S TUYERE WORKS   p.101, 244
MAYNARD, Rev W.S.F.   p.247
MILLSTONE   p.73
MOOR   p.140
MOORGATE   p.68
MOOR-GATE ALEHOUSE   p.34, 180, 198, 226, 231, 241
MOOR GATE ROAD   p.193, 249
MOOR PLATT   p.87, 246
MOOR SIDE ROAD   p.192

NAIL ROCK   p.99
NEVETT, Mr   p.252
NEVY FOLD   p.161
NEW CHAPEL   p.64, 85, 86-89, 92, 206
NEW CHAPEL SICK SOCIETY   p.251
NEW HOUSE ESTATE   p.161
NICHOLLS, Rev R   p.96
NIGHTINGALE, R - advertisements p.3
NORCROSS, Rev John   pp61-63, 87, 126

ODDFELLOWS   p.73, 251
OLD CHAPEL   p.221
OLD LORD'S   p.164
OLD MARLED EARTH   p.140
ORANGEMEN   p.73, 251
OVERSEERS   1683-1883   pp158-161

PACE-EGGING   p.239
PASS, Mr   p.203
PATRIOTIC FUND   p.248
PEAK, Mr   p.249
PEAK, A   p.250, 251
PEAK, Tom   p.197
PEAK'S TUYERE WORKS   p.103, 244
PEARL BROOK TUYERE WORKS   p.243, 244
PEARSON, Thomas   p.245
PENDLEBURY, Henry   p.42, 43
PENDLEBURY, William   p.162
PIGOTT, Mrs   p.247, 248
PIGOTT, Rev H. S.   p.83, 246, 247, 255
PILKINGTON, Dr   p.203
PILKINGTON, James   p.121
PILKINGTON, Richard   pp.63-66, 88, 205-207
PILKINGTON'S ESTATE   p.190, 203
POLICE   p.240, 241

POPULATION p.70
PRIMITIVE METHODIST CHAPEL, Bottom-of-Moor p.161
PRIMITIVE METHODIST CHAPEL, Horwich Moor p.103
PUBLIC HALL pp.254-256, advertisements p.6

QUARRIES p.192

RACECOURSE p.18, 230
RAMMOCK HILL p.140
RAVEN PIKE see RIVINGTON PIKE
RAVENTON see RIVINGTON: Origin of name
RAWLINSON FAMILY p.208
REDMAYNE, Rev. Leonard p.94, 95, 99, 100
RED ROW BRIDGE p.156
RENSHAW, Ellen p.206
RIDGMONT p.191, 194, 221, 243, 246
RIDGMONT LODGE see INDEPENDENT ORDER OF ODDFELLOWS
RIDGMOUNT p.75
RIDGWAY, Cecily p.201
RIDGWAY, John p.182, 183
RIDGWAY, Joseph p.71, 75-79, 83, 183, 191, 192, 194-203,
                                          216, 225, 253
RIDGWAY, Mary p.81, 175
RIDGWAY, Thomas p.71, 73, 81, 149, 182, 183, 191, 192, 194-196,
                                          200, 201, 220
RIDGWAY, Thomas Hastings p.201, 202
RIDGWAY BRIDSON p.241
RIDGWAY CHARITY p.251, 252
RIDGWAY FAMILY p.181, 184, 185, 189, 190, 194, 196, 203, 221,
RIDGWAY HUNT p.194, 195
RIMMER, Thomas p.216
RIVINGTON p.35, 39, 185
RIVINGTON: Origin of name p.18, 39
RIVINGTON CHAPEL p.92, 93, 100
RIVINGTON GRAMMAR SCHOOL p.62
RIVINGTON HALL p.249
RIVINGTON OLD GRAMMAR SCHOOL p.18
RIVINGTON PIKE p.29, 33-36, 39, 67, 70, 93, 231, 236-239
RIVINGTON PIKE FAIR p.237, 238, 246
ROBBERS' WALK p.10, 18-21   ROCKHAVEN 229
ROBERTSON, Dr Medical Officer of Health p.252
ROPER, Edward p.197
ROPER, Ellen p.241
ROSCOE, Amelia p.206
ROTHWELL, James p.96
ROUND CROFT p.140
RUNWORTH p.11, 12
RUTTER, W p.197
RYECROFT p.140

SALFORD   p.32, 33
SCHOLE BANK   p.165, 177
SCOTT, John   p.242
SCOWL BANK see SCHOLE BANK
SCULLARD, Rev. H.H.   p.88
SEPHTON'S   p.162
SEWERAGE   p.250
SHARPLES   p.11, 13, 35
SHARPLES, John   p.241
SHARPLES, Mary Ann   p.241
SHARPLES FOLD   p.161
SHARROCKS FARM   p.161, 165, 243
SHAW, John   p.243
SHAW BROOK   p.189, 242
SICK SOCIETIES   p.251
SILVERWELL STREET   p.99
SMITH, Mr   p.250
SMITH, W   p.250
SMITHILLS   p.33, 35, 38
SQUIRREL INN   p.9, 73
STEAD, Mr   p.250
STOCKS   p.167, 183
STOCKS ESTATE   p.186, 203
STONES, James   p.250
STONE PIT ROAD   p.192, 193
STORM, 1850   p.242, 243
STUBBS, Jos - advertisements p.6
STUBBS, Joseph   p.247
SUNDAY SCHOOL   p.75, 247
SUTTON TUNNEL   p.243

TAYLOR, Henry   p.256
THIEVES' GRAVE see ROBBERS' WALK
THREE LANE ENDS   p.165
TIGERS, the   p.242
TIGERS IN THE WOOD ALEHOUSE   p.21
TOTTERING TEMPLE   p.177
TRIBBLE, William   p.245
TURNER, Mrs   p.241
TURNER, Noah   p.216
TURTON   p.35
TUYERES   p.243, 244
TUYERE WORKS   p.101, 103, 243, 244
TWO LADS   p.29, 33-37, 224, 227

UNITED ORDER OF ODDFELLOWS   p.251
URMSTON HOUSE   p.161, 160.

VAUSE, Elizabeth   p.125
VAUSE, George   p.197
VAUSE, Margaret   p.125

VAUSE, Mary   p.88
VAUSE, Thomas   p.88

WALKER, Rev J   p.86
WALLSUCHES   p.183, 184, 189, 194, 195, 199, 253
WALLSUCHES BLEACHWORKS see BLEACHWORKS
WALLSUCHES ROAD   p.192, 249
WALMSLEY, Thomas   p.241
WALTON, James   p.43, 45
WARD, Mr   p.243
WARD FAMILY   p.208
WATER SUPPLY   p.250
WATKINS, Rev J   p.96
WATSON, Rev George   p.87
WELLESBIE, Thomas   p.92
WESTHOUGHTON   p.29, 116
WETTENHALL, Mrs   p.243
WHITE GATE   p.192, 193
WHITE HOUSE   p.190, 203
WHITTAKER, G - advertisements p.6
WHITTAKER, George H. Medical Officer of Health   p.252
WHITTLE, Hugh   p.47, 133
WHITTLE, James   p.224, 225
WHITTLE FAMILY   pp.139-144
WHIT WALKS   p.246
WHOWELL, Thomas   p.225
WILDER LADS - see TWO LADS
WILDERSWOOD   p.100, 162, 181
WILDERSWOOD MILL   p.98, 176, 179, 243
WILKINSON FAMILY   p.208
WILLIAMS, Rev D   p.96
WILSDEN, Rev William   p.86, 88
WILSON, Charles   p.240
WINTER HILL   p.29, 34, 35, 37
WINTER LADS   see TWO LADS
WITTENHALL, Annie Maria   p.194
WOOD, Rev John   p.86
WORTHINGTON, Richard   p.162

www.ingramcontent.com/pod-product-compliance
Lightning Source LLC
Chambersburg PA
CBHW032135230426
43672CB00011B/2339